D1187770

The Secret History of the Roman Roads of Britain

For Prof. D.L. Kennedy, who showed me the way

The Secret History of the Roman Roads of Britain

M.C. Bishop

Pen & Sword
MILITARY

First published in Great Britain in 2014 by
Pen & Sword Military
an imprint of
Pen & Sword Books Ltd
47 Church Street
Barnsley
South Yorkshire
S70 2AS

ISBN 978 1 84884 615 9

A CIP catalogue record for this book is available from the British
Library

Typeset in Ehrhardt by
Mac Style, Bridlington, East Yorkshire
Printed and bound in the UK by CPI Group (UK) Ltd, Croydon,
CRO 4YY

Pen & Sword Books Ltd incorporates the imprints of Pen & Sword
Archaeology, Atlas, Aviation, Battleground, Discovery, Family
History, History, Maritime, Military, Naval, Politics, Railways, Select,
Transport, True Crime, and Fiction, Frontline Books, Leo Cooper,
Praetorian Press, Seaforth Publishing and Wharncliffe.

For a complete list of Pen & Sword titles please contact
PEN & SWORD BOOKS LIMITED
47 Church Street, Barnsley, South Yorkshire, S70 2AS, England
E-mail: enquiries@pen-and-sword.co.uk
Website: www.pen-and-sword.co.uk

Contents

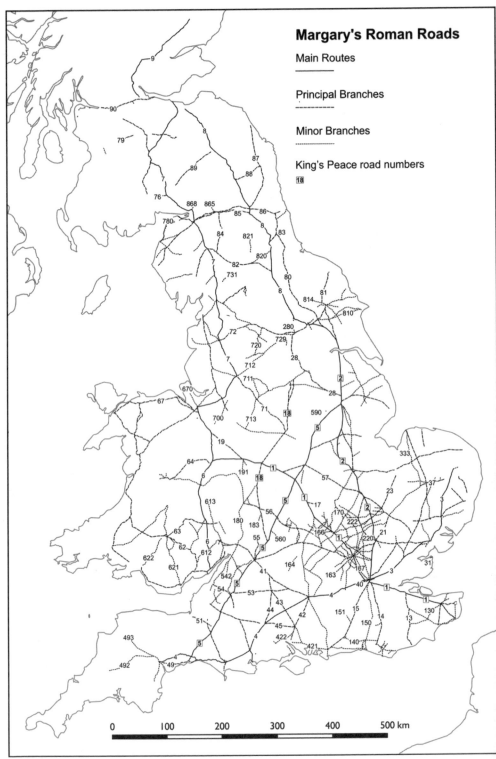

Margary's (1973) network of Roman roads in Britain.

List of Figures

List of Plates

Acknowledgements

Many people have aided me in one way or another during the writing of this book, a process that took nearly twenty years, off and on. Various individuals, groups, and societies listened politely to me talking on the subject of the roads of south-eastern Scotland and it was from that work that my wider interest in the Roman road system in Britain sprang. The Trimontium Trust and the Border Archaeological Society are just two of many who had to endure me harping on about roads, but I always found a sympathetic hearing in the company of Walter Elliot, Bill Lonie, and Donald Gordon, all motivational luminaries of the former society.

The late Raymond Selkirk showed me great kindness when I enquired about his speculative fort discovery at Press Mains in Berwickshire, whilst a casual comment of his about the neighbouring road led me on to pursue his line of thinking about a road continuing the Devil's Causeway north of the Tweed.

A decade and a half of excavating for Northern Archaeological Associates Ltd and AOC Archaeology has provided many friends and colleagues who have tolerated my fixation about all things Roman, and even supplied the occasional road for me to dig (including several previously undiscovered ones).

Prof. David Kennedy first marched me across the Roman roads of Jordan, showed me recumbent milestones, cleared Severan tracks, and sportingly evinced a measure of tolerance and understanding at my poor efforts to keep up. He has gone on to be a source of wisdom, (sometimes impenetrably) dry wit, and useful contacts. What more can you ask of a person?

The wonderful Rupert Besley very gracefully allowed me to use his marvellous cartoon (Plate 1) about Roman road construction, first spotted as a card which I then carefully hoarded for many years with the intention of one day using it. That day has arrived. Plate 3 of Mastiles Lane was kindly provided by Neil Sheridan, whilst David Graf generously provided me with colour photos (one of which is Plate 9) of the painted milestones he discovered in Jordan. Plate 17 is © RCAHMS (Aerial Photography Collection), licensor www.rcahms. gov.uk. Plate 18 is © Crown copyright: Royal Commission on the Ancient and Historical Monuments of Wales.

Particular, bejewelled thanks are due to Jon Coulston and John Poulter, both of whom read closely and commented insightfully upon an early draft of the text. I harbour no doubt that, without them, this would have been a much poorer book. However, whilst I have benefitted from and sought to incorporate their many suggestions, it is inevitable that I should stress that I alone am responsible for the doubtless many faults, idiocies, and inaccuracies remaining.

My long-suffering editor, Phil Sidnell, deserves a special award for his patience and his faith in me. I only hope he feels the wait, like the text, was justified. As a copy-editor myself, I think it is only fair also to thank my copy-editor, since I know how important (but seldom acknowledged) a job it can be. This book will inevitably be better for their gentle mistrinations (just testing).

Every book seeks to achieve a level of perfection, although few attain it. This one is doubtless just happy to be launched into the daylight, blinking and bedazzled, by its ungrateful and ridiculously tardy author, finally able to tell its tale.

Preface and Introduction

When light begins to glimmer, day to break, on the Dark Ages... when daylight begins to flow, wavering, and spreads for us over the Dark Ages, what is the first thing we see? I will tell you what is the first thing *I* see. It is the Roads... I see the Roads glimmer up out of that morning twilight, with the many men, like ants, coming and going upon them; meeting, passing, overtaking; knights, merchants, carriers; justiciars with their trains, king's messengers riding post; afoot, friars – black, white and grey – pardoners, poor scholars, minstrels, beggar-men; packhorses in files; pilgrims, bound for Walsingham, Canterbury, or to Southampton... I see the old Roman roads... hard metalled, built in fine layers... I see the minor network of cross-roads. *Arthur Quiller-Couch*[1]

This morning, I travelled along the Roman road from Corinium to Cunetio (Plate 19). The stretch south of Chiseldon is as straight as an arrow, unerringly dipping and soaring over a series of low hills. However, just 4.5 km from its target, which is now an open field next to the village of Mildenhall in Wiltshire, its course is suddenly abandoned and the modern road departs, wriggling across the landscape to arrive, finally, at the medieval market town of Marlborough, Cunetio's successor. The Roman road blithely continues as a lane, a track, a path, and then a lane again. So, although a short length of it is no longer a major route, it continues to make its mark upon the landscape.

We all owe much to Roman roads, but I have long harboured the suspicion that most people do not realize quite how much. It has become customary to dismiss the Roman contribution to British history as minimal. Their sidelining in the National Curriculum is perhaps symptomatic: fun for kids, but not serious, formative history. I disagree.

This book has been written partly from the conviction that this assumption is quite simply wrong, but partly also to draw attention to what I have come to recognize as common threads that link us today with the Romans and – beyond them – to our prehistoric past. For, just as we underrate the Roman contribution to our heritage, we appear to be completely ignoring part of our prehistoric legacy: in both cases, it is the gift of an ever-evolving road network.

Roman roads affect the lives of everybody living in the British Isles in a way that more prominent monuments, such as (to take a deliberately provocative example) Stonehenge, never have done and never will. They are hardly romantic, nor are they likely to inspire much beyond the occasional ramblers' guide book. However, a road system is quintessentially practical: it was the skeleton of the Roman province of Britannia, just as it was before the Romans even arrived, and just as it was to continue to be after their brief sojourn – in terms of British history, at least – was over. These roads have witnessed the wanderings of kings and scholars, the tramp of passing armies, and commerce between settlements that could not have existed without them. Our modern communication network, the siting of many of our cities and towns, even the very nature of who we are is linked to those roads. Unlike most monuments, many of them are still fulfilling their original role, one of which – as we shall see – was not new when the Romans arrived.

In writing this book, I have unashamedly drawn heavily upon my own experiences in fieldwork and excavation, largely because I know what I saw and find myself to be reasonably trustworthy most of the time. This may give a particular and unexpected viewpoint but why else write a book other than to share an opinion? So this volume is not a catalogue of roads, like those of Codrington or Margary (although it owes much to their labours), nor is it a detailed technical or technological analysis of the system in Roman times (others have done that better than ever I could). Instead, as befits a road, it offers a brief glimpse of the complexity of origins and destinations, where Roman roads came from, where they went, and what they were for. Much that is here has already been said, but never marshalled under one cover nor, I feel, said sufficiently loudly: the Roman heritage (to steal back an overly abused word) of our road system is not only profoundly important today, but provides a direct link back to our even more distant ancestors, and it is in this respect that I feel it is a 'secret history'. Thus the book is my poor attempt to descry some unity within the study of the past: by examining a chronologically distinct subject – Roman roads – we can see how what went before and what happened afterwards are every bit as much a part of the story, and that the whole is perhaps more important than any one element. So it was that I started this book as a Roman archaeologist and appear to have finished it as a faux landscape historian. However, like every reader, I remain a road-user; one with an enormous debt to the past.

Chapter 1

The Prehistory of Roman Roads

Preamble

What did the Roman find when he arrived in the first century AD? He found a trackway already 2,000 years old. It was not engineered, and would have abounded in hollows, ruts and obstructions of all kinds. At intervals along the route there were the banks and ditches of the Early Iron Age period, demarcating the territorial boundaries. Here was a route which he could use. From the several more or less parallel tracks he chose that which was most direct and most suitable, and straightened it where necessary. *The Viatores*[1]

Compare and contrast that view with this:

It is sometimes said that most main Roman roads in Roman Britain are based on pre-existing British tracks. While it is, indeed, certain that there were such tracks, and that they had clearly developed widely before the Roman conquest, even a general account would be uselessly fragmentary, since virtually nothing is known of them in detail. The well-attested examples, however, do not coincide in general with the Roman roads, which were unquestionably designed as instruments of conquest, as in other provinces. *Collingwood and Richmond*[2]

There is a popular misconception that the Romans brought the idea of roads to Britain (Plate 1), but nothing could be further from the truth. Every few years, scholars rediscover the idea of pre-Roman roads in British archaeology and then seemingly forget about it again. Dramatic headlines greeted the recent discovery of what appeared to be Iron Age road surfaces at Sharpstone Hill (Staffordshire); likewise, at the time of writing, a brand new book makes dramatic claims about the prehistoric origins of 'Roman' roads. However, earlier generations of historians and archaeologists had little trouble in dealing with the concept of roads before the Romans. Indeed, this very notion led Alfred Watkins to propose his Old Straight Track theory which, for all its flaws, recognized the importance of roads in prehistory. One of the most interesting approaches to Roman road studies in recent years has been a diachronic study of Akeman Street from the prehistoric into the Roman periods. What Sharpstone Hill provided was convincing archaeological evidence brought to the attention of a wider public.[3]

However, it is not necessary to cite large numbers of excavated examples of prehistoric roads in order to show that roads were not a Roman invention. To demonstrate this, we need only consider what might be termed Plautius' Dilemma, which (hypothetically expressed in the modern form of a multiple choice question) is this:

You are the commander of the Roman invasion force of about 40,000 troops. Arriving at the coast of Britain in AD 43. Do you

a) begin building all-weather roads to move your troops towards their ultimate goal of Colchester,
b) start marching them (and their baggage train) across country towards that destination, or
c) make use of existing roads to achieve the same ends?

It does not take a genius to work out that a) will take too long (see below page 19), b) will take almost as long and be completely impractical for wheeled transport (historically, armies have *never* marched across country when it can be avoided), and that c) implies and requires the existence of pre-Roman roads of some sort. Assuming – for the sake of argument, as it is by no means universally agreed upon by scholars – that Plautius landed on the south-east coast of Kent at Richborough, was there an existing route available to him?[4]

The so-called Pilgrim's Way was a ridgeway along the North Downs. Originating at Winchester, it passed through Guildford, Farnham, Snodland, Charing, to Canterbury, and originally continued as far as Dover (Figure 1). Despite its name, this was probably *not* the route used by Chaucer's pilgrims in the *Canterbury Tales* (who will more likely have followed the metalled Roman road – Margary 1). Four of the five places mentioned by Chaucer (Deptford, Greenwich, Sittingbourne, and Boughton) are indeed situated on the Roman road (as is the point of origin, Southwark) and another (assuming Bob-Up-And-Down to be Harbledown) probably was. However, the ridgeway does provide the most natural route from the south-east coast to the lowest Thames crossing and its use by the Roman invading force has long been accepted as a possibility by modern writers.[5]

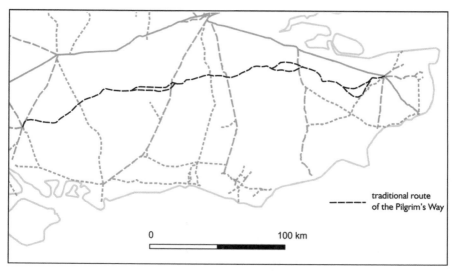

Figure 1: A ridgeway? The Pilgrim's Way (and its Roman successors).

So how did the Roman conquest of Britain progress from that point? It is not unreasonable to suggest that it continued in the same vein – using existing routes. Therefore, before we consider the Roman network, we must examine this prehistoric system and how it relates to its Roman successor.

Types of prehistoric roads and tracks

The existence of prehistoric trackways (Figure 2) is certainly accepted and referred to by modern writers – although the antiquity of the so-called ridgeways has been called into question – and in recent times some have even been excavated, most prominently the wooden trackways of the Somerset Levels. There are indeed writers on the subject of Roman roads who acknowledge the debt the Roman system owes to its native predecessor, including Hillaire Belloc. Nevertheless, the idea that roads that could be used by wheeled transport were already in existence at the time of the Roman conquest is seldom voiced, despite the fact that such early vehicles are indeed archaeologically attested: the earliest wooden wheel from Scotland (and, it so happens, Britain), for instance, dates to c. 1255–815 BC. However, one scholar (who had better remain nameless) remarkably even went so far as to suggest that wheeled Bronze Age vehicles were purely for the purposes of display, since no roads existed, so it seems clear that the role of the road in prehistoric Britain has not been overemphasized.[6]

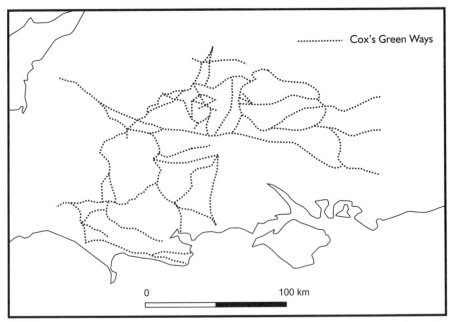

Figure 2: The prehistoric trackways of central southern England according to Hippesley Cox (1944).

Given that excavation of them is so rare, proving that a route is prehistoric is by no means easy. It is not as if one can trace the outline of a footprint and identify it as pre-Roman. Some of the upland trackways and ridgeways in Britain have a fairly obvious antiquity if they can be identified over long distances but have not been made into modern roads. Moreover, in the case of both such 'obvious' candidates and their less-obvious brethren, close association with prehistoric monuments may be a good indicator of a direct and tangible relationship (although it does tend to beg the question 'which came first: route or monument?'). Matters are made even more complicated by the tendency of all roads to 'creep' laterally across the landscape, and we shall be returning to that problem later in a Roman context (below, page 104). Nevertheless, it is probably true that we ought to be thinking more in terms of prehistoric 'routes', with often more than one track running parallel and their use perhaps dictated by seasonal conditions.[7]

Fortunately, some trackways are demonstrably prehistoric. As we have just seen, wooden footpaths across the Somerset Levels have been excavated and, by means of dendrochronology, these can be dated very accurately to the Bronze Age and even into the Neolithic. Although not used by wheeled traffic, they nevertheless demonstrate a familiarity with routes and the need to produce them where they did not already exist. It would surely be unreasonable to believe that these were the only such tracks in prehistoric Britain. Indeed, in Ireland, a 3.5–4 metre-wide wooden plank trackway (at Corlea in County Longford), dating to 146 BC, appears to have been specifically designed to take wheeled vehicles. It is difficult to avoid the suspicion that trackways preserved by exceptional environmental conditions – such as bogs – may be just the visible component of a largely invisible network of trackways and routes across the British Isles. Possible (but by no means certain) Bronze Age and Iron Age bridges have been identified on the Thames at Eton and Vauxhall.[8]

In fact, rural pre-Roman roads are known and, once again, some have even been excavated. A track has been identified crossing the Bronze Age landscape of Holne Moor in Devon. Further north, a type of Iron Age settlement, known as a 'ladder settlement', was in fact a linear landscape focused on a trackway of some kind (which happens to look like a ladder laid out on the ground when viewed from the air). Excavation of an example at Melton (E Yorks) failed to find any evidence of metalling but did locate roadside ditches and confirmed the complex nature of this Iron Age and Romano–British rural settlement. At Mount Pleasant, near Crambeck (N Yorks), a similar settlement showed such continuity from the Iron Age into the Roman period (Figure 3), laid out along a side road leading to the main Roman road from York to Malton in North Yorkshire (Margary 81a). Not only was the surface metalled (albeit using the living rock), but wheel ruts were evident in the pre-Roman surface. The fact that the road served as a link to the Roman-period road points to it having served the same purpose in the earlier period: clearly, one might conclude that not only the side road but the road from York to Malton itself pre-dated the Roman invasion. Minor roads like these were certainly a feature of the Romano-British landscape, but it is becoming clear that these are the legacy of an earlier period. It is perhaps worth noting that examples of such pre-Roman roads associated with rural settlements tend to be slightly sinuous and not straight. In this, they contrast with formally-constituted 'Roman' roads (although many evidently continued in use into the Roman period) and, crucially, with the proposed ley line routes favoured by Watkins as prehistoric roadways.[9]

It has already been mentioned that a number of long-distance trackways are known that are commonly presumed to be prehistoric in origin. These include famous routes like the Ridgeway (now formalized as a National Trail from Overton Hill in Wiltshire to Ivinghoe in Buckinghamshire) and the Icknield Way (from Ivinghoe to Knettishall in Norfolk). As Rackham has pointed out, a principal reason for identifying these as prehistoric used to be the rather misguided notion that early people only settled (and travelled) on

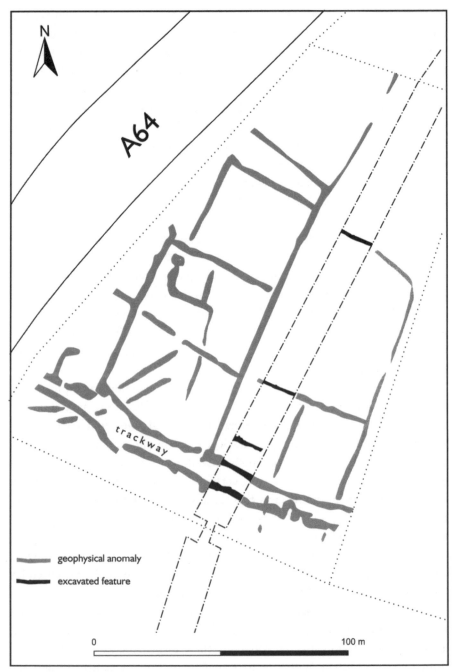

Figure 3: Trackway with a ladder settlement at Mount Pleasant, Crambeck (after Abramson et al. forthcoming).

high ground, since all the valleys would be full of woodland and impassable rivers. We now know this to be untrue (not least because of evidence like that from the excavations in the Somerset Levels), but as most of them do pass close to prehistoric monuments, the claim that they are prehistoric is probably true. At the same time, it might be argued that it would be very difficult indeed for a route to pass through much of Britain without passing close to at least a few prominent monuments (Plate 2).[10]

At least two trackways in the Peak District have been identified, passing a number of prehistoric monuments, including henges and hillforts, such as Arbor Low. The connection between prehistoric (and Roman) routes with prehistoric monuments is prominent and probably more than coincidental, as we shall see.[11]

Deduced examples

In some instances, the existence of a prehistoric route is indicated by its partial re-use by a Roman road. At Roecliffe, near Boroughbridge in North Yorkshire, a Roman fort guards a probable river crossing for a north–south route running parallel to the Roman Dere Street (Margary 8b), which itself crossed the Ure a mile to the east, where a fort (and later a town) was built at Aldborough (*Isurium Brigantum*, Figure 4). Interestingly, the Roecliffe crossing appears to have been indicated by a group of four standing stones, the Devil's Arrows; the coincidence of standing stones with Roman roads is not unknown in other locations (see below, page 14). To the north of Roecliffe, on what might be termed the Great North Route, there is an impressive series of prehistoric monuments (including several henges, notably those at Thornborough) and, once again, their proximity to the road is striking.[12]

A similar situation can be identified near Corbridge in Northumberland, where an earlier Roman fort (Beaufront Red House) guards a crossing to the west of that later used by Dere Street (Margary 8d) and subsequently guarded by another fort overlooking a stone Roman bridge over the Tyne.[13]

A further example of Roman roads using prehistoric routes may be provided by Badbury Rings in Dorset, where two Roman roads meet at a hillfort (Figure 5). Field (1992) has gone further and suggested that other hillforts in the area may have been linked by a network of Roman roads, but if this was indeed the case, it is possible that these routes also had a pre-Roman origin. Across the Channel in France, just such a network of roads between hillforts has been identified in Burgundy, so the likelihood that something similar existed in Britain must be considered. There was a time when the proximity of a Roman fort to a hillfort would be remarked upon as a likely reason for the existence of

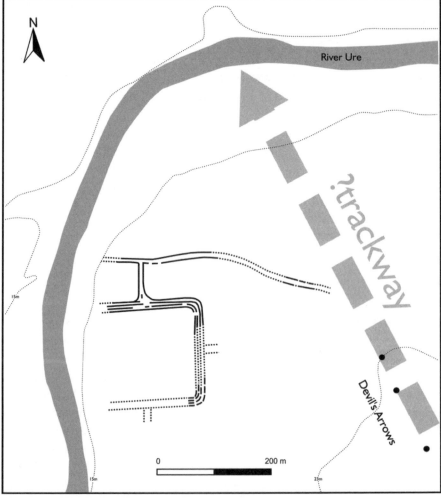

Figure 4: The east–west road (and north–south trackway?) at Roecliffe (after Bishop 2005).

the Roman fort (despite the fact that many such sites could not be shown to be contemporary), but it might be more credible if we see them both in the context of the same thing – their respective road systems. It is conceivable that later, more sophisticated, prehistoric *oppidum*-type settlements, such as Colchester-Camulodunum, St Albans-Verulamium, and Silchester-Calleva, may have anticipated their Roman successors and have lain at the heart of polity-centred networks of trackways.[14]

Yet more evidence of the Roman use of prehistoric tracks may be provided by the locations of temporary camps. Two series in particular are of interest here.

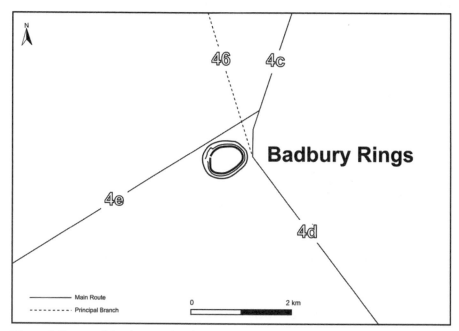

Figure 5: From nodal point to redundancy I: the Roman roads at Badbury Rings.

The first runs up the south bank of the River Tweed between Tweedmouth (Northumb) and Maxton, near St Boswells (Borders), and is difficult to explain if it is not utilizing an existing route. The second, and probably the best known, is the line of camps that runs up the east coast of Scotland, representing multiple campaigns. Scholars have attempted to classify and date these, but for our purposes what matters is the fact that a metalled Roman road has only been traced as far north as just beyond Cardean (Tayside), whilst the camps continue about 140 km further up to the shores of the Moray Firth. This last route was also probably exploited by Edward I, once he too had exceeded the limits of the Roman system.[15]

Mastiles Lane in North Yorkshire was a monastic route which used to communicate between the estates of Fountains Abbey on either side of the Pennines. As it crosses Malham Moor, it passes through the Roman temporary camp at Malham (Plate 3), suggesting that the route not only pre-dates the monastic period, but already existed when the Roman army was campaigning in the area (after AD 71). It also hints at the fact that the Romans were interested in east-to-west movement in this area during this time (perhaps in concert with the use of the A66 route (Margary 82) during the advance on Carlisle (Cumbria)). Mastiles Lane went on to be used as a drove road after the Dissolution and survives today as an enclosed 'green lane' (and is still used by walkers, horse-riders, and until recently off-road vehicle enthusiasts). It was never officially adopted into the road system of any period, but nevertheless remained important from the prehistoric period onwards.[16]

Dating

Other than those few wooden trackways that can be dated by dendrochronology, the dating of prehistoric routes must – with the exception of rare examples such as Shapstone Hill – usually derive from the monuments associated with them. Hillforts, tumuli, henges, and standing stones all fall within this group and it is not hard to produce examples of each. What is lacking, at the time of writing, is any sort of statistical analysis of this apparent relationship. It is possible that we are seeing some routes that date back to the earliest occupation of the British Isles by mankind, but it is equally possible that each age has added to this proto-network to meet its own particular needs, and the invention and spread of the wheel must have had a key role to play here.

We might presume that the first people to move across Britain will have followed animal tracks, and that some of these will have broadened with use, others fallen from favour. That the routes of some of these are still in use to this day seems at least a possibility. In the American West, animal trails were used by the native Americans pursuing prey, adopted as waggon trails by settlers, and later followed by both railways and modern paved roads. The bulk of the prehistoric road system may well have come about during the Neolithic period in association with an increasingly settled lifestyle and the concomitant need to engage in trade.[17]

Function

This brings us to the question of how prehistoric roads were used. It is only too easy to assume that, from our modern perspective, they functioned in the same way in the past as they do now, but that would be naïve at best. Mankind's fondness for ritual led other civilisations and cultures to exploit roadways in ceremonial and such a function has been suggested for the Avenue at Avebury and at Arbor Low. Archaeologists are only just beginning to understand how the people of the past interacted with the spaces around them. A road need not be just a road, but it could be a route for ceremonial processions. If this seems vaguely ridiculous to those unencumbered by the archaeologist's obsession with 'ritual', we need only recall the *Via Sacra* in Rome, used in triumphal processions from the Republic right through the Imperial period. Roman Republican history provides hints at a darker side to the ceremonial use of roads, with the rebels of Spartacus crucified along the road from Capua to Rome. Roads have a place in ritual that is only dimly remembered now in the final ceremony of the cutting of a ribbon to open a new road (along which the celebrants will, of course, duly process).[18]

Roads facilitate travel. It is not impossible without them, and many bush peoples may have travelled vast distances all their lives without the benefit of any sort of road, but they do undeniably make travelling easier. As a direct result of their existence, trade will flourish. Some of the great prehistoric roads were trade routes – the Amber Route, the Silk Road – but what was true on an international scale was certainly even more so at a national or regional level. Travelling by ship or boat along coasts and up rivers was natural, but not all rivers are navigable, and do not always lead to where they are needed, so this could be supplemented and complemented by trade along roads.

Roads help armies. Just as it is true in later periods, it is important to remember that roads in the prehistoric period will have had a role in warfare. After all, the inhabitants of pre-Roman Iron Age Britain were given to using wheeled vehicles in war as well as other forms of wheeled transport. The Romans certainly borrowed their technical terminology for carts wholesale from the Celtic language, the clear implication being that the 'Celtic' peoples of Europe were pre-eminent in the construction of wheeled transport. In Britain, one of the earliest eye-witness accounts (that of Caesar) makes special note of the British use of chariots in warfare in the first century BC. They are mentioned again in the context of the Battle of Mons Graupius under Agricola, over 100 years later. Excavation has produced evidence of such vehicles, most famously from the chariot burials of East Yorkshire, amongst the Parisi, where their timber structure was preserved as 'ghosts' in the soil. The recent discovery of a chariot at Newbridge, near Edinburgh, demonstrates a further northern British example of their use and confirms Tacitus' account. Four-wheeled waggons or carts are also mentioned in relation to the final battle of the Boudican revolt in AD 60/61 and what must be similar vehicles are shown in relief on the metopes of the *Tropaeum Traiani* at Adamclisi in Romania. It is a fundamental law of wheeled transport that it always moves faster on a road of some kind than if it has to move off-road or cross-country (little has changed in that respect and even the most powerful off-road vehicle, whether it be a wheeled Land-Rover or a track-laying tank, will invariably travel faster on a road). The wheeled vehicles of the Britons were no different.[19]

Prehistoric roads will also have been used for transhumance. Drove roads existed in the medieval period for taking animals to market (Dere Street providing an important route for Scottish cattle going to Stagshaw Fair near Corbridge) and may well be earlier in date in some instances. In areas of Britain with upland pastures, there will also have been transhumance routes between summer and winter pastures. Elsewhere in the empire, the Romans sought to control (but not stop) such movements of livestock and people and in Britain the Knag Burn gateway through Hadrian's Wall – not itself on a Roman road – has been suggested as having been placed on just such a route.[20]

Early roads may also have served the dead as much as the living. The Roman use of roadside burial places is well-known (see below, page 34), but it is not beyond the bounds of possibility that this association between burial and roads may reach back beyond the Roman period in Britain. The linear distribution of tumuli in some regions has been commented upon before now and in some places the use of burial mounds continued into the Roman era (as at High Rochester and Great Chesters). Possible Bronze Age mounds called Coney Hills lie next to a Roman road near Gilling in North Yorkshire. In later periods, dedicated 'corpse roads' carried the dead to their final resting place; an example in the Lake District led from Mardale Green to a church at Shap (both Cumbria), some 11 km.[21]

From a practical point of view, whilst it is acceptable to manoeuvre war chariots over a field of battle, off-road use for long-distance travel was simply not practicable. Therefore, mustering a chariot army and deploying them to the scene of battle will have required some sort of road system over which they could be moved, always assuming that they were not in some way transported to battle (like modern tanks, which use specialized low-loader vehicles), perhaps being disassembled and carried on pack animals.

Relationship to monuments

The apparent proximity of Iron Age hillforts to Roman roads has already been mentioned. In Burgundy, a network of pre-Roman roads has been identified linking hillforts; in this case it is distinct from the Roman road network, whereas in Britain, the frequent association of hillforts with Roman roads suggests a higher degree of integration of the pre-Roman and Roman networks. At Badbury Rings in Dorset, two Roman roads (Ackling Dyke from Old Sarum to Dorchester, and the Hamworthy to Bath road) crossed immediately to the north of the hillfort (Figure 5), and other examples of hillforts close to road junctions can be cited. Old Sarum lay at the junction of three roads, as

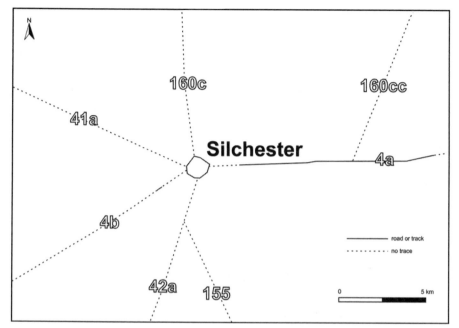

Figure 6: From nodal point to redundancy II: the Roman roads at Silchester.

did Silchester (Figure 6). The fact that both of these were major pre-Roman settlements which later developed into important Roman sites cannot negate the coincidence between their location and the Roman road network. That coincidence is obviously more prominent at sites that did not continue into the Roman period, but it does not make the observation any less significant because they did not have a later existence. Thus it is scarcely surprising that the junction of the Fosse Way (Margary 5b) with the road from Winchester to Charterhouse-on-Mendip (Margary 45b) is marked by the hillfort at Beacon Hill, a few miles to the east of Wells, nor that the east–west road is paralleled by a line of round barrows.[22]

What is by no means clear is whether the course of pre-Roman roads determined the placing of monuments, or if they merely served to join existing settlements. Logically, if we are to accept that elements of the road network pre-date the Iron Age, then the location of hillforts must, to some extent, have been determined by the course of roads (although other factors will obviously have been equally or more important). From that assumption, we can project the same determining effect backwards to earlier times. When might such roads have been formalized? The possibility that some at least were in use in the Neolithic period (and, given the existence of Neolithic wooden trackways, this does not seem unreasonable), when settled farming first became a feature of the British landscape, must at least be considered. If they were that old, then doubtless many of them marked even older routes used by man when traversing the land.

Standing stones are another class of monument that can be associated with Roman roads (and, presumably, with their antecedents). Taking just southern Wales, Maen Madoc next to Margary 622 is one such example, Bwlch y Ddeufaen by Margary 67c another, and Gelligaer (Margary 621) another.[23]

Major prehistoric ceremonial sites also cluster around Roman roads – even Stonehenge is situated near the junction of the Mildenhall/Old Sarum road (Margary 44) and the Winchester/Charterhouse road (Margary 45). On a lesser scale, there is Arbor Low in Derbyshire and Y Pigwyn stone circles next to Roman roads (Margary 71 and 62 respectively). Avebury too is linked to the main road from London to Bath (Margary 53) by the stone-lined Avenue, the junction being marked by Silbury Hill (which the Roman road swerves to avoid) to the north, West Kennet long barrow and The Sanctuary to the south. It is now known that Silbury lies adjacent to a major Roman settlement. Monuments of various ages are thus seen to be respecting a route that is adopted by the Roman road.[24]

It is tempting to agree with Rackham when he suggests that the majority of minor roads in Britain may be prehistoric in origin. The similarity between the sinuous trackways of ladder settlements and the meandering British country lane is undeniable. However, for our purposes, the most important observation is that many of our major trunk roads are not just Roman in origin, but probably pre-Roman. The Romans did not invent roads, but they certainly knew how to improve those that already existed.[25]

Ghosts of former roads may even be preserved in anomalous Roman roads. The outpost fort of Bewcastle, some 10 km north of Hadrian's Wall, has been suggested as guarding friendly local territory and it is nowadays thought unlikely that it and its fellow outpost forts (Birrens, Netherby, Risingham, and High Rochester) were placed on likely routes for incursion into Roman territory. However, three of these lay on Roman roads into Scotland (Margary 7f and 8e), Netherby on a short spur of road (Margary 868), and Bewcastle on a similar spur linked back to Birdoswald on the Wall itself (Figure 7). It seems fairly likely that all of these routes are therefore prehistoric in origin, that some were completely reused in the Roman period, others (like Margary 865 to Bewcastle) partially adopted and given an all-weather surface, but only so far as was necessary for logistical purposes. However, recent geophysical survey has shown a road running north out of the fort which may well reflect a continuation beyond Bewcastle, at least in part.[26]

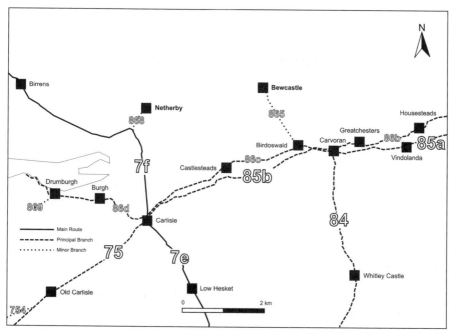

Figure 7: Netherby and Bewcastle on dead-end spur roads north of Hadrian's Wall.

Chapter 2

Conquest and Construction

Existing winding trackways were sometimes utilized by the Romans, and were straightened somewhat and metalled. This is noticeable especially in Hertfordshire, the heart of the Catuvellaunian territory, where some parts of the roads have obviously been based on pre-existing Belgic tracks. *The Viatores*[1]

Roman Britain before Roman roads

So it was that when the Roman army landed on the coast of southern Britain in AD 43, they were immediately faced by a major logistical problem – how should they advance? Of course, this only seems like a problem from our point of view. The Romans themselves clearly had only limited choices, the most obvious and convenient of which was to use the existing native 'trackway' system. As we have seen, this need not have been as crude as has sometimes been assumed, but it is certain the army could not wait for even the simplest all-weather roads to be constructed, as this would have taken far too long. The presence of a large baggage train – both pack animals and wheeled vehicles – restricted the movement of the army, and travel without it could usually only be accomplished for a short period. Movement along the existing system of trackways and routes would have presented few problems during the campaigning season (traditionally March to September) and it would have been easier than travelling cross-country, although it would have meant the progress of the Romans could to some extent have been anticipated.

Surviving accounts of Roman armies on the march show how they sent detachments ahead with the specific duty of clearing the way for the main body of troops. They were evidently not meant to construct roads, merely improve existing ones. Indeed, the usual term seems to have been 'to open up' a road (*aperire*) and we find this being used of Tiberius in AD 10 and Germanicus in AD 14 when campaigning in Germany. In AD 9, the unfortunate Quinctilius Varus tried to march his army along inadequate tracks through dense woodland (some clearance was apparently required) and in foul weather, leading to the infamous *clades Variana* in the Teutoburg Forest. Not surprisingly, the use by the military of existing routes is attested elsewhere in the Roman Empire. In Arabia, the *Via Nova Traiana* followed an earlier Nabataean caravan route and presumably reflected part of the Roman advance into that province in AD 108.[2]

The formalization of a road network

So it seems that we must accept that the Romans did not, indeed could not, build roads at the same speed as they advanced. Properly constituted, all-weather roads, even if they were begun at the time of the invasion (and there is good reason to argue that there were better things for troops and engineers to do), would have followed far behind the marching army. Tacitus records how, when Germanicus was campaigning across the Rhine in Germany, the general despatched Lucius Apronius with a detachment to conduct road and bridge building behind his main force.[3]

Once they arrived in Britain, the Romans needed to establish an efficient infrastructure as quickly as possible. During the campaigning season (from spring to autumn) the existing tracks would have served, but once winter set in and the routes became wet and the rivers swollen, then lines of communications would definitely have been threatened. Constructing temporary 'campaign' roads along the native routes was one possible solution to this pressing problem and calculations published by John Peddie give some idea of the speed at which this minimalist exercise could have been accomplished. With the help of the Royal Engineers, he calculated it would have taken a force of 1,000 men fifteen weeks to construct one of his 'assault roads' from the Kent coast at Richborough to the Thames at (what was later to be) London. Such calculations (which would equate to approximately one yard per man per day) are, at best, 'guesstimates', but they nevertheless serve to provide some idea of what would be possible (and it has to be remembered that these are not proper surfaced Roman roads, but effectively cleared trackways). In reality, it is more likely that most Roman work of this kind was focused upon improving the existing road network, allowing the army to progress somewhat faster than Peddie's figures suggest.[4]

An alternative system of roadways might have been provided by the use of log corduroy roads. This method was used very effectively by General Sherman to move his army through the Carolinas during the campaign of 1865, and he was reportedly able to achieve a rate of construction of twelve miles a day. We cannot completely rule out the possibility that the Roman army could have constructed similar roads *de novo* on occasion – there may even be a case for arguing that examples of such constructions survive beneath existing roads at Ambleside

(Cumbria), Southwark (London), or Scaftworth (Notts) (see below, page 36) – but we can suspect that it was not their normal method of movement.[5]

The process of all-weather road construction during consolidation would need to have been followed rigorously as the Roman army advanced throughout Britain. In Germany, Germanicus realized the vulnerability of his lines of supply to adverse weather conditions and that was why he had Apronius work on road and bridge construction. It is extremely unlikely that forward bases could be maintained during the winter if they were not accessible by road, even if water transport was available. Later in the Roman period, outpost forts beyond Hadrian's Wall and the Antonine Wall always had good roads linking them to their mural barriers.[6]

Campaign roads may be detectable in the archaeological record in some instances, although they will usually be concealed by later, more permanent roads. In Arabia, some broad paths were cleared through the basalt boulder fields of the Hauran but were never surfaced. They were marked by milestones, showing them to have been 'constructed' under the Emperor Septimius Severus, the cleared rocks piled on either side of the track. In Britain, parts of the Dere Street appear to diverge from an original prehistoric route which was only in use by the Romans between their conquest of Brigantia in AD 71 and the construction of its Roman successor, probably some time after AD 85. Likewise, the temporary camp at Rey Cross is bisected by the later trans-Pennine Roman road which clearly post-dates it, and this suggests that the force which constructed the camp – presumably in the early days of the Roman conquest of the north – were using an earlier trackway, the course of which was later followed (evidently not slavishly) by the new Roman road.[7]

Thus, it might seem logical that, once the campaigning season was over in the autumn, the army would withdraw to winter quarters and send out detachments to undertake road building on the grand scale. The Romans knew that idleness is the greatest enemy of the professional soldier, and road construction was one way of avoiding this problem. However, the Highland military roads of the eighteenth century were normally built during the summer season, usually between April and October. There is certainly good reason to suspect that, although Petilius Cerialis invaded Brigantia in AD 71, the final form of Dere Street was not constructed until at least AD 85, when Roman forces were starting to retreat from Scotland. This would allow fourteen years to construct 140 km of road between York and Corbridge.[8]

Practicalities of road building

Wherever possible, local materials would have been used. They could be obtained from most river valleys, and quarry pits can often be seen lining roads where the right geological conditions to supply gravel prevail (Plates 17 & 18). The timber used in the log corduroy between Scaftworth and Bawtry (S Yorks) included alder, a common tree in the carr landscape found in such a waterlogged river valley. Other corduroy-founded roads have been found on the south bank of the Thames at Southwark, approaching the Roman bridge to London and at Ambleside, in the Lake District, near the Roman fort.[9]

We have already examined Peddie's calculations for the construction of 'campaign' roads, but it is much more difficult to guess how long a proper road would have taken to build. This is not only because we do not know the speed at which the Romans worked, but we have no idea of the proportion of their available manpower they might have been willing to devote to the task. We do have some brief details of how contemporary roads were constructed, thanks to the poet Statius (although even his account is sometimes dismissed as poetic fancy). Here he is describing the construction of the Via Domitiana, between Sinuessa and Puteoli:

> The first task was to prepare a trench and open a route, excavating a deep hollow in the ground; the next to re-fill the open trench with other material, and prepare a base upon which the cambered surface of the road might be laid, in case the ground should subside or provide an unstable bed for deep-set blocks. *Statius*[10]

The picture gained from his short description can be fortified by analogy with the mural barriers of Hadrian's Wall and the Antonine Wall. Both were built by gangs of soldiers, traverse the terrain in a similar way to roads, but – crucially – are accompanied with fairly detailed epigraphic records of their construction, even down to the amount built by each gang, allowing scholars to work out how they have been constructed. Using these as our guide, we can postulate how (and, importantly, how fast) a Roman road could be built. The mural barriers show clear evidence of having been constructed in stints assigned to particular units. Construction of a stretch of, say, Hadrian's Wall might be allotted to a particular legion, and within that particular cohorts and, again, within that particular centuries. Although there was once believed to have been an overall movement of the construction process from east to west (albeit with possible variations), doubt has now been cast upon it being such a linear process. So, once a sector was constructed by the legions apportioned to it, they would have moved to their next allotted section and started the process all over again. A similar model may have been used in road construction, particularly for the major arterial highways, such as the Watling or Dere Streets. However, as was the case with the Walls, surveying and laying out need not necessarily have been undertaken in the same direction as actual construction. Nor, indeed, need the actual construction process have been sequential from one end to the other.[11]

We can also compare our conclusions with a later historical example of military road-building, fortunately better-documented than those of the Roman period. The subjugation of Highland Scotland in the eighteenth century saw a massive campaign of road construction under Marshall Wade and Major Caulfeild specifically aimed at facilitating the movement of troops. The military roads of Scotland were constructed in a similar way to the average Roman road: a broad trench with flanking drainage ditches dug, rubble foundations inserted, with finer gravel compacted on top. They were also constructed using more or less the same tools as were available to the Romans. Direct comparison is obviously difficult, not least because there would inevitably be special circumstances surrounding the construction of roads in highland terrain, but it can at least provide some hints as to what would have been possible in the Roman period. The expected rate of construction was 1½ yards (1.35 m) per man per day (at 16 ft – 4.8 m – most roads were just over 5 yards wide), and in at least one case 2 yards per man per day was achieved. This can usefully be compared with the Royal Engineers' figures (of one yard per man per day) for clearing campaign tracks, but it is difficult to know where between these two sets of data one should place a Roman army detachment in terms of road building ability.[12]

At the sort of rates Wade and Caulfeild expected (and, as we have just seen, sometimes surpassed), we might hypothesize the 140 km of Dere Street between York and Corbridge to have taken approximately 285 man–years to construct. Taking this to extremes, if the entire British invasion force of approximately 40,000 men were put to road construction, they could produce slightly less than 21,000 km of road per annum, assuming they had nothing better to do. Absurd though this might at first seem, it at least provides a ceiling figure for the maximum achievable by the army in terms of road construction. It might be more reasonable to assume that a Roman commander might be willing to detail a proportion of his force – say a tenth – to consolidating his infrastructure. Thus, if his men were as good as Caulfeild's, he might expect those 4,000 to lay 160 km of all-weather road in a month.

If work gangs were used to construct the road at several points simultaneously, this would obviously be quicker than one or two teams working from either or both ends towards each other. Comparison with the construction of linear barriers is obviously tempting here, particularly in the light of recent theories concerning the construction of Hadrian's Wall (Hill noting evidence for several gangs at work simultaneously). Unfortunately, whilst construction records of linear barriers like the Antonine Wall preserve the distances built by particular units, they do not supply any details of the time taken and this has consequently become a popular academic guessing game. Wade worked with teams of around 500 men between April and October. Caulfeild increased these numbers substantially – in 1749 he had 1,350 men from five regiments involved in road construction (largely because he was building more roads than Wade), plus a further eighty on repair and maintenance. Tacitus refers to *manipuli* (pairs of centuries) being used to construct roads and bridges in the Balkans, prior to the army mutiny of AD 14, but it is not clear how much reliance should be placed on his choice of words (since it may just have been used in the sense of 'detachments'). It might therefore be speculated that the 160 men of two centuries could construct 216 m per day at Wade's rate of work, and thus about 650 days for the York/Corbridge stretch (or 478 days at Caulfeild's rate). So, given a working season of seven months, it would take a force of that size three years to complete it.[13]

Surveying

Before a Roman road could be built, as has been mentioned, its course would require surveying. Surveyors (*mensores*) had always been an integral part of the Roman army, primarily being involved in the layout of overnight and campaign camps, as well as more permanent bases, but also skilled in the construction of roads, bridges, and tunnels. It was their task to lay out the course of a road in such a way that it could easily be built by the army. The equipment they used is well-known and fairly basic: ten-foot measuring rods, flags (which served like ranging poles), and an instrument called a *groma* which allowed the siting of ninety- and forty-five-degree angles. They had no means we know of for measuring distance by line of sight (which requires precision optics or, increasingly nowadays, electronics). Nevertheless, all of the surveying operations necessary to construct a fully serviceable and long-lasting road were available to them.[14]

Although it might have been useful for the purposes of comparison, it is not known precisely how the eighteenth century Highland military roads were surveyed. Taylor has suggested that similar teams to those used by Watson and Roy during the Military Survey of Scotland would have been employed (an engineering officer, an NCO, and six men). We do know something of the survey that was undertaken in 1749 prior to the construction of the Military Road between Newcastle and Carlisle, since two copies of the plan survive, as do records of the operations of the surveyors. Two officers, Dugal Campbell and his deputy Hugh Debbeig, were assigned to the task and seem to have had enough time to note details of the Roman remains during their month in the country. Paradoxically, when the road came to be built, construction was contracted out to civil companies.[15]

Much is often made of the straightness of Roman roads (Plate 1). Many of the best-known do indeed have long straight sections, but most roads have frequent (if slight) course changes to allow for variations in the terrain they are traversing. What makes them so distinctive is that the sections of road – however short – are usually straight and not curved, unlike so many more recent British roads. This means that Roman roads make sudden adjustments of course of only a few degrees, rather than the sort of smooth gentle curves preferred for modern motorized transport. This is primarily due to the difference between a surveyed road (where its geometric origins are betrayed by angularity) and one formed by 'line of desire' (where lack of planning is revealed by a sinuous nature).[16]

Roads traversed long distances in this fashion, only varying from the pattern when they had to tackle a particularly demanding obstacle such as a river crossing. Often a sudden diversion would take the road down one side of a valley obliquely (sometimes down an engineered ramp), across the obstacle, then up the other side and resuming the old course, as happened at the crossing of the Haltwhistle Burn by the Stanegate in Northumberland.[17]

Interestingly, roads often maintained a general bearing, despite making deviations for various purposes. These were so-called 'aligned roads'. It has been suggested that this implies that some form of long-distance directional surveying was used, perhaps utilizing the position of the sun or stars. Stane Street, as it leaves London, for instance, is said to be aligned exactly on the east gate of Chichester (*Noviomagus*), although such accuracy has long puzzled scholars. Some find it difficult to see how surveyors could have achieved this (particularly when the two endpoints were not intervisible), and some of the more ingenious methods proposed are less than convincing. However, if it is assumed that the road pre-dated the settlement, the position of which was thus determined by the road, then it all becomes much easier to understand. Crude cartesian coordinate systems were employed in the Roman period, as is shown by Ptolemy's map of Britain, but it is not clear whether these were merely derived from a map or actually determined on the ground in some way and there is nothing to suggest their employment in the planning of roads.[18]

Of course, projecting a more-or-less straight line over long distances is relatively simple with even the most basic of surveying equipment – essentially all that is needed is a series of ranging poles along which the surveyor sights the alignment (a technique understood by Watkins) and it can be no accident that the major roads of southern Britain radiate from London; this would certainly seem to imply that the roads were surveyed *from* Roman London and might also be thought to give some indication of the fact that this did not happen until after that town became provincial capital during the first century AD. However, implicit in such an assumption is the notion that there were no pre-existing roads to use as models. Was a nodal point Roman or earlier?[19]

One interesting hypothesis has been advanced about the precise way in which Roman roads were surveyed in Britain. Davies advocated the use of maps by surveyors in their planning of routes to account for the accuracy of some roads in maintaining a general bearing (citing the example of Stane Street between London and Ewell pointing directly at Chichester). It is questionable whether sufficiently accurate maps were available to the Romans (certainly none have come down to us on a large scale that would fit the bill). More seriously, Davies does not allow for the possibility that there were already roads existing, which would conveniently provide the necessary (albeit approximate) alignments. To some extent, the hard work had been done for the Roman surveyors and all they had to do was cope with local requirements.[20]

With Davies' scheme, the characteristic use of straight lengths is seen as a product of the way in which a road is surveyed and planned by transects, whereas earlier scholars have tended to opt for a 'line of sight' explanation, but both are, to some extent, flawed. In the case of Davies', it is because of an over-technical reliance on planning and accuracy for which there is little supporting evidence; with 'line of sight', it has to be pointed out that for every course adjustment on a high point, there are a dozen that are not. If straight sections are a feature of planned roads, it is legitimate to ask why Wade's and Caulfeild's roads did not end up resembling Roman roads more closely (they often do, but not invariably). The missing element has to be the relationship to the pre-existing route, how it picked its way across the terrain (and most especially avoided obstacles which may, in the succeeding centuries, have vanished or changed) and, importantly, how it could be used to service the construction of its new, all-weather, straight-sectioned Roman successor.[21]

An alternative, and perhaps more practical, explanation has been advanced by Poulter. His examination of both roads and mural barriers (Hadrian's Wall and the Antonine Wall) in Britain has suggested that the Romans often did survey (and, presumably, mark out) their alignments from hill tops, but that they tended to place their survey points on the far side of a crest. This more often than not allows their direction of survey (but not necessarily construction) to be identified.[22]

The course of a Roman road thus derived from several factors:

1. overall heading would be provided by an existing route, almost certainly already in use by the army, and possibly even improved to some extent to prevent it deteriorating too much;
2. the local course would then be a product of the line taken by the prehistoric route across the terrain, the Roman road approximating it (perhaps paralleling it, repeatedly crossing it, or a combination of these), but executed in straight lengths;
3. particular topographical obstacles might cause slight adjustments in the line to avoid them, such as a dogleg to cross a watercourse or a zigzag to climb a hillside.

This still does not explain why straight lengths were used, and the answer here must be the same as it was for the mural barriers in northern Britain: it was easy for the army to accommodate. The Roman military surveyors could certainly cope with curves, both in terms of surveying and construction (each military base had at least four, one at each corner, and sometimes more in complex-shaped defences), but straight lines were fundamental to the army's way of setting anything out. It would always be quicker to mark out an angular turn than it would be to describe an arc, and speed must have been a major consideration in laying out the new network. Moreover, an arc has a tactical advantage over a right-angle in castrametation; in road construction, such a benefit was absent and it would be an unnecessary flourish.[23]

Accuracy would always be a problem, since measurement could be haphazard in the Roman world. Without the benefit of precision engineering, small errors could occur in the transmission of the formal standards kept at Rome (in the temple of Juno Monetalis) by the time they reached the provinces. This situation was further complicated by the use of regional forms of measurement in some provinces – the league in Gaul and the *pes Drusianus* in various parts of the west including, it has been argued, Britain – and finally compounded by what appears to have been a slapdash attitude amongst the bureaucracy to the enforcement of 'standards'. Thus, whilst a mile (*mille passus*) was always 1,000 paces, a pace (*passus*: technically two modern paces) was always five feet (*pedes*), the actual length of those feet was most definitely variable. The distance that is usually cited for a Roman mile is 1.48 km, but this can be found to range from 1.68 km to 1.89 km in Arabia (the last possibly due to a Roman surveying error!). In Britain, very few contiguous milestations survive, but in one or two places it is possible to reconstruct the original distances.[24]

On the Stanegate (Margary 85), the road that runs from Corbridge to Carlisle, three milestations survive near the fort at *Vindolanda*, two of these with in-situ (if truncated, in one case) standing milestones (Plate 4). Two more neighbouring milestations can be reconstructed and these seem to confirm a mile of about 1,550 m, implying a *pes* of 0.31 m – close to the *pes Drusianus* of 0.33 m. The next milestation to the east of Vindolanda – at Crindledykes Farm – includes a stone with the distance 'XIIII', presumed to refer to Corbridge which, even allowing for uncertainties over the exact course of the Stanegate to the east of the North Tyne, lies some 21 km to the east (and so close to a distance of 14 Roman miles, calculated on the basis of the *Vindolanda* mile of 1.55 km). A possible milestone was identified at Corbridge during the 1911 excavation there, the stone in question reported as being 2 ft 6 in (0.76 m) high and with a diameter of 1 ft (0.3 m), and two more milestones are known from the site, so it is possible that this is the point from which the XIIII was measured.[25]

On the Stainmore Pass (Margary 82), a group of three milestones at Spital in County Durham (so probably in situ at a milestation) were located 4.26 km from another stone at Old Spital to the west, equating to a distance of less than three Roman miles, which suggests the western stone has been moved, regardless of whether the *pes Monetalis* or the *pes Drusianus* was used. Sure enough, it was seen at a turnpike toll house in 1776 and may actually have come from slightly closer to Rey Cross camp. That camp derives its name from an early medieval cross erected within it. This was a marker stone, supposedly commemorating the site of the death of Eric Bloodaxe (the Norse king of Northumbria) or the boundary of the Diocese of Glasgow, originally located next to the southern side of the road on a small mound. Whilst there is no suggestion of a Roman origin for the stone, it is tempting to see it as set up close to a Roman milestation, from which the Old Spital milestone had been removed.[26]

More detail of British standards of mensuration can be gleaned from the *Antonine Itinerary* (see below, Chapter 3). This document gives distances between the various stations on each *iter* and thus allows us to compare the quoted with the known distance. If it is assumed that the distances in the document were measured by some means like the cart known as a hodometer mentioned by Vitruvius, which mechanically recorded distance travelled, then the error between the quoted and the known distances ought to be standard, at least within any given *iter*. In the past, scholars have assumed numerical discrepancies to be due to scribal errors in the manuscript tradition for the

Itinerary (very easy with Roman numerals), but that does rather assume a standard mile (5,000 *pedes* = 1,000 *passus* = 1.48 km) was widespread in Britain. It seems at least as plausible to consider the possibility that not all Roman miles within Britain were the same length: mistakes might easily have occurred when recording the details on milestones, or even when laying out the road in the first place. Scribal errors are therefore just one of several possible causes of error in the recorded distances. Indeed, the spacing of the post-medieval turnpike milestones along Stainmore around Rey Cross suggest a mile of *c.* 1650 yards being used in 1743, despite the fact that the statute mile had been declared at 1,760 yards in 1593, providing a curious coincidence with the possible Roman milestations and showing just how flexible a mile could be.[27]

Comparison of the *Antonine Itinerary* with the small surviving British portion of the *Tabula Peutingeriana* relating to the south coast provides some interesting detail (Table 1). This suggests, at the very least, that neither document is a copy of the other. Moreover, the tendency to underestimate distances appears to be present in both at some points, supporting the idea of some variability in the measurement of the mile.

Table 1. The Peutinger Table and the Antonine Itinerary compared

	Peutinger Table	*Antonine Itinerary*	*True distance*
Durovernum to Durolevum	7	12 (Iter II)	?
Durolevum to Durobrivae	7	13 (Iter II)	?
Durobrivae to Noviomagus	17	17 (Iter II)	17
[break]			
Caesaromagus to Canonium	12	12 (Iter IX)	13
Canonium to Camulodunum	8	9 (Iter IX)	10
Camulodunum to Ad Ansam	5	6 (Iter IX)	7
Ad Ansam to Combretovium	15	15 (Iter IX)	15
Combretovium to Sitomagus	15	22 (Iter IX)	23
Sitomagus to Venta	22	32 (Iter IX)	32

The *Antonine Itinerary* has even been used to argue for the utilization of a 'Celtic mile' of 1.665 km (as opposed to the usual 1.48 km), suggesting that this could explain the repeatedly shorter distances cited in the *Antonine Itinerary* than should have been the case if measured on the ground in standard Roman miles.[28]

Construction of all-weather roads

Varieties of construction types

Basic road construction in Roman Britain consisted of a number of components: foundations, surfacing materials, some form of drainage, and associated ancillary structures (like bridges) and roadside furniture such as milestones. The first stage in the actual construction of a road was to mark out the borders of the road by digging ditches and then stripping the topsoil. Statius, with a hint of poetic licence, describes this as the 'excavation of a trench'. Opinions of his description of the construction of a road vary. Elsewhere, marking-out stones have been noted, during the excavation of the Roman Ridge (Margary 28) near Aberford (W Yorks) and in examining a *vicus* road at Inveresk. These consisted of stones set vertically before the foundation was laid and which, once the road surface was added, were no longer visible.[29]

An important element in the construction of a good Roman road was always its foundations. This normally consisted of coarse rubble or boulders, but under special circumstances other techniques were employed. Across low-lying boggy land, for instance, a log corduroy might be laid upon which the upper layers of sand and gravel would, in effect, float. An example of such a road has been excavated crossing the flood plain of the River Idle near Bawtry (see below, page 36). In the eighteenth century, Highland military roads were successfully 'floated' across boggy areas in a similar way, using metalling placed upon brush and log corduroys.[30]

The Roman roads of Hollywood films with neatly paved surfaces are a standard visual cliché, drawing on familiar images such as the Via Appia south of Rome or the streets of Pompeii. Such roads were not common in the provinces, not least because the resources were harder to come across, but they also required more work to produce. In Britain, there are a few suggested examples of paved roads, as at Blackstone Edge near Manchester or Doctor's Gate, crossing from Brough-on-Noe to Melandra in the Peak District, but the identification of the surfaces (if not the courses) as Roman has been questioned. These had kerb stones and a central spine, with neatly-shaped setts like a nineteenth century cobbled street filling the space between, all enclosed within the customary ditches.[31]

By far the most common surface on a Roman road was one of compacted sand and gravel and such metalled roads are often found. The materials needed were easy to acquire (see below). In some areas, industrial waste was exploited to provide road metalling. In Sussex and the Forest of Dean, the debris from iron-making was used for this purpose and an example of a road surfaced in this way is still visible at Hoylte in Sussex.[32]

Regardless of the type of metalling employed, it was important that the road surface should have a camber on it to assist with run-off into the lateral ditches. Roads varied greatly in width and no 'standard' width seems to have been employed. The Stane Street was typically 6.45m wide, whilst Doctor's Gate was 1.45m wide within its kerbstones, just wide enough for one waggon (perhaps another reason to doubt that it was Roman). The standard axle width was 1.4m, a fact that is evident from wheel ruts in the gateways of Roman forts and was a product of the most convenient width for a vehicle drawn by two animals yoked side-by-side.[33]

The various types of surface were primarily designed to take military traffic – the feet of the soldiers, the hooves of their pack animals, and the wheels of their baggage trains, as well as the infrastructure of the commissariat – so wear would have been light by comparison with modern macadamized metalling and the volume of wheeled transport which that has to cope with. The greatest enemies of a Roman road were probably the weather (with frost damage a major problem) and the encroachment of vegetation (especially on seldom-used routes). Milestones make reference to repairs conducted under various emperors and it is likely that the repair and maintenance of stretches of highway were the responsibility of the nearest town council (see below).[34]

Many roads that are found now have lost their original surfaces and only the foundations survive – this is probably the case on Wheeldale Moor (Plate 5) and in the *vicus* outside the fort at Brough-on-Noe in Derbyshire (Plate 6). Whilst the date of Wade's Causeway on Wheeldale Moor has also been doubted, the road at Brough was undoubtedly Roman. The road leading out of the east gate of the fort at Inveresk was rebuilt (not just resurfaced) three times in the space of about twenty-five years, each time with a new foundation and new surfacing.[35]

Some roads have been found which do not conform to the model of fine surfacing material resting on coarse foundations. In these cases, metalling – often of fairly small pebbles – would be laid directly onto the existing subsoil (turf and topsoil having first been stripped away). Such a system would have the advantage of being very much faster to lay than a 'proper' road, less demanding in the amount of materials required, and adequate under most weather conditions. Examples have been noted at a number of places, notably Brough-on-Noe (Derbyshire) and Roecliffe (N Yorks) and it seems likely that this is a characteristic of early, conquest-period roads.[36]

Many Roman roads have their origins in major settlements like towns, but few actually pass through Roman military bases, it being far more normal for a site to be situated next to a road and a short branch road to lead to one or more of the gates. It is not hard to see why this should have been so: a large army marching along a road could have caused havoc by marching through the centre of a base, since it might take several hours to pass. Towns, on the other hand, would have been keen to attract visitors passing through. Corbridge is one of the notable exceptions to this, with the *via principalis* of the base forming the Stanegate once it left the western gate, which may well indicate that Corbridge was intended as the eastern terminus of the road (although it later extended further eastwards). Then, as Corbridge was developed from a fort into a town with a small military presence, things changed. Whilst Dere Street appears originally to have passed to the west of the *castra*, it was diverted across its old site and up the eastern side of the burgeoning town. At the same time, the Stanegate seems to have extended eastwards at least as far as the modern settlement.[37]

Once within settlements, roads very seldom had flanking open ditches but tended instead to use covered stone-lined drains and the Stanegate just to the west of Corbridge provides a perfect example of this (Figure 8).[38]

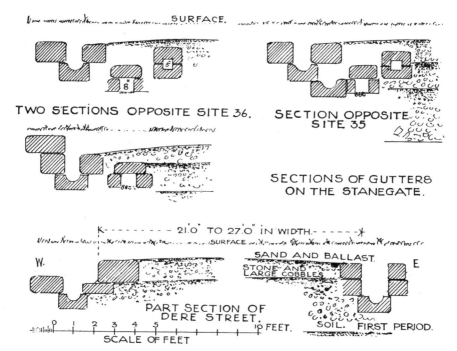

Figure 8: Sections through the Stanegate at Corbridge (from Forster and Knowles 1912).

The elements of a Roman road

The metalled surface

Crucial to the maintenance of a road was the prevention of standing water on its surface, and to avoid damage from running water. The first goal was achieved simply by the use of camber, shaping the profile of the road so that its centre was slightly higher than its edges. In most circumstances, water would then simply run off. Central stone spines – without a gutter – are also sometimes found, as at Wade's Causeway on the North Yorkshire moors or on the Via Nova Traiana in Arabia.[39]

The margins

Nearly all roads were accompanied by drains along either side, serving to carry away the run-off from the camber. These might range from simple ditches to formal stone gutters, and perhaps even covered drains, as at Corbridge, the latter types especially in the vicinity of settlements. Roadside ditches were not universal, however, possibly because some well-drained soil types rendered them unnecessary. Ponding of standing water next to a road (which might eventually cover it) was undesirable, so culverts were sometimes set into the structure of the road and these have been noted on Wade's Causeway. The road through the civil settlement outside the fort at Inveresk had no lateral drains, whilst that at Roecliffe did. However, the former was equipped with a culvert to carry water away and down the neighbouring hillside.[40]

Milestations

Roman roads were typically marked at intervals of a Roman mile (however that was defined) by inscribed mileposts or milestones, set up at what are nowadays termed milestations. These are important as they mark the surveyed distance from a point of origin on a road. The provenance of a milestone is of course no guarantee of the proximity of a milestation, however. Since most have quite plainly wandered away from their original locations, those that have been found may also have done so. There are in fact at least four in Britain that can lay claim to being in their original positions: two near Vindolanda fort in Northumberland, one at Temple Sowerby in Cumbria, and one near Stinsford to the east of Dorchester in Dorset. We can to some extent rank the reliability of milestation identification: the least reliable is obviously a re-used solitary milestone, which may have been carried an unknown (and probably unknowable) distance from its original location; next comes a recumbent single milestone, usually excavated during construction or agricultural processes; finally, the most reliable has to be a group of milestones from one location. Even in the last case, the possibility cannot be excluded that milestones have been collected for re-use in the post-Roman period. One of the most plausible milestations in Britain has to be Crindledykes on the Stanegate (Margary 85), just east of Vindolanda. A group of five complete and two fragmentary milestones was found during field-drain digging here in 1885 (Plate 7). What makes it particularly noteworthy is that it lies only one mile east of the milestone opposite the fort at Vindolanda, and two miles from the in-situ milestone at Smith's Shield.[41]

Milestones were usually (but not exclusively) cylindrical stone columns, often with square pedestals set into the ground. Fewer than 100 inscribed examples are known from Britain (Figure 9), but there must originally have been many more. Other provinces show how milestations could accumulate a succession of milestones (up to nine examples, at one milestation in Jordan), older ones simply being pushed over when a replacement was erected (Plate 8). At Gallows Hill, south of Carlisle, a stone with an inscription to the usurper Carausius was inverted and a dedication to Constantine placed on it, which suggests milestones were as much about display as they were about record and that it mattered whose name they bore. The seven Crindledykes milestone inscriptions have a date range from AD 222 to 337, although the Stanegate was originally probably built in the early second century AD. In a perfectly predictable world, this would equate to a mean of one milestone every seventeen or so years, so we might expect another eight milestones to await discovery at this site alone![42]

Unlike the milestones of more recent times, Roman ones probably existed primarily to mark out the mensuration and did not always include an actual distance to a neighbouring destination (unless, of course, they were added in paint and have since disappeared). We do not know precisely how they were used: perhaps a tally was maintained by travellers wishing to record the distance covered or, perhaps, the army may have used them to judge their speed when marching. Some did give useful distances, however. One such example comes from Derbyshire, where the distance of 11 Roman miles to *Navio* (the fort at Brough-on-Noe) is noted whilst a stone from the Crindledykes milestation with a distance of fourteen Roman miles ('MP XIIII', presumably measured from Corbridge) has already been mentioned. The honorific inscriptions upon them record the names of the emperors under whom the construction or repair work was carried out, and most British examples belong to the third century AD (Figure 10). In Britain these are all carved, but painted inscriptions have survived elsewhere (Plate 9), which leads to the suspicion that some 'uninscribed' milestones, such as the one still standing near the fort at Vindolanda (Plate 4), may originally have borne a painted record. Moreover, there is an inference that

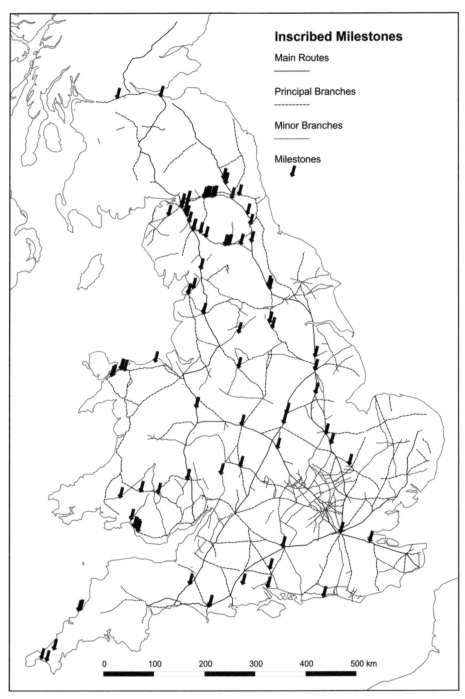

Figure 9: The distribution of inscribed Roman milestones in Britain (based on location data in *RIB* I and III).

Milestones

Diachronic distribution

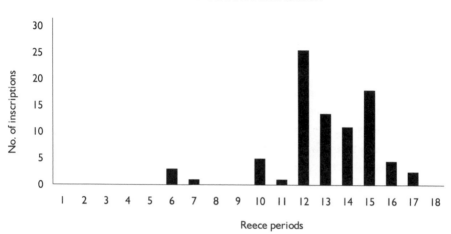

Figure 10: The dates of Romano–British milestones (Reece periods: 1: AD 1–41; 2: 41–54; 3: 54–68; 4: 68–96; 5: 96–117; 6: 117–38; 7: 138–61; 8: 161–80; 9: 180–92; 10: 193–222; 11: 222–38; 12: 238–60; 13: 260–75; 14: 275–96; 15: 296–317; 16: 317–30; 17: 330–48; 18: 348–64).

can be drawn that carved inscriptions need not be primary, for there is now no way of telling whether they had been placed on what was previously a painted milestone that may, in its turn, have borne more than one painted inscription.[43]

Thus the 100 or so inscribed milestones of Roman Britain probably present a highly biased picture of road construction and maintenance. Our dating for the milestones is, as we have seen, predominantly third century or later and may well be skewed. We can either assume from this that roads needed little maintenance from the time of their construction to the erection of the milestones or, as seems more likely, the practice of carving inscriptions on them only became popular in this period. This need not mean that they were not inscribed, since – as we have seen – they could have been painted.

Milestones were unlikely to travel far from their milestation after the Roman period, but manuports cannot be completely discounted. Since they were quite clearly an attractive resource for the acquisitive medieval builder, it is little wonder that most have now disappeared (Plate 10). Nevertheless, if every milestation was equipped with a milestone, then our 100 inscribed stones represent only 1.24 per cent of the original assemblage in Britain, based just on Margary's suggested road network of approximately 11,938 km (8,067 miles). That, of course, can only represent a proportion of the original Roman network.

If we then assume, on the evidence of Crindledykes Farm and milestations elsewhere in the empire, that more than one milestone may be expected at many British milestations, then that percentage will drop even further. At the very least, we may have to think in terms of upwards of 20,000 milestones throughout Roman Britain, in which case those 100 milestones form a mere 0.5 per cent.[44]

Junctions

As was mentioned above, the junction of Dere Street and Stanegate at Corbridge has been excavated and was shown to have been of one build. This is not surprising, since the northerly course of Dere Street appears to have been diverted to pass through the settlement along the Stanegate, once the fort had been demolished in the second century AD. Roman roads tended to meet at an angle, if not at a nodal point such as a settlement. In such cases, there might sometimes be a short cut allowing a traveller to 'jump' from one road to another without having to go all the way to the apex of the junction. For example, traffic heading south on the Dere Street (Margary 8) could cut across to the Stainmore Pass by using Margary 820 to avoid going all the way south to Scotch Corner before heading north-west again (see below, page 43).[45]

Wayside shrines are still a common sight in Catholic countries and this is a practice that has almost certainly been continued from antiquity. Few examples have been identified in Britain (probably because they lie away from settlements and thus tend not to be excavated). Crossroads were thought to have supernatural associations and were the traditional burial place for suicides.[46]

It was a requirement of Roman law that all cemeteries should lie outwith the boundaries of a settlement. Cemeteries usually began by lining the roads outside settlements and then spread as the settlements grew and time passed. Many funerary inscriptions even appeal to passers-by and travellers, showing that proximity to roads was thought important for the dead and the need to remember them. Excavation on Roman burial grounds around London has shown how early ones were later encroached upon by the spreading town. The unusual barrow cemeteries outside the forts at High Rochester and Great Chesters in Northumberland carry interesting echoes of an earlier time and remind the visitor of the many prehistoric barrows that can be found close to Roman (and presumably prehistoric) roads.[47]

Bridges, fords, and landscape engineering

Modern authors have an inexplicable fondness for fords as an explanation for how Roman roads crossed rivers. In reality, Roman roads usually crossed rivers and streams by means of bridges; fords seem to have been much less common than they were in the medieval period (see below). Bridges were always preferred for the eighteenth century Highland military roads, not least as the passage of artillery was an important consideration, although in some cases the roads predated the final stone bridges (perhaps implying earlier, timber, temporary ones). Common strategic sense would demand that any river, or even stream, that was impassable when in spate would need to have been bridged, for as soon as a river became unfordable, it would have blocked the lines of supply and negated the whole rationale behind engineering a system of all-weather roads. This would almost certainly have been unacceptable for the army. The Roman military certainly knew how to ford a river – Vegetius gives a vivid description of how the cavalry would be strung out across the river to catch any who were swept away – but this was in campaign situations during the summer months when rivers would be at their lowest, and there were simply not enough cavalry in Britain to screen every river crossing in this way. Fords must have existed, but they will logically have been the exception, rather than the rule, where an all-weather road was required.[48]

So far as it is possible to tell, the most common Roman bridges were probably built of timber, so it is not surprising that few are known. Natural decay and the ravages of even the smallest watercourse can soon remove most traces of such structures, but there are exceptional circumstances where the remains of timber bridges have been found or where indications of their former presence have been noted. Even stone-founded bridges could have a timber superstructure, as appears to have been the case with Trajan's Bridge across the Danube. The best known account of the construction of a timber bridge is that of Caesar describing the one he constructed over the Rhine. Trajan's Column attempts to depict bridges of various sizes in its reliefs, including pontoon bridges, although its accuracy on such matters is questionable. Coins of the emperor Septimius Severus suggest that a pontoon bridge was used at least once in Britain, possibly either to cross the Forth or the Tay during his Scottish campaigns, and they may well have made sense on some tidal crossings.[49]

Where timber bridges crossed a stream flowing over bedrock, sockets for upright timbers can sometimes still be seen, as at Alfoldean on the Stane Street (where there were also traces of wood preserved). Squared timber uprights were also identified at Rossington Bridge. The discovery of the remains of a timber bridge over the River Nene at Aldwincle (Northants) has provided further useful insights into Roman bridge-building in Britain, but undoubtedly the most important find to date has been that of the Roman bridge over the Thames at London.[50]

At Aldwincle, a revetted, rectangular timber abutment 5.5 m wide has survived together with three phases of timber uprights, the whole structure apparently reinforced by angled buttress struts. There were indications that spans of about 3.5 m were used to cross the river. To the east, the road surface survived to approximately 6.5 m between ditches 10.5 m apart. The bridge evidently collapsed three times (at the end of the first century and again in the later second or early third century, then finally at some subsequent date). Each time it fell down, it deposited the actual road surface into the river, causing the level of the river bed to rise slightly at that point.[51]

Archaeologists have long sought the Roman bridge across the Thames at London, and strong hints were found to its likely location, but in 1981 the first major indications of its exact location were found during excavations on the Roman quayside at Pudding Lane. A substantial structure 7 m wide was revealed, which (it was thought) might be one of the piers of the bridge. The squared timbers interlocked to form a near-square box and at the time of its construction it was free-standing within the water (although later engulfed by the development of the quayside). The bridge probably employed both piers and piles to cross the full width of the Thames, for it has been pointed out that piering would not have been practical in the deeper parts. Constructed in the first century AD (after AD 78 according to dendrochronological dating), it was abandoned during the second century AD, probably in favour of a new bridge on a different site. It has been noted that there must have been both an earlier and a later bridge nearby and this seems wholly reasonable.[52]

A timber causeway, probably leading to a bridge, has been excavated at Scaftworth, where the main road from Littleborough to Doncaster (Margary 28a) crossed the River Idle, negotiating the marshy floodplain by means of a road surface laid upon a timber corduroy fastened in place with vertical piles. The bridge over the River Idle at Rossington Bridge has been examined in situ a few kilometres further north on the same road.[53]

It was thought at one time that the remains of the timber bridge at Newcastle (*Pons Aelius*) on the River Tyne had been found, but that idea has since been disproved and the precise location of the Tyne bridge remains uncertain, although the fact of its existence is not doubted.[54]

As in so much Roman construction, both timber and stone were used for bridges, although the former seems to have been more common on most Roman roads in Britain. There is a fine series of stone bridges associated with Hadrian's Wall, two of which (Corbridge and Carlisle) carried important roads heading north (Margary 7 and 8), whilst others (Chesters and Willowford) carried both the Wall itself and the Military Way (Margary 86) across major rivers. There is some suggestion that these structures were – in part, at least – monumental in function, rather than just purely practical.[55]

References to stone bridges in Anglo-Saxon charters may in some cases refer to old Roman bridges. There is at least a possibility that some '-bridge' place-names owe their existence to a surviving Roman bridge and Corbridge (which, it is often argued, did not receive a medieval bridge until the thirteenth century) may be one example of this practise. However, further along the Stanegate, near Chesters fort, the settlement of Chollerford lay next to the Roman bridge that carried Hadrian's Wall across the North Tyne and that too had a medieval bridge so an Anglian bridge at Corbridge cannot be ruled out.[56]

The Romans did not just run their roads straight across the terrain but, where necessary, were quite willing to indulge in landscape modification. Where roads remain in use, such details are usually obscured or even obliterated, but the state of roads no longer in service can be more productive.

Roman roads often ran on an engineered embankment known as an *agger* and these are still to be seen in many places (Plate 11). They are not just restricted to low-lying or poorly-drained ground, as might be expected, and may have been due to the individual whim of the engineer responsible for any given stretch of road. It has even been suggested that insufficient excavation has been undertaken to be sure that some may not in fact represent an accumulation of successive surfaces, rather than one dump of material designed to raise the line of a road. Striking examples of an *agger* can be seen on Dere Street (now the A68), first as it heads south towards Corbridge (Plate 12), although part of it has been removed (possibly during the construction of the neighbouring turnpike road), and further north, at Ox Hills, where the modern road veers off the Roman course. A particularly impressive embankment survives at Roman Ridge, north of Castleford (West Yorkshire). The prominence of an *agger* may be one reason why later peoples showed a fondness for using Roman roads as boundaries.[57]

Roads that ran along the side of a hill would usually be terraced into it, which would involve cutting into the upslope side and depositing the spoil on the downslope side, thereby producing a platform for the road surface. At Haltwhistle Burn, the Stanegate is terraced into the hillside as it passes the fortlet, before continuing on the other side of the stream on an *agger* (Plate 13). Cuttings could also be used to cross a sudden break of slope, and may be found in approaching a river crossing. To illustrate the scale of some such operations, Trajan's cutting at Pesco Montano (Italy) sliced through 38m of rock, requiring the removal of 13,600 m^3 of stone.[58]

In mountainous areas, roads could be cut into the living rock, sometimes with 'tramlines' cut into the surface to help guide the wheels of vehicles. No examples are known in Britain as yet, but they are well-known in continental Europe – with examples at Bacharach in Germany and Langenbruck in Switzerland – and it is not impossible that some still remain to be found in Britain. Tight turns or hairpin bends were avoided by Roman roads except in such mountainous circumstances.[59]

So much for the 'nuts and bolts' of the road system. This has been covered by many writers before, but what is most significant about Roman roads tends to get overlooked: what can be deduced about their development and use and it is to this that we turn next.

Chapter 3

Development and Use

Even the Lines of Communication by Means of Military Roads, in some parts of the Highlands, have been productive of Benefit to the Country, though the Motives that gave rise to their Formation, having no Relation to Objects of Commerce or Industry, the Advantages derived from them are very imperfect and the Want of further Roads has been the greatest Obstacle to the Introduction of useful Industry. *Reports of Commissioners for Highland Roads and Bridges*[1]

Phasing the network

Most of the time, it is not easy to date a road archaeologically. The dating of Dere Street at Corbridge to *c* AD 85, for instance, is based upon the assumption that its construction coincided with that of the first Roman fort on the site. An earlier fort, at Beaufront Red House, slightly to the west, may mark the course of the original prehistoric route used by the army during the initial push north in the first century AD, which was then probably abandoned when the new road arrived. That is, however, a deduction based on limited evidence. To actually date a road archaeologically requires an understanding of the archaeological process, especially stratigraphy, and how an artefact found on a road surface provides a *terminus ante quem* (*TAQ*) for the construction (or repair) of that surface, and a *terminus post quem* (*TPQ*) for any surfaces above it, but sadly no guarantees of its contemporaneity with either act (how old are the coins in your pocket?). Moreover, as any excavator of Roman roads will tell you, finds are not exactly liberally scattered on their surfaces. Nevertheless, finds do occur occasionally and can be of assistance, but it would be a mistake to think that they are common.[2]

Although the major Roman roads of Britain are known by certain names of some antiquity (Figure 11), none of them date back to the Roman period. In most cases, these names seem to derive from the Anglo-Saxons. Dere Street (York–?Inveresk), for instance, is first recorded (as *Deorestrete*) in the early twelfth century *History of St Cuthbert*, describing the lands around the church at Gainford in County Durham. The name also occurs in various charters from

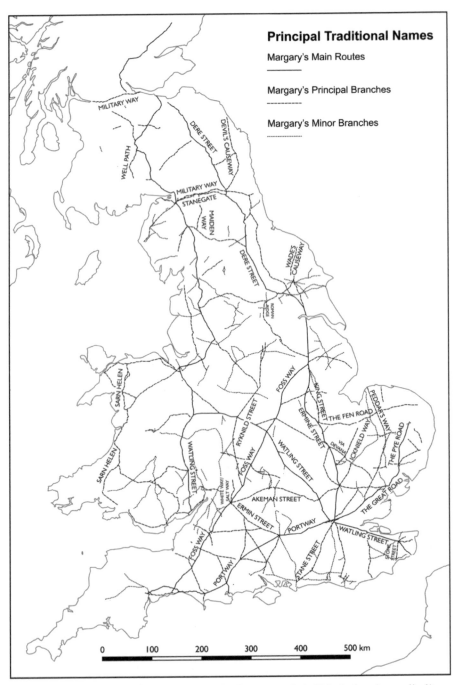

Figure 11: The principal traditional names for Roman roads in Britain (see Appendix 1).

the twelfth century onwards, notably in Scotland. Watling Street (London–Chester) is mentioned even earlier (as *Wæcelinga Stræt*), in the treaty between Alfred and Guthrun that establishes the boundaries of the Danelaw. Although only surviving as a fourteenth century copy, the treaty nevertheless dates back to 886–90.[3]

Whilst we do not know any of the Roman names for their British roads (the Via Julia between Bath and Bristol, Margary 54, was a very obvious antiquarian invention) – nor even if they actually had any – we can guess that any that did will have been named after the emperors associated with their initial construction (e.g. *via Claudia*, *via Flavia*). Thus in Arabia, the *Via Nova Traiana* and the *Strata Diocletiana* bear the names of their imperial progenitors. It is unlikely that roads of Britain will have been named after provincial governors as was the practice in Republican times, since this would be seen as offering dangerous competition to the ruling emperor: the British governor Sallustius Lucullus succeeded in offending Domitian simply by naming a new weapon after himself, so an eponymous road would seem to have been out of the question. Additionally, we may be justified in suspecting that, by the Late Roman period, most roads in Britain were known as *strata* (like the *Strata Diocletiana*), rather than *via*, if for no other reason than the word entered the Anglo-Saxon language as *streat*.[4]

Since most of the major roads in Britain probably had their origins in the military campaigns of the conquest period, it is not unreasonable to suggest that the various components of the network can be dated to the aftermath of the earliest military activity in each area (Figure 12). Moreover, it may be possible to attempt to deduce the various stages of the development of the road network in Britain. In this, we must assume that the surfaced Roman roads more-or-less followed the courses of their native predecessors but, as has been outlined above, we can take comfort from the fact that this is not an unreasonable assumption. To some extent, what we must be witnessing is the selection of key components of the existing network that best suited Roman military needs. Indeed, in one or two instances early forts are overlain by a later metalled road, as at Baylham House.[5]

First there would be routes derived from the main line of advance in a campaign. In this category we could include the roads from Richborough to London (Margary 1), London to Lincoln (Margary 2), London to Colchester (Margary 3), London to Wroxeter (Margary 1), and London to Exeter (Margary 4). Although these probably originated as pre-Roman routes, they would have been formalized as all-weather roads in the way outlined above. This first stage would have been military in origin.

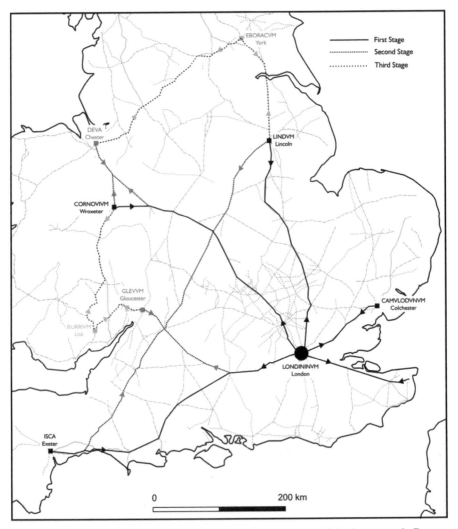

Figure 12: A hypothetical phasing of the principal components of the known early Roman road network in Britain.

Next, cross-routes would have been provided, linking the lines of advance. Their function would have been strategic, facilitating the lateral movement of men and supplies, linking bases along the main roads. Roads like the Fosse Way (Margary 5), that from Chester to York (Margary 7, 712), or the Stanegate (Margary 85) fall into this category. Again, pre-Roman routes would have been exploited and formalized, and this stage would also be set out by the military.

It is at the third stage that we start to see the interaction of the civilian sphere with the military. Civilian use of roads will probably have followed rapidly after the initial military construction and exploitation, as trade and social interaction led to the development (or, more likely, continuation and expansion) of movement around the province by the indigenous inhabitants and the many non-military occupants of (or visitors to) Britannia. This is a similar phenomenon to that commented upon by the Highland Commissioners in the quotation at the head of this chapter, for they were noting that whilst the eighteenth century roads of Wade and Caulfeild were military in purpose, they also had a commercial effect (and one which could have been greater). With regard to the Roman network, however, it will probably have been at this stage that elements of the existing (pre-Roman) network will have been tied into the formal military structure, perhaps not even as a deliberate or planned act.

The fourth and final stage will have been the natural and gradual evolution of the network, with some roads (both formal and informal) going out of use as needs changed, and new ones added where appropriate. Thus, it is a mistake to look at a map of the Roman roads of Britain and think of it as unchanging. All roads systems are dynamic, evolving to meet the developing needs of their users and any such map is inevitably a palimpsest.

Roads can to some extent be phased by their structural relationships, just as an archaeological site can be phased by its stratigraphy. What does this mean? Quite simply, a side road that joins a main road at an angle of ninety degrees almost certainly postdates the main road (otherwise there is no reason for it to exist). Elements of the system can therefore, to a limited extent, be identified as earlier or later than other components. In this way, the road from High Rochester to Learchild (Margary 88) provides a link between the Dere Street and the Devil's Causeway, but it is a road that cannot exist without the other two having first come into being. It is, of course, possible that it is a fossilized part of a much longer pre-Roman route that has been incorporated into the Roman system to meet a very specific need, but that must remain speculative.

Similarly, some roads appear to run counter to the natural development of the system from the south-east northwards. Margary 820 links the two early conquest routes of Dere Street (Margary 8) and the Stainmore Pass (Margary 82) by forming a short cut from Bowes to a point south of Binchester that would obviously facilitate traffic moving between the two, since it removes the need to travel south-east to Scotch Corner and then effectively double back on the other road, shortening the journey between Bowes and Binchester by some 20 km. Once again, however, this could easily be an earlier route which has been fossilized in the middle and lost either end. Thus Margary 8 is for north to south travel, Margary 82 for south-east to north-west movement, and Margary 820 is provided to facilitate travel from the north-east to the western side of the

Pennines, avoiding the need to go via the Stanegate. On the western side of the country, Margary 731 may well have provided the complementary link between Margary 82 and that other early conquest route, Margary 7, for those wishing to travel between the two without visiting their junction at Brougham (Figure 13).

Inevitably, tied in with the question of a road network in any province of the Roman Empire is the question of centuriation. This is the term used to refer to the regular (even rigid) division of land for settlers, frequently veterans in *coloniae*, marked out by a regular grid of roads in rural areas. Many attempts have been made to identify instances of centuriation within Britain, largely unsuccessfully. Examples have been suggested in the region of Colchester and Gloucester, *coloniae* that had been legionary bases. Margary suggested that a network of roads he had identified in Sussex might demonstrate it, although nowhere near an established *colonia* and, some would suggest, within a possible imperial estate that was devoted to industry rather than settlement. Genuine cases of centuriation are based upon a land unit of twenty *actus* in length (710 m) and cases are known in other provinces, such as Gaul, from both documentary evidence as cadastres, like those from Orange or Béziers, and from aerial

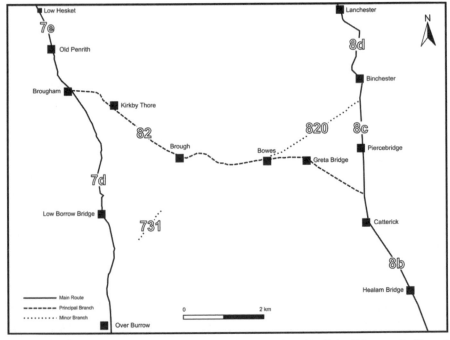

Figure 13: Main east- and west-coast routes with trans-Pennine links (Margary 8, 82, and 820 with routes 7 and 731).

photography. A cadastre is a document, usually surviving in the form of an inscription, recording the apportioning of land. No cadastral documents survive for Britain, but claims for evidence on the ground for centuriation continue to be made periodically. Amongst the most recent are assessments of the evidence from a number of suggested implementations in the landscape in the northern home counties of England (Hertfordshire, Middlesex, and Essex) and in the Weald. The existence (or lack of it) of centuriation in the British landscape is only really significant because, if it did occur, it has proved surprisingly difficult to trace, whereas continental examples are normally readily apparent. As such, it may be indicative of the complexity of landscape development in Britain, even in rural areas, rather than the genuine absence of centuriation.[6]

Who built, maintained, and used the roads?

By and large, roads were built by the army, maintained by civil authorities, and used by everybody. As such, their financing was partly hidden, insofar as the army's input – technical skills and manpower both for labour and the acquisition of the necessary raw materials – was its to dispose of as it saw fit. The Roman army were and are famed for using their troops in engineering tasks: this not only aided them in their preferred form of engineering warfare, but served to keep a vast standing army from becoming bored through idleness. Thus the 'costs' of road construction are largely irrelevant. A minor consideration might have been ownership rights over the land through which routes passed (Plate 1), but more recent parallels, such as the construction of railroads in America, suggest that, at one extreme, scant attention might be paid to the rights of indigenous inhabitants, whilst at the other they could be bought through more-or-less valuable deals.[7]

Maintenance required real money, however. Town councils in Roman Britain operated by making officials increasingly personally responsible for the debts of a council. Taxes would need to be raised, a portion of which would have to have been allotted to the upkeep of roads in the region for which they were responsible. In many of the frontier regions, where there were no local town authorities, maintenance must effectively have been the responsibility of the army.[8]

Whilst it was normal practice just to resurface roads that had become worn out, at Inveresk the road through the civil settlement was also given new foundations at the same time, resulting in three successive roads built on top of each other within approximately twenty-five years (c. AD 140–c. 165) when the nearby fort was occupied. Most of the surviving inscribed milestones from

Britain record repairs to roads, rather than their actual construction, and the majority of them date to the third century AD or later (Figure 10).[9]

Although wear and tear from use will have taken a toll on road surfaces, the example of the military roads of the Highlands suggests that the climate will have had a much more significant effect. Ironically, therefore, lack of use may have been more detrimental than frequent use, as weathering and the encroachment of vegetation slowly tore a road to pieces. The sort of rutting and flooding reported from Roman roads still in use in the medieval and later periods was a result of long-term use; roads constructed at the same time but no longer used will have long since vanished.[10]

One of the functions of a state road network was to provide remount and accommodation facilities for officials or those travelling with their approval. This system was known as the *cursus publicus* and, amongst other things, made it possible for couriers to travel overland as rapidly as possible, given the contemporary constraints on speed. The remount system was based around *stationes* and *mansiones*, examples of the latter being identified, although not proven, from a number of sites. These would typically be large buildings with a number of rooms for accommodation, a bath suite, and stables and other outbuildings. Important travellers would almost certainly be put up as the guests of local officials or army unit commanders, so it would be the many minor bureaucrats who would have been found at *mansiones*. Examples of these structures in Britain have been suggested at a number of sites, such as Chelmsford, Vindolanda, Corbridge, and Catterick, although it has to be said that most are *deduced* as being *mansiones* and lack any intrinsic, indisputable evidence of their function. Many of these were courtyard structures with associated bath buildings (Figure 14). Often set towards the edge of settlements, they would usually be placed near the roads they are thought to have serviced.[11]

Although Roman roads were probably not built for anything other than military use, that did not mean they were not exploited by civilians for the purposes of travel and trade. Of course, long distance travel and heavy haulage were often much easier and cheaper by sea or, in some cases, by river craft, but there could be no escaping the fact that for short distance travel and trade, the roads could not be surpassed. Study has shown how the distribution of pottery over a region can be linked to the road network, whilst shipments of pottery over long distances (such as 'army contracts' for particular wares, such as black-burnished or, more obviously, samian, pottery) would depend upon sea transport. The comparison of costs of land and sea transport from the limited available evidence shows why this should have been so.[12]

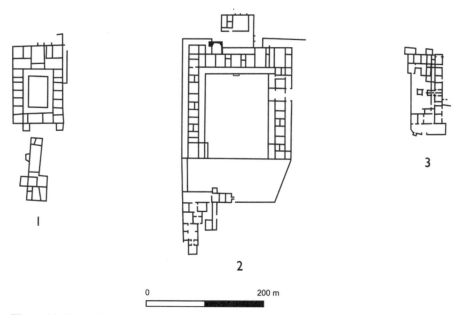

Figure 14: Examples of *mansiones*. 1: Godmanchester; 2: Silchester; 3: Caerwent.

Evidence from better-documented provinces, such as the Palmyrene Tax Law from Syria, shows how taxes and tolls were imposed on the movement of goods into and out of the province and for these reasons customs posts were set up near borders, usually manned by troops outposted from units. There would also have been 'police' posts manned by *beneficiarii*, responsible for keeping a watchful eye on movement along the road system. It must be remembered that brigandage and petty pilfering would have been endemic within the empire, particularly on those parts of the network remote from major troop concentrations or civilising influences such as towns.[13]

In literate societies, road systems invariably end up being mapped. A large map of the road system in the Roman Empire, now known as the *Tabula Peutingeriana* (or Peutinger's Table) records the major roads and waystations throughout the empire, complete with distances between places. Unfortunately, only a small part of the British road system survives, mainly that from south-east England and East Anglia. The document survived only as a medieval copy in the monastery at Worms in Germany and was given to Konrad Peutinger of Augsburg in 1508, hence its name.[14]

Although the *Tabula Peutingeriana* is the only surviving graphical representation of the road network in Roman Britain, another document is arguably of greater importance, and that is the so-called Antonine Itinerary

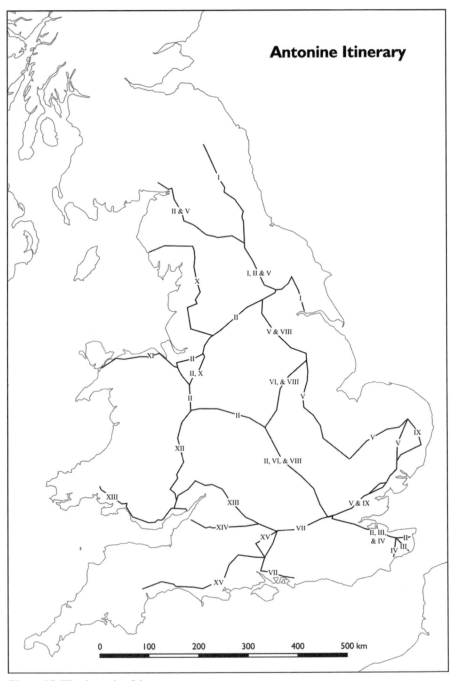

Figure 15: The Antonine Itinerary.

(*Itinerarium Provinciarium Antonini Augusti*). Navigation by map was probably rare, given the cumbersome (and presumably expensive) nature of Roman cartography, but itineraries – simple lists of places with distances between them, equivalent to the sort of information modern motoring organisations (or even Google) provide for drivers – may have been more widespread. Although purely textual in form, the Antonine Itinerary also covers the whole empire and provides a series of *itineraria* (routes), fifteen of which relate to the road system in Britain. Recording place-names and distances between them, they appear to be a record of a series of journeys, rather than any sort of recommendation of approved routes to take, and in this they resemble the medieval royal itineraries (see below page 110). Iter II, for example, from *Blatobulgium* (Birrens) to *Ritupiae* (Richborough) crosses the country three times unnecessarily (Birrens across the Pennines to York, back across to Chester, down to Wroxeter, then across once more to London and thence Dover). It would have made much more sense to either cross to York and proceed southwards down the east coast, or head southwards on the west coast and only cross upon reaching Wroxeter. The suspicion that this is not just a list of routes is heightened by comparing Iter V with Iter VI and Iter VIII. All three go from London to Lincoln (V continuing on to Carlisle and VIII to York), but take very different and, in the case of V, indirect routes (Figure 15).[15]

Some clue to the date of the Antonine Itinerary can be gleaned from the places mentioned, only two of which are not south of Hadrian's Wall, whilst the title of the document itself is suggestive of a connection with one of the Antonine emperors (the first being Antoninus Pius, who came to power in AD 138). At least one scholar has argued for an association with Caracalla (or Marcus Aurelius Antoninus, to give him his formal name) and Septimius Severus, whilst others have pointed out that inconsistencies in the text may indicate that the routes have been accumulated over time.[16]

Strategic function

Even a cursory glance at a map of Roman Britain shows a scattering of forts, fortlets, and signal stations. The problem with an undifferentiated distribution lies in the fact that not all sites were occupied at once and that the sites demonstrate both a broad and a specific phasing. The two principal concentrations of post-Hadrianic sites lie in Wales and in the north of Britain. Earlier sites tend to lie in the Midlands and the south of England, for fairly obvious reasons (the Romans invaded the south and progressed northwards: the narrative of this progress may be disputed in fine detail but never in doubt in its overall scheme). The forts are linked by roads. Indeed they often occur at nodal points in the road network, which is only what would be expected if a logistical, rather than strictly strategical, interpretation were to be placed upon their distribution.

Perhaps the mistake scholars have made is always to think in terms of frontiers rather than networks. The distribution of the Roman army along certain elements of the road system in Britain was certainly a strategic placement in the sense that it was a logistical necessity – an army cannot be concentrated in one place for too long without straining its supplies – but by spreading it out in a network of strong points, it could also guarantee the security of its own supply chain. Thus it could be that these sites are as much inward- as outward-looking.

One writer at least noticed the illogicality of the frontier mode of thought when looking at fort networks in the East of the Empire. This was Edward N. Luttwak, a modern strategist and historian, who went on to formulate the theory of Defence in Depth when looking at that eastern Roman distribution of sites. In this, he suggested that the network of forts seen in provinces such as Syria was a response to the inadequacies of the peripheral frontier way of thinking and that by spreading troops into what was effectively a buffer zone, an invading enemy would be worn down, prone to attack from a number of sides, rather than free to roam in the hinterland once they had penetrated the hardened outer 'casing' of the frontier. His ideas attracted a considerable following at first (in what might be termed the 'Invasion and Response' phase of Romano-British studies), but fell into disfavour as a more critical eye was cast over his interpretation of the available evidence. Luttwak's chief shortcoming (if such it be) was that he had viewed the ancient world with a modern eye. It must be understood that this was not necessarily a bad thing and that his rethinking of the situation was a refreshing breeze through the more cobwebby areas of Roman frontier studies. Nevertheless, it can be argued that he saw a genuine phenomenon but misinterpreted it from a modern perspective, influenced perhaps by the contemporary strategic situation pertaining in Western Europe.[17]

Frontier systems exhibit an intimate relationship with roads and not just because one usually accompanies the other. In order to understand the distribution of forts (and fortlets) along roads, it is illuminating first to examine a rather famous frontier. Romanists have long railed against interpreting Hadrian's Wall as being defensive in nature, stating that it was never designed to be a fighting platform (despite the resolute silence of Roman authors on this fact; many seem quite happy with the concept of wall-top defence in other contexts). Luttwak could not help but take a strategic view of it and similar frontier works as 'base lines for mobile striking forces, which operated against large-scale attacks in a tactically offensive manner'. Another modern writer, David Divine, former defence correspondent with *The Sunday Times*, went so far as to draw up a theoretical plan for how Roman forces could be concentrated in the field to the north of the mural barrier, so great was the Roman abhorrence of wall-top defence thought to be. This was the doctrine of open field conflict writ large: Hadrian's Wall would never be defended by soldiers on top of it, but rather had to be managed by units in the field in front of it. The difficulty with such a model is the absence of the command and control element in the Roman world. Whilst radar made it possible for the Royal Air Force to defend Britain against the Luftwaffe by having advance intelligence of their approach, as well as an idea of their strength, the best historians could manage for Hadrian's Wall was that the outpost forts (Birrens, Bewcastle, Netherby, Risingham, and High Rochester) might have been designed to gather intelligence and give similar advanced warning of enemy incursions. Units of scouts (*exploratores*) are attested from the last three of those sites. They of course lacked the facility to convey sufficiently detailed information quickly enough: signalling with smoke or fire could certainly communicate the fact that there was an incursion taking place, but little in terms of the necessary detail needed to decide how big a force should be deployed to deal with it. Nowadays those advanced forts are thought more likely to have served to protect friendly local populations.[18]

If Hadrian's Wall was not a defence against invading armies, what was it? Over the past few years, archaeological work has shown how important the tactical component of the Wall was, with an increasing number of instances of berm obstacles being identified, mainly in the east so far. This, taken with the adjustments made to the system as it was built – milecastles adjusted from their hypothetical measured positions, additional towers included to cover blind spots, the careful use of terrain (notably the use of re-entrants and short stretches of ditch to cover gaps in the crags) to enhance the defensive qualities of the Wall, mean it is increasingly possible to view the Wall as a tactical, as well as, or even instead of, a strategic system. So what were all those forts doing along the Wall? There has been little serious questioning amongst writers that they provided the garrison for the eighty-one milecastles and upwards of 162 turrets it contained. Even if each milecastle contained only, say, twenty-four men on detachment (and assuming no permanent detachments within the turrets), a figure that fits within the estimates of between eight and thirty-two men for each milecastle, that would still have been a permanent drain of nearly 2,000 men from the theoretical maximum of 10,000 that those Wall forts could muster. How, then, a pre-emptive defensive system of the sort Divine envisaged was supposed to work is open to question. It is much less complicated to see the forts as the logistical hubs for the garrison of the Wall, facilitating the supply of men for its operation, and linked by a road (the Military Way) which ran from one end to the other.[19]

Such a view of Hadrian's Wall helps explain why the Stanegate 'system' continued to operate in tandem with it and why the Stanegate forts could never have fulfilled what has been suggested as the original scheme for the Wall. Scholars have little doubt that the Wall as designed allowed only for the linear components (ditch and curtain wall), with milecastles every Roman mile and two equally spaced turrets between each of them. Troops would be supplied by the Stanegate forts, it is thought, but that the shortcomings of that proposal were soon evident, given the distance of some Stanegate forts from the line of the Wall and the additional time that would need to be taken to address an emergency such as an assault upon it. However, another interpretation might be that the Stanegate forts, designed to service the road and protect the movement of convoys along it, could not provide the additional capacity also to man the Wall. The Vindolanda Tablets provide penetrating insights into the operation of one of these pre-Hadrianic Stanegate forts, and a surviving *pridianum*, a document summarizing unit strength at a given point in time, makes it clear that the *cohors I Tungrorum*, whilst having a paper strength of 752 men, could only actually count on 265 fit for duty within its walls, since so many were either outposted or sick. The additional impact of having to provide more troops to man the new frontier can only be imagined. Hence the so-called 'forts decision' can be seen as a pragmatic recognition that road forts could not be expected to undertake additional tasks and that dedicated forts were needed for the Wall to act as resource centres for its operation.[20]

So, given the possible tactical nature of Hadrian's Wall, keeping low-intensity threats to the northern inhabitants of Roman Britain at bay, why were forts needed to protect convoys to the south of it? The answer must lie in the fact that the two systems were dealing with different problems: one looking outwards, the other inwards. Brigandage was endemic in the Roman world but increased to epidemic proportions during the instabilities of the third century AD, with large numbers of individuals, including renegade soldiers, dropping out. It was clearly never envisaged that supply trains would be safe to move about without the protection offered by the army in its fortified strong points and also, presumably, by virtue of its patrolling the fortified roads. Naturally, if towns were included amongst the strong points, this would hold true of the whole province, not just the 'military zones' defined by the distribution of forts. Effectively, the whole of Britain was a military zone so the problem (the lack of security for supply convoys) was a universal one.[21]

So it is that Luttwak's identification of the importance of fort-and-road networks should not be dismissed, but for different reasons from those proposed by him. He saw their distribution as strategic in the defensive sense, but it is equally feasible to view them in a logistical light. Moreover, these networks are not, as he thought, a feature of just the High or Later Empire, but can certainly be seen operating in Britain from the very beginning of the conquest. Early forts have now been identified at many sites in Britain to the south and east of the later military zones of the North and Wales. Some lie beneath later towns and have been identified from structural or, less certainly, from artefactual evidence. Others remain on what are still greenfield sites, rendered redundant by the advance of the army north and westwards. A series of sites along the Trent valley – Broxtowe, Osmanthorpe, Newton on Trent, and Marton – would seem to demonstrate this as a series but there are other isolated examples which must reflect changes in the perceived strategic requirements of the road network. Thus the overall network of forts that can be plotted from the map of Roman Britain (Figure 16) is inevitably a palimpsest of networks, stretching from the earliest Roman occupation right through to the latest forts, such as the Saxon Shore system. We can crudely phase it into pre-Flavian (Figure 17), pre-Hadrianic (Figure 18), and Hadrianic and Antonine (Figure 19) in order to see just how the networks change with time (it can, and has, been phased more finely many times). Once towns are factored in (Figure 20), it becomes clear that an evolving system can be made out, but it seems likely that this is only a crude approximation of the realities of the situation, since we may suspect a military presence at smaller sites like villas, wayside stations, and *beneficiarius* posts too. A case can therefore be made that Roman Britain was thoroughly militarized.[22]

One reason for this militarization, often overlooked, is the absence of a police force to provide civil security. Although we know the city of Rome had the *vigiles*, a watch force that combined policing and fire-fighting in its duties, and there is even a *numerus vigilum* attested from Britain, it has to be doubted whether these operated countrywide, rather than on just a per-settlement basis. Security in all its manifestations had to be provided by the army (and the *beneficiarii* were of course outposted soldiers). Modern armies tend to be uncomfortable with policing roles but there were no such scruples in the Roman world. The military were integrated into the justice system (military officials passed judgement in civilian spheres, military officials such as the regionary centurions had a role to play in provincial judicial administration) and thus their role in security was as much to deal with the enemy within as with the invading barbarian.[23]

Throughout it has been stressed that most major roads in Britain were used by the army, but it is worth asking how a campaigning army actually exploited

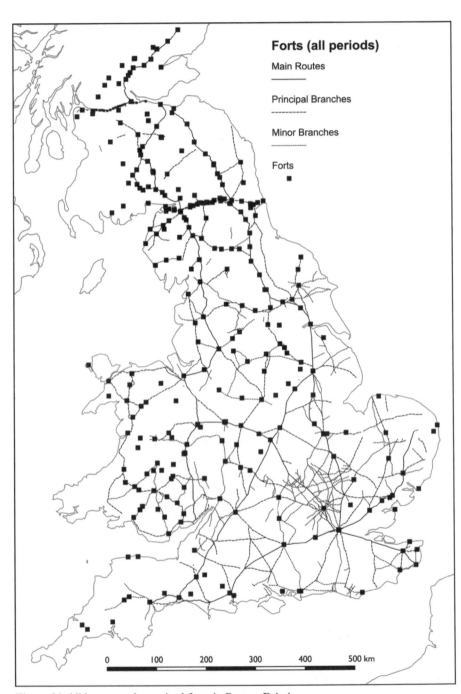

Figure 16: All known and surmised forts in Roman Britain.

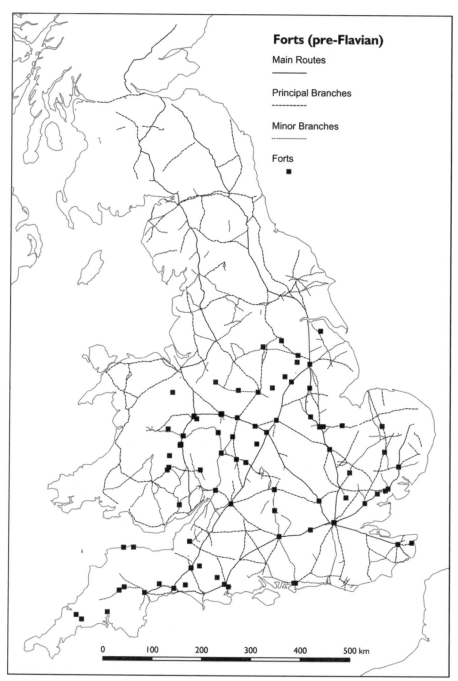

Figure 17: Pre-Flavian forts in Roman Britain. It is likely that more remain to be found.

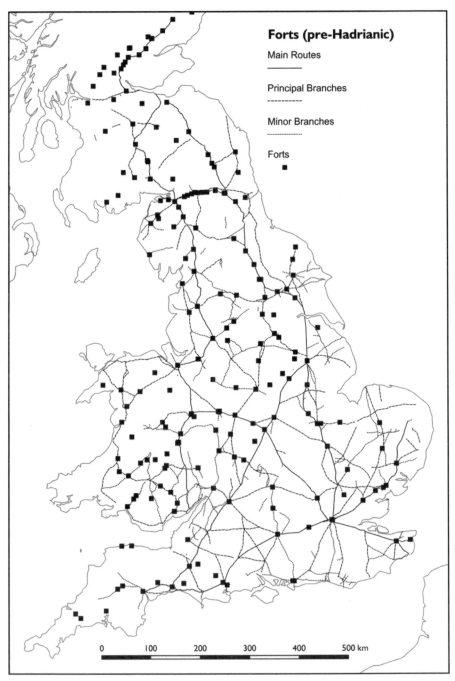

Figure 18: Pre–Hadrianic forts in Roman Britain.

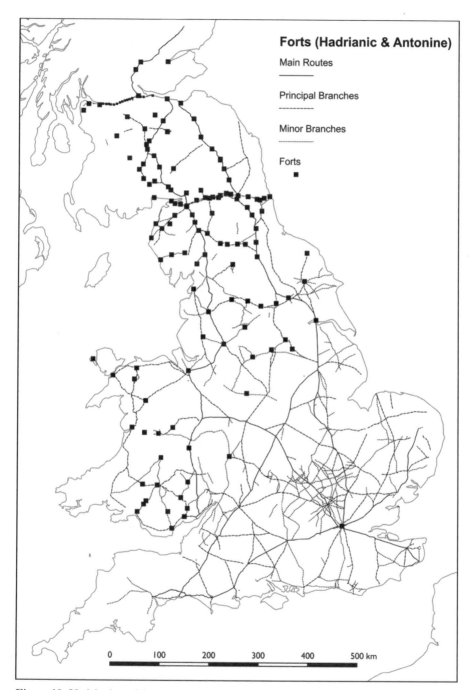

Figure 19: Hadrianic and Antonine forts in Roman Britain.

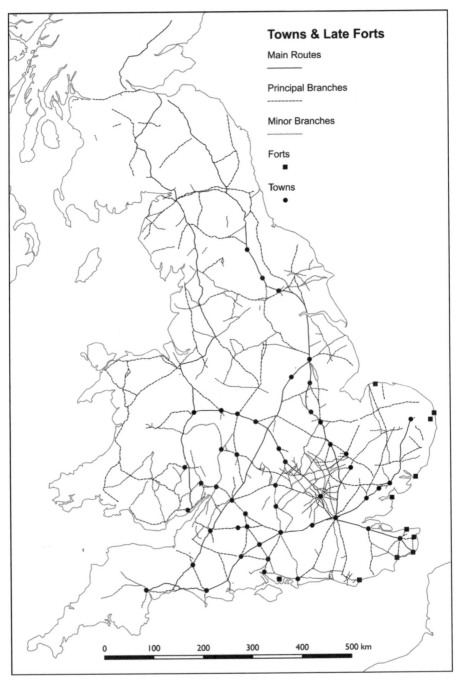

Figure 20: Towns (and later forts) in Roman Britain.

a road. It is clear from contemporary accounts of army movements that no attempt was made to fit all the personnel and baggage onto the metalled surface. Roman cavalry were unshod so almost certainly did not use metalled roads. This meant that a marching army would have had its infantry and baggage train moving along the surfaced road, but its cavalry (and perhaps a screen of infantry scouts) operating to either side of it, so a proper military road was in fact not just the surfaced area, but also the cleared zone on either side of it. Accounts of Roman armies on the march confirm that this was often the case.[24]

On a more mundane and everyday level, the army had to move supplies between its bases, and collect taxes delivered in kind (Tacitus mentions an abuse of the system whereby farmers might be made to transport goods long distances for this purpose), but probably also used roads for the shipment of bullion to fund their activities and coin to pay soldiers.[25]

Vegetius provides an important insight into the way the system operated, recording that troops had to be placed in fortified locations, either towns or forts, in order to safeguard the movement of supply convoys:

> Amongst those things the commander will provide, whether based in camp or in a city, are grazing for the animals, transport of grain and other things, water collection, wood gathering, and foraging, made safe from attack by the enemy. Because otherwise it is not possible for our supply convoys to pass back and forth, if garrisons are not distributed at certain points, whether these should be cities or walled forts. For, if not already fortified, forts are quickly set up in suitable places, surrounded with large ditches (forts are named from the diminutive term for camp). Living in these, moderate numbers of outposted infantry and cavalry keep the route safe for convoys. For an enemy only dares to approach such places with difficulty, where his adversary provides support in front and to the rear to delay him.[26]

This is something of a chicken-and-egg situation. However, as such posts would themselves need supplies, so the very fact of establishing the network would have ensured its continuation. Inevitably, it is easier to supply a distributed army than a concentrated one and it can be argued that the 'network' of Roman military bases throughout Britain (and, indeed, other provinces) is as much a product of supply requirements as it was defensive or offensive. It is at this point that scholars start to think in terms of frontiers or frontier zones, and fortified roads such as the Stanegate come to be discussed in terms of a frontier system without any clear evidence that the Romans themselves viewed them in these terms.[27]

Moreover, that passage in Vegetius – usually at least partially dismissed as a late epitomist – bears closer scrutiny. Careful analysis of the text, combined with Vegetius' own cursory list of his sources, allowed Dankfrid Schenk to suggest that it comes from a section of the work thought to be derived from the lost *De Re Militari* of Sex. Iulius Frontinus, formerly the governor of Britain (or, more accurately, as *legatus Augusti pro praetore*, the commander of the army in Britain) during the first century AD. Comparison of Frontinus' text in his surviving *Strategemata* (originally an appendix to the *De Re Militari*) revealed telling stylistic similarities. Frontinus' credentials as both a tactical and strategic writer are therefore of the highest quality and lend weight to Vegetius' words.[28]

Not only does this passage tell us what forts were for – protecting convoys – but it also reveals that they must be seen in the context of garrisoned cities. Analysis of the finds from the towns of Roman Britain has revealed a consistent pattern of items of military equipment from the second and third centuries AD. Now, whilst there are several possible explanations for the presence of such artefacts at sites, the combination of the distribution of towns and forts in Britain from the second century onwards would appear to support Vegetius' (or Frontinus') claim (Figure 21). Earlier writers thought in terms of a 'military zone' in Britain, in simple terms seen as the North of Britain and Wales, but it may well be that this was a misunderstanding of reality: the whole of Roman Britain was 'militarized'.[29]

By comparison, it is interesting to note how the Bozeman Trail in the American Mid-West, linking the Oregon Trail with the towns of Bozeman and Virginia City, was watched over by a series of forts – C.F. Smith, Reno, and Phil Kearney – all dismantled when the treaty of Fort Laramie was signed (Figure 22). The Myos Hormos road in Egypt provides a documented Roman example of a militarily protected route elsewhere in the Empire, with fortlets and towers protecting both army interests and those of civilian trade along it from tribal attacks.[30]

The picture we gain of Roman Britain, therefore, is one of a province that lives with an element of insecurity (perhaps crime would be a better term to use), the effect of which is ameliorated by the presence of the army at crucial points along key routes. The statement recorded by Vegetius makes it likely that these routes were the ones in which the army had a direct interest, since they comprised at least a part of their lines of supply (allowing for the fact that transport by sea must have been an important component in the overall resupply picture).

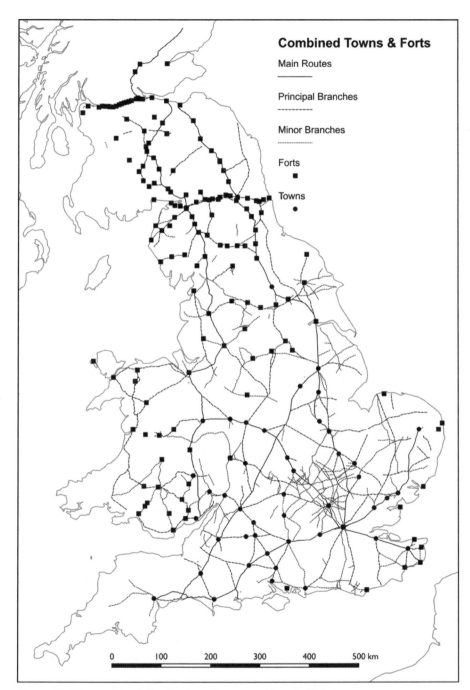

Figure 21: The combined distribution of towns and forts in Britain.

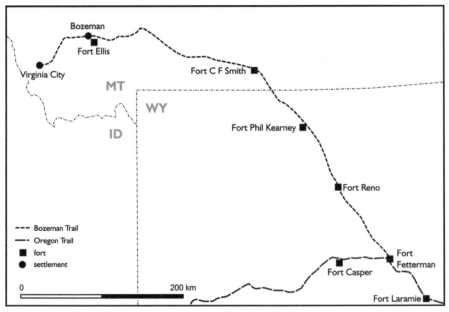

Figure 22: The Bozeman Trail and its forts (after Waldman 2009).

So what was being moved in these convoys? During the civil war of AD 69, Tacitus relates how rebellious troops intercepted a convoy carrying money to pay some allied troops. This tale reflects upon what must have been a regular occurrence, the shipment and escorting of pay for the army, which most units would have had to have received by road. Wherever possible, they would probably have exploited water transport, but it was inevitable that the road system had to be used at least part of the time. An impression of the extent of its usage may come from the distribution of lead 'pigs' around Britain, since they are almost invariably found next to roads (Figure 23). These were the product of the silver- (and lead-) producing mines, which were of course directly controlled by the government. Mines under state control within Britain were producing a range of important raw materials, but few are more prominent in the archaeological record than the silver/lead mines (a state-controlled monopoly). Pigs of lead, often with their silver content already removed, were taken to coastal ports, possibly for shipment abroad. These cast (and often inscribed) pigs were so heavy that a Roman waggon could probably only take two at a time. A number of these ingots have been found, sometimes leading to suggestions of skulduggery on the part of some of those involved in the production or shipping of the lead.[31]

What cannot now be judged is the extent to which the precautions suggested by the fort network were actually needed: could the perception of threat have

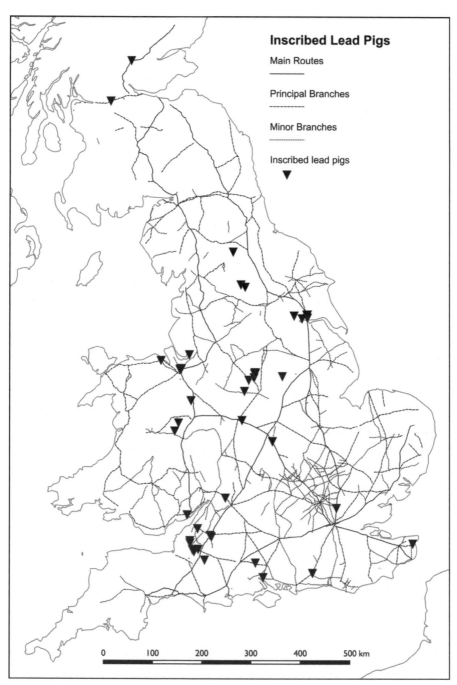

Figure 23: The distribution of lead pigs (based on location data in *RIB* I and III).

been greater than the reality? One possible insight into this problem can be gained by that same distribution of lead ingots, or pigs, around Britain (Figure 23). Surviving pigs carry official stamps moulded into their tops that clearly identify them for what they are. Nevertheless, a proportion of these were 'lost' during transport. Given the size and weight of each one, accidental loss is scarcely plausible in all instances as an interpretation for their presence in the archaeological record, particularly since the government will have had a direct interest in (and almost certainly a record of) their existence and movements. Some have come from sites next to water (as with two bars from Bitterne), perhaps as a result of sunken ships, whilst others come from mine sites (like Charterhouse), but a significant number have been found near roads, but far from either a likely source or a probable destination. It is at least possible, therefore, that the surviving items are the result of successful raids on convoys which were not subsequently retrieved by the villains concerned. As with coin hoards, what is unknowable with caches of pigs is how many were retrieved and thus do not survive for us to find; we can only suppose that it was a greater number than those actually recovered.[32]

Lead pigs also raise an interesting point about the manner of freight transport on roads. One lead pig weighed in the region of 60–70 kg. Whilst that is within the capabilities of a mule, it would be difficult to pack as a balanced load. Two pigs, however, is beyond the capacity of most mules, so balancing a load with two pigs would be out of the question. This might seem to suggest that wheeled transport was necessary to move lead pigs, but we cannot rule out the possibility that some form of secure pack harness was used to hold one pig in place in the centre of the animal's back (although it would entail an alarmingly high centre of gravity for the load).[33]

The Vindolanda writing tablets provide further evidence on the operation of Roman military supply. One Octavius, writing to Candidus (at Vindolanda), bemoans the fact that a shipment of hides from Cataractonium (Catterick) has been delayed 'because the roads are bad' (*dum viae malae sunt*) and he does not want to injure his draught animals (*iumenta*). He evidently has a financial interest in this material, although the status of the two is unclear. Major supply shipments must also be seen in the context of the personalized trickle of items moving around the Empire, often accompanying travelling soldiers. Letters home asking for socks or pieces of equipment are known from Egypt and Britain, and this trade was evidently inter-provincial and was all presumably at the very least assisted by the *cursus publicus*, the official posting system.[34]

Just as Roman roads facilitated the movement of the army, both on a large and small scale, and helped it supply itself, they would also have had an important symbolic function (whether intentionally or not is open to debate). Comparison of an all-weather, metalled post-conquest road with its native predecessor must have been a powerful indicator of how much things had changed since the arrival of Rome. As for the native British attitude to the roads, there are certainly stories of Highland Scots refusing to use the eighteenth century military roads, even to the extent of avoiding setting foot on them and wading streams next to new bridges. Nevertheless, since much of the Roman system appears to have re-used native predecessors, if similar obstinate token displays were undertaken, it must be wondered to what degree they were followed by any more than a small minority of the population, given the eventual longevity of the roads. Similarly, as was noted by the Commissioners for Highland Roads and Bridges (above), the unintentional effect of an enhanced road network on civilian trade may have been considerable too. There are, nevertheless, theoreticians who see Roman all-weather roads as a manifestation of Roman imperialist ambitions and decry pragmatic interpretations of the network, and there may even be a kernel of truth to that assertion, but it ignores the link with the pre-Roman system outlined above and inevitably underestimates and downplays the capabilities and intentions of the native Britons.[35]

The road system of Roman Britain was by no means perfect. As has been pointed out by a number of authors, some sections may have been impassable to draught animals due to impracticable gradients (see below, page 105). Moreover, even though Britain presented fewer challenges than many of the continental provinces, extreme weather conditions would have rendered many sections of road useless at times. North of the River Tees, Dere Street (Margary 8) enters the Pennine foothills and even today, its modern successor (the A68) is often blocked by snow when coastal roads (such as the A1) experience no such difficulties.

Such problems were vividly highlighted by the discovery of the *dum viae malae sunt* letter from Octavius about that cargo of hides from Cataractonium. Such a load would, of course, have been required to come up Dere Street (Margary 8) to Corbridge and then along the Stanegate (Margary 85a) to Vindolanda, a total distance of around sixty-six Roman miles (98 km). Interestingly, Octavius' letter contradicts some writers who have seen all freight transport as having used waterways and confirms the views of those who see evidence for the use of a more balanced mix.[36]

Available transport and its limitations

The range of modes of transport available to users of the Roman road system in Britain was fairly limited. They could ride, walk, or be pulled and those options more or less reflect the range of speeds, from fastest to slowest.

Riding on horseback would have been the preferred means for government couriers, supported by the remount system at way stations. There is anecdotal evidence for the speeds that might be attainable in this way, as in the case of the future emperor Tiberius riding from Mainz to Drusus' death bed in twenty-four hours, covering a distance of about 200 miles at an average speed of eight miles per hour. However, it is difficult to see this as anything other than an extreme case which cannot be used for anything other than to show the limits of what was possible.[37]

Walking was of course the way the bulk of the army moved around, covering about twenty – in extreme circumstances twenty-five – miles a day. Undoubtedly, a large proportion of those who were not military who used the roads would have chosen this way to get around. Being carried in a litter was a possibility for a select few, but probably reserved mainly for use in town.[38]

Freight, and any official users of the *cursus publicus* who did not merit the use of the remount system, would probably have gone by draught or pack animal. Two- and four-wheeled carts might be pulled by horses, mules, or oxen, the last of these probably only achieving an average of two mph. This produces a figure of around sixteen miles per day travel, assuming eight hours of travel, which interestingly approximates with the spacing between many neighbouring military bases in Northern Britain. Octavius' shipment of hides would have passed from Catterick to Vindolanda via Piercebridge, Binchester, Lanchester, Ebchester, and Corbridge, in other words a five-day journey by cart. The *Antonine Itinerary*, on the other hand, breaks the journey into three sections: Catterick to Binchester, Binchester to Ebchester, and Ebchester to Corbridge (the section Corbridge to Vindolanda is not included in any of the *itinera*), each of around twenty miles. Given that an acceptable speed for pack animals might be around 4 mph, then three days for the journey from Catterick to Vindolanda was easily achievable and even two days not impossible.[39]

Fort spacing from Iter I

From / to	Antonine Itinerary (Rmiles)	Actual (km) / (Rmiles)
Catterick / Binchester	22	32.6 / 22
Binchester / Ebchester	19	29.6 / 20
Ebchester / Corbridge	9	14.8 / 10
Corbridge / Vindolanda	–	22.2 / 15

Diocletian's *Edict on Prices* suggests that the preferred capacity for waggons was 1,200 Rlbs (393 kg), but such ideals almost certainly did not reflect actual practise, merely what the state hoped would be done. Some writers have cast doubt upon the ability of draught animals to haul loads up some of the inclines on the road system of Roman Britain. Anderson, on the other hand, has shown how actual loads carried could differ widely from those legislated for under Diocletian's *Edict on Prices*, by perhaps as much as a factor of three in magnitude. He suggests that it would only have taken 143 ox-carts of grain per year to supply a cohort-sized military base. Since Anderson's work, des Noëttes' seminal work on the limitations of Roman draught harness has been questioned further, suggesting loads of 1,000–1,500 kg would not have been impossible. Nevertheless, whilst the various claims and counter-claims in this debate remain unproven by any pertinent scientific data or experimental archaeological work, it is probably best to suspend judgement on just how steep a hill a Roman ox-cart could negotiate when laden. To get to Vindolanda, Octavius' shipment of hides would have had to come by a route that required a total height gain of some 279m, with maximum slopes in the region of 9 per cent, but since he was intending to use pack animals (*iumenta*), this would have been less of an obstacle than it would to waggons. Pack animals are attested elsewhere in our sources and could have been used to carry a range of goods, providing they were not too bulky. They are also the obvious solution to objections to Roman roads being too steep in places for draught animals pulling wheeled vehicles, although evidence suggests that the Roman army would have used both pack and draught animals when moving around – they are certainly featured on Trajan's Column (Plate 14).[40]

It has recently been suggested that the role of water transport has been seriously underestimated by scholars in the past. Whilst this is almost certainly true as a generalisation, some of the more extreme claims, such as the widespread use of damming to enhance navigability of natural water courses, have been thoughtfully challenged. Some Roman military sites (such as the bases at Whickham or Housesteads) defy any sane attempt to get a barge anywhere near them for purely topographical reasons. Exploitation of coastal transport, along with the navigation of major rivers, is beyond doubt and well-attested by the evidence, but the use of an intensive local canal system is sadly unproven. This means that short-haul freight transport will have to have used the available wheeled transport or pack animals.[41]

Which side of the road did the Romans use?

A perennial favourite, the question of which side of the road the Romans used says much about modern perceptions (and misconceptions) of the past and much ink has been spilled on this subject, notably in the letters pages of *Current Archaeology*. It has even been suggested that 'proof' that the left-hand side was favoured has been excavated (although the idea that such a concept is capable of proof is, to say the least, open to question). Ruts were found to be deeper on one side of a road leading to a quarry than the other, from which it was inferred that laden carts travelled on the left, empty ones on the right.[42]

Although the British use the left-hand side of the road when driving, there is seldom a comparable rule for pavement areas or pedestrianized zones; the nearest to such a rule for non-vehicular traffic can be found in some rail and underground stations in London, where pedestrians are advised to keep to one side or the other when using the stairs or a corridor. Such suggestions are frequently disobeyed. Nevertheless, practical considerations tend to make those on foot use one side of a pavement going one way, one the other, but there will invariably be individuals who dodge around as they do not wish to move at the same speed as the mass.

In reality, the main user of the roads – the army – used the whole road when on campaign, a column being flanked by its cavalry on the softer unmetalled margins (Roman cavalry were unshod; see above, page 59): any other road-user would simply have had to get out of the way.

Chapter 4

After the Romans

But the Romans long exercised a beneficent influence on the development
of the country, as when they went away they left their roads behind them.
J W Gregory[1]

So what happened at the end of Roman rule in Britain? It is very far from the end
of the story of Roman roads. Just as we saw with the question of the existence
of pre-Roman roads, scholars disagree about what happened next, some seeing
the Roman road network rapidly decaying to the point of uselessness. However,
others stress that the evidence points to continuity in many parts of the system,
whilst at the same time other elements were deliberately abandoned. Put simply,
if a Roman road is still in use today, it has been in use since the end of Roman rule;
those stretches that were not needed soon being abandoned and succumbing to
nature. This is, of course, no more and no less than the Romans seem to have
done with the existing prehistoric road network when they arrived. The process
almost certainly went on during the three-and-a-half centuries of Roman rule,
so not all roads that were active in the first century AD would still be in use in the
early fifth century. Road systems adapt to meet current needs.[2]

The speed and efficacy of plant colonization, even on modern road surfaces,
can nowadays be seen in rural areas where modern single-track roads have
been given tarmac surfaces. Whilst the wheels of vehicles using the road keep
two strips on either side clear, the central area between the wheels begins to
decay fairly rapidly and, with the aid of weathering, soon turns into a grassy
strip (Plate 15). If this happens even on modern tarmac surfaces, which are
far more resilient than the rammed gravel used for most Roman roads, it
does not take much imagination to appreciate how long it would be before an
unused Roman road disintegrated to the point of being unusable. Indeed, one
of Thomas Codrington's published works concerned the upkeep of pre-tarmac
roads. Rackham points out that the earliest colonizing species was likely to be
blackthorn and this goes some way to explain why Roman roads can survive as
hedgerows and other boundaries. Where they were abandoned to cultivation,
however, they were (and are) vulnerable to ploughing, particularly once more
heavily mechanised forms of agriculture were introduced. It is all too easy to

look at a modern road preserving the line of its Roman predecessor and imagine them to be indestructible. They are not and that is why some sections of road appear to disappear completely.[3]

Moving medieval armies

The English historian G.M. Trevelyan clearly recognized the true value of the contribution of Roman roads to the subsequent history of the British Isles. In effect, they were to provide a framework for that history: the skeleton and arteries of a medieval state.[4]

The Romans may have gone, but armies still needed roads. In 1993, N.J. Higham published a map illustrating the association of Anglo–Saxon battlefield sites with Roman roads. Although it went almost uncommented in his text, the significance of his observation is obvious: early medieval armies used Roman roads to move around. Could this have remained true in later periods? Road building in medieval Britain was unusual, even rare, and it is difficult to find examples of it having been undertaken on anything other than a local scale, although one man was fined for having constructed one from Yarmouth to Winterton in Norfolk. In 1235, a road was built to link the new bridge at Corbridge with the existing Roman road. It has been suggested that Edward I may have undertaken some limited road construction (more likely clearance: see above page 16), but this was very unusual. He certainly ordered a thirty-mile road cleared from Chester to the River Conwy, via Flint and Rhuddlan, in 1277. Almost exclusively, the Roman road system continued in use, often heavily repaired, sometimes slightly diverted, but it remained the core of medieval British infrastructure. At the same time, the large number of -*ford* place-names in Britain may indicate that, whilst the roads remained in use, bridges were often allowed to fall into disrepair. Roman bridges that survived into the Middle Ages are rare anywhere in the Roman empire and almost non-existent in Britain. We now know that bridges were being built in the post-Roman period: an example at Cromwell Lock was assumed to be Roman and marking the line of a road (Margary 590), but dendrochronological study of a surviving timber has shown it to be eighth century in date. An early date might be true for a medieval bridge at Corbridge on the Tyne, too, despite the fact that general opinion seems to be that it was a ford until the thirteenth century and gained its name from the proximity of a Roman bridge. Chollerford, a few miles away on the North Tyne, has the -*ford* component in its name, despite being close to the Roman bridge at Chesters. Were there no early medieval bridge at Corbridge, we might expect that too to have been Corford, rather than Corbridge, but its name appears in the form *Et Corabrige* as early as AD 786.[5]

So why were so few roads built after the Romans? The medieval kings of Britain were every bit as organized as their Roman predecessors and their engineers just as accomplished. The answer may simply lie in the availability of the existing Roman network. For all its faults, it was there and worked after a fashion, whilst its slow decay seems to have led to piecemeal responses rather than a massive construction initiative. Hence provision of a new road in the medieval period became worthy of comment precisely because it was so unusual.

The Romans had used their road network to move their armies around and there is a substantial body of evidence that indicates they were far from the last to do so. Even today, the modern British army is garrisoned along the major Roman roads. In fact, the military history of Britain was often enacted along those same roads. There is an undeniable broad correlation between battle sites in Britain – especially England – and the Roman road network. This is true of major conflicts like the Scottish War of Independence, the Wars of the Roses, and the English Civil War, as well as countless other smaller military adventures right down to the 1745 rebellion under the Young Pretender. When William Wallace defeated the English at Stirling Bridge and Bannockburn, he did so on a Roman road; when Richard III allegedly offered his kingdom for a horse, it was beside a Roman road (Margary 57b, regardless of which battle site is favoured); and when the Royalist forces met the Parliamentarians at Marston Moor, they did so less than two miles south of a Roman road (Margary 8). Roman roads thus played both a strategic and even tactical role in later warfare. Examples are not hard to find from any age, but are perhaps most striking in the earlier periods. As Barrett (1896) noted, 'Nearly all the battles on English soil have been fought either across one or other of the old Roman roads, or in close proximity thereto'.[6]

Early Medieval (AD 410–1065); see Appendix 2
Soon after the Roman period, the road network will have most closely resembled that of the latter stages of the Roman occupation of the island. Priorities had changed, however, and some major components fell out of use whilst others, such as the ridgeways, may have assumed a new importance. It seems highly unlikely, however, that any construction of new roads took place. There may well have been the beginnings of a process that has been termed 'roads making themselves' (see below, page 104), but it is unclear how widespread this was, or even if in fact the old, pre-Roman network continued to be used and thus became fossilized in the landscape. The battles changed from being between the

native British (or 'Welsh', a word derived from the Anglo-Saxon *wealas*, meaning 'foreigner') to between rival Saxon kingdoms, then between the Saxons and the invading Danes, and finally between the Saxons and the invading Normans.[7]

It is hardly surprising that earlier battles are usually harder to locate than later ones. As such, their strategic, as opposed to tactical, use of Roman roads will be harder to detect. In 508, the battle of Natanleaga, identified with Netley Marsh in Hampshire, was fought between Saxon Cerdic (later the first king of Wessex), with his son Cynric, and a British force, and this is one of the earliest post-Roman battles where a location seems likely. It is situated just over 2 km south of Margary 422, which branches off from the Winchester/Bitterne road (Margary 42b) and heads in a south-westerly direction through what was to become the New Forest towards Ringwood and perhaps on to Poole Harbour. The Battle of Cerdicesford in 519 (possibly to be equated with Charford, south of Salisbury) is intriguing as the suggested site is near some street place-names that are not on an identified Roman road. After succeeding his father, Cynric is reported fighting the British at Searoburh (identified with Old Sarum) in 552 and Beranburh (possibly Barbury Castle, south of Swindon) in 556. The first of these lay at a strategically important junction in the Roman road network, where Margary 4, 44, and 45 met. Barbury, if the identification is correct, lies on the Ridgeway, just 5 km from its junction with the Cirencester/Winchester road, Margary 43.[8]

Amongst these late fifth or early sixth century battles, that of Mons Badonicus, often associated with Arthur/Artorius (but not by Gildas), attracts the attention. Its location is unknown but there has been much speculation, suggested sites including one of the hills around Bath, Liddington Castle near Swindon (and not far from the above-mentioned Barbury), and Badbury Rings in Dorset. All of these are close to Roman roads, a fact that adds little to the debate. Nevertheless, place-name evidence and Gildas' use of the term *obsessio*, implying a siege and therefore a place that could withstand an assault – such as a hillfort – is intriguing. Most hillforts, as we have already seen, sit comfortably within the Roman and pre-Roman road network.[9]

Another battle connected with Arthur (supposedly his last), was Camlann, assigned to 537 but not attested in a source before the tenth century. Nevertheless, a number of sites have been identified with it, a recent favourite being Birdoswald on Hadrian's Wall (assuming the identification of the site with Camboglanna is correct). The proximity of the Stanegate (Margary 85), the Military Way (Margary 86), and, slightly further away, the west coast road (Margary 7) and the Maiden Way (Margary 84) to the east would do nothing to hamper the identification.[10]

The Battle of Catraeth (*c*. 600), the subject of the poem *Y Gododdin*, is often assumed to have been fought at Catterick, and thus would have been located on the Great North Road, Margary 8b, if this association is indeed correct. Whilst not a major nodal point, it was the site of an important river crossing, over the Swale, at the Roman town of Cataractonium so it is easy to see why the identification is appealing. A battle that was fought at a nodal point was Cirencester in 628, between Penda, king of the Mercians, and Cynegils and Cwichelm of Wessex. Once again, this was a Roman town, Corinium, acting as a focus for activity.[11]

Heavenfield (Heofenfelth) in 633/4 marked the triumph of Christian Northumbria over heathen Britons, but despite the chapel at the site associated with the battle, there is little beyond tradition to pin it accurately to the accepted location adjacent to Hadrian's Wall, 5 km west of the point where Dere Street (Margary 8) crossed the Wall. The added complication of the involvement of the place-name Deniseburn, suggested as lying south of Hexham, makes it difficult to interpret the battle, unless there was an episode of pursuit down the Roman road.[12]

Although not actually a battle site, the Viking use of Repton as winter quarters during the years 873–7 not only provided them with sea-going access for their ships via the Trent, but also placed them less than 3 km from Margary 18. This was crucial in the subsequent division of the army in 875, half going north to Tyneside, the other heading south to Cambridge. The activities of the Vikings were responsible for the decision to remove St Cuthbert's body from Holy Island and it was taken all the way south to Crayke (on Margary 80) – a property originally given to Cuthbert for when he was travelling to York – for four months before venturing back up the road to Chester-le-Street.[13]

Two (some scholars think only one) major battles were fought at Corbridge in Northumberland during the tenth century. This again involved Dere Street, but this time at its junction with the (east–west) Stanegate (Margary 85); its strategic significance (like its fellow site at Carlisle) did not end with the Romans. So it was that the Bernician noble Ealdred and the Scottish king Constantine intercepted (and were sent packing by) a marauding party of Danes (travelling from west to east, and thus in all likelihood along either the Stanegate or its medieval successor, the Carelgate) at Corbridge in (probably) AD 914. Dere Street (which was a *via regia* of the Scottish monarchy) was a favoured route for Scottish incursions into England – it was often the case that when the English (like Edward I or III) went up the east coast (see below, page 81), the Scots would travel down Dere Street.[14]

In 934, Athelstan, the king of Wessex, marched north and invaded Scotland, apparently reaching as far north as Dunnottar. On the way, he stopped at the sepulchre of St Cuthbert which, at the time, was in Chester-le-Street, betraying the fact that Athelstan was heading north on Margary 80. The fact he was accompanied by a fleet suggests he kept to a coastal route in his progress north. His best-known battle, Brunanburh in 937, where he defeated a combined Scottish and Danish army, is commemorated in a poem but, unfortunately, unlocated, although many candidates have been proposed for its site. One of the most favoured, Bromborough on the Wirral peninsula, would lie close to Margary 670, but another candidate, Burnswark in Annandale, is situated on Margary 7, whilst a further site, Brinsworth, is near the junction of Margary 18 (which actually crosses the village) and 710.[15]

As we have already seen, when Eric Bloodaxe (the Norse king of Northumbria) died in AD 954, he did so traditionally at Rey Cross, on the trans-Pennine Roman road (Margary 82) that is nowadays followed by the A66 (and where there also happened to be a Roman temporary camp surviving as an earthwork). He had no army with him, but nevertheless chose to flee on a Roman road. The likely site of the Battle of Maldon in 971, unusual in being both precisely located and commemorated in a poem, was more than 9 km from the London to Colchester road (Margary 3). However, the identification of a short length of road to the east at Bradwell (Margary 31) hints at the possibility that it may in fact have lain close to or even on an as-yet-unidentified stretch of that Roman road.[16]

Amongst our final Early Medieval battles, Carham was fought between Malcolm II of the Scots and Uhtred of the Northumbrians in 1018 on the putative Tweed Valley road (see below, Appendix 5), although only the location is cited and thus the significance of the road can only be inferred. Dunsinane Hill took place in 1054 between Macbeth and Malcolm Canmore, and is situated only 6 km from the main road (Margary 9) running up the eastern coastal plain of Scotland. They fought again in 1057, this time at Lumphanan, resulting in Macbeth's death. This last is some way north of the nearest known paved Roman road but a number of camps stretch even further north than Lumphanan (which is 22 km south-west of the 110-acre camp at Kintore), suggesting the existence of tracks which both the Romans and their successors were using.[17]

Medieval (AD 1066–1539); see Appendix 3

AD 1066 is a useful, if arbitrary, point at which to begin our consideration of the role of Roman roads in the battles of medieval Britain. In terms of a road network, the point at which national, rather than regional, states came into being might have been a better point at which to draw a line, had there actually been any change in policy towards roads, but there was no such modification. Such legislation as there was for maintenance of the existing system tended to be haphazard and generalized, as with Edward I's requirement in the Statute of Winchester of 1285 that roads be kept clear on either side to prevent ambush. The importance of the Roman road system in the medieval period has already been underlined by other writers, as well as the informal mechanisms by which roads might come into being (such as 'roads that made themselves'), but an additional factor that should be stressed is the hidden, yet potent, role of pre-Roman roads and trackways in helping along those self-made roads. Settlements followed roads, rather than being created *de novo* in the middle of nowhere, so if there was no formalized Roman road there, it may be presumed that some sort of pre-Roman track or road would facilitate foundation and growth. Only then could additional 'self-made' links form. Conversely, failure or removal of a settlement could kill a road, as we have seen for the immediate post-Roman period for sites like Silchester or Mildenhall.[18]

So it was that the system was continuing to evolve, albeit without the agency of a direct government contribution. To the pre-Roman tracks and roads and the all-weather Roman roads were added streets in settlements and even the occasional local stretch of road outwith, as well as tracks between new hamlets and villages.

The period certainly opens with a famous example of the post-Roman use of the road system which serves to underline their continued importance. In 1066, the invading Norse army of Harald Hardrada was met in battle at Gate Fulford by a Saxon army commanded by Walcar and Waltheof, between Riccal (where the Norse army had encamped) and York. Margary has no numbered road running south from York, but the place-name, incorporating as it does a *Gate* element, together with a -*ford* component, is at least suggestive of a Roman road. This would have been a branch from Margary 2, which at first adopts a southerly course out of York, before turning to the east. In fact, within his section dealing with route 800 (which heads north-east from York) he refers to the discovery of a Roman road running from Heslington down to Pool Farm, crossing the Germany Beck on its way. The Saxon army, which must have marched down this road from York, was defeated and the remnants retreated back to the city, whilst Hardrada and his ally Tostig moved to Stamford Bridge at the junction of Margary 80 and 810. There, they were soon met in battle and defeated by the army of Harold Godwinson, who had marched from London in order to intercept them. Whilst in the north, Harold must have received word of the Norman invasion of Sussex on 28 September, and promptly marched his army back south.[19]

The accomplishments of Harold Godwinson and his army in that fateful year would not have been possible without the Roman road system. In a comparatively short time, he had to march an army from the south of England to York, fight a battle at Stamford Bridge, then march south again to tackle the invading Normans at Senlac.

His march north involved his gathering levies as he went. Setting out from London on 20 September, he reached Tadcaster (315 km, using Margary 2 and 8) on 24 September, and so achieved a scarcely believable average speed of 79 km (53 Roman miles) per day. Harold's march back to the south of England was slightly more leisurely, involving another 400 km (250 miles) in just twelve days (an average speed of 34 km – 21 miles – per day, closely matching that claimed for a Roman army on the march). There is an inevitable compromise between the speed of forced marches and an army's combat-readiness at the end of such ordeals. In 1942, the Second Battalion of the 506th Parachute Infantry Regiment of the US army set a record by covering 190 km (118 miles) in 75 hours during a march from Camp Toccoa to Fort Benning. This, it has to be remembered – at an average speed of 63 km (39 miles) per day – was neither preceded nor followed by combat.[20]

Although there were to be many complaints about the decaying condition of the Roman system in centuries to come, Harold's extraordinary achievement demonstrates that a shoddy road system remained better than no system at all so far as an army was concerned. Hastings, fought 4 km from the Roman road (Margary 13) that would ultimately give William access to London, was not the final battle of 1066, however. When William marched from Canterbury to London in December to claim the capital and be crowned as king, he did so along Margary 2. Reluctantly admitted to the city, there was then unrest that resulted in the deaths of Londoners.[21]

The Battle of Stafford in 1069, when William took to the field again and defeated the troublesome Mercian earl, Eadric the Wild, is of particular note because it seemingly occurred nowhere near a Roman road. The close correlation which we have so far witnessed between early battlefield sites and the Roman road network as we understand it renders this more than a little surprising, but for the time being it need only be noted. At the end of the year, William was in the north laying waste the region around York after some local difficulties. This is of less interest in itself than the fact that it directly led to the all-too-mobile body of St Cuthbert being returned to Holy Island to avoid this 'harrying of the north'. Simeon of Durham even preserves detail of its route (via Jarrow, Bedlington, and Tughall) which appears to demonstrate the use of Margary 80. William's marches from the Tees to Hexham and then from York to Chester in

1070 are described by Orderic Vitalis in terms that suggest the Roman roads proved quite challenging. Malcolm III 'Canmore', the Scottish king, caused additional problems for the Normans in the north, but was finally killed at the Battle of Malcolm's Cross, near Alnwick, in 1093. This was another battle supposedly far from a Roman road which, like the peripatetic St Cuthbert's route, will be discussed later, since both seem to have utilized what is probably a Roman route between Newcastle and Tweedmouth (see below Appendix 5).[22]

The first half of the twelfth century is dominated by the civil war between Stephen and Matilda and continued conflict with Scotland; the two are not unconnected. David I invaded in 1136 in support of Matilda, attacking sites on the east coast between Berwick and Newcastle. When a peace treaty was signed he retreated but returned again in 1138, arriving at Corbridge after besieging Wark Castle, so presumably travelling down Dere Street. Stephen followed him up to Roxburgh, then headed back south via Bamburgh. It was not long before David was heading south again, this time down the east coast, ending up at Newcastle. Then, sending his army on to ravage as far as Teesdale, he returned to lay siege to Norham Castle. Meanwhile, part of his army under his nephew William had marched west and met and defeated an English force at Clitheroe in Lancashire (on Margary 72). Once the Scottish army was reunited they marched south via Bamburgh and Mitford, crossed the Tyne and on into Yorkshire. There they met an English force near Northallerton in the so-called Battle of the Standard, on the road to York (Margary 80). This resulted in a Scottish defeat and David retreated to Carlisle, presumably using the Stainmore Pass (Margary 82).[23]

In the second half of the century, a confrontation between forces loyal to Malcolm IV of Scotland and the would-be invader Somerled, the Lord of the Isles, at Renfrew saw the defeat and death of the latter. Fragments of a road south of the Clyde, running towards the Roman fort at Whitemoss and the fortlets at Lurg Moor and Outerwards, were known to Margary (route 780) but more has since come to light and it is clear that a road ran around the peninsula towards Largs. Renfrew is situated on this route, some 8.5 km from Whitemoss, and it may have been Somerled's intention to use it. Malcolm's son, William the Lion, having laid siege to Prudhoe Castle in Tynedale, had the misfortune to be captured at a second Battle of Alnwick in 1174, during the revolt against Henry II, once again betraying the use of the east coast route by the Scots. Henry himself took his siege train from Huntingdon towards Framlingham Castle, intending to besiege the rebel Hugh Bigod there, but before he could reach his goal, Hugh came to him and they met at Syleham. This is only 3.6 km from Margary 35, a length of road on a north-west to south-east heading which may have linked in with a route to Huntingdon that incorporated Margary 37, towards which it is heading. [24]

The thirteenth century saw John venturing north and exercising his acquisitive tendencies and a nascent archaeological bent by digging at the Roman site of Corbridge, looking (unsuccessfully) for treasure. Undeterred by a lack of success in February 1201, he apparently repeated the exercise in August 1208 and June 1212. What is of interest to us is that he was travelling along the line of the Stanegate (Margary 85) or possibly along the line of its successor, the Carelgate. In 1201, he ventured up from Newcastle to Belford and Bamburgh, before cutting back to Hexham through Rothbury and then west to Carlisle, whilst in 1208 he travelled from Newcastle to Carlisle via Hexham. In 1212, his route was from Richmond, up the line of the Stainmore Pass (Margary 82), via Bowes and Appleby, before heading up Margary 7 to Plumpton with a brief detour to Kirkoswald. His next move, to Calder and then Wigton, has no known Roman road, but it may indicate that a route from Brougham to Old Carlisle has yet to be found. He then goes to Carlisle and across to Hexham, before looping back down to Durham, presumably on Dere Street (Margary 8), on his way south to York on Margary 80. In these adventures (Figure 24), it is of course his visits to Hexham that afforded him the opportunity to explore Corbridge.[25]

John inevitably became involved in the affairs of Scotland, but a confrontation at Norham in August 1209 was avoided when William backed down once the English king sallied north from Newcastle, presumably using the east coast Roman road (see below, Appendix 5). His problems came nearer to home with the revolt by his barons in 1215–17. This saw the French King Louis coming over to Britain and installed in London. The barons, meanwhile, are recorded as having moved from Dunstable to Mountsorrel on the way to Lincoln, utilizing two of the major Roman routes, Watling Street (Margary 1) and the Fosse Way (Margary 5), rather than going straight up Ermine Street (Margary 2). The decision to go on to Lincoln apparently only occurred after the besieged Mountsorrel had been relieved but, when they reached there, their army was defeated and the survivors fled south to London, completing the triangle, presumably by using the most direct route: Margary 2.

The Second Barons' War saw the Battle of Lewes of 1264, with Simon de Montfort surprising Henry III and his son, who were based there. Simon had marched by the London to Lewes road (Margary 14), staying overnight at Fletching, less than 3 km from the Roman road. The events that led to the downfall of Simon in the following year saw some frenzied movements after he left his home at Odiham Castle in Hampshire for the last time. Proceeding to Northampton, he then made for Coventry and then Gloucester. His next move,

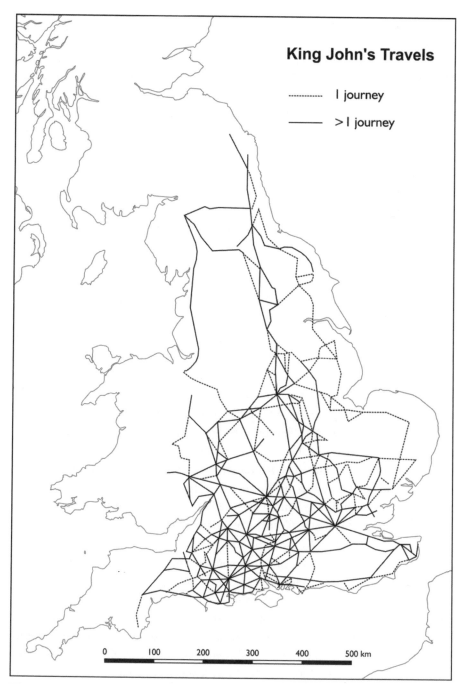

Figure 24: The travels of King John (after Hindle 1998).

to Hereford, is unhelpful, as there are several routes he could have taken, but his march to Monmouth, in an attempt to break out of the blockade his enemies had instituted along the Severn, can only have been undertaken on Margary 6. From Monmouth, he took routes 612 and 62 down to Newport, but failed to cross the channel and had to retrace his steps to Hereford. He finally managed to cross the Severn at Kempsey, to the south of Worcester. Kempsey has produced a milestone, although that could come from Margary 180 which runs just to the east of the village. However, his route 63, which passes to the north of Hereford, is pointing in the right direction and a Roman road is reputed to run from east to west through Kempsey, the two crossing at Palmer's Cross. If this road did exist it would presumably have led to Evesham and would thus complete his fated journey. This untidy end only serves to underline how inadequate our knowledge of Roman roads can be, as does the aftermath of the revolt, where Simon's supporters retreated to the Isle of Axholme, an area devoid of Roman roads (although this particular gap in our knowledge did not stop the young prince Edward reaching it, even building wooden bridges in the process, and signing a treaty at Haxey).[26]

August 1274 saw the coronation of Edward I, one of the most interesting English kings from the perspective of Roman road studies. Not only are his movements known in some detail, but he was one of the few medieval monarchs who actually undertook some limited road construction of his own. As early as 1277, he was campaigning in north Wales against Llewellyn ap Gruffudd, de Montfort's former ally, clearing a route from Chester to Flint (20 km), a task which only seems to have taken ten days. Having made Flint his base, the route was then extended to Rhuddlan, evidently taking from 26 July to 20 August to do so. There was no Roman road for some 17 km of his preferred coastal route from Flint to Rhuddlan (*c.* 27 km), or he would not need to have cleared this route (Margary 67 turns inland at Holywell and stays to the south of his preferred route). In fact his 'road' turns out to have been little more than clearance through wooded landscape, reminiscent of the Roman practice of sending out an advance guard for the same purpose (see above page 16). The final stage, to Deganwy on the Conwy (*c.* 25 km), took only nine more days. The fact he undertook this route clearance is noteworthy for occasioning mention in the sources, as if a measure of how unusual his campaigning style was thought to be. Between 1,500 and 1,800 woodmen were employed for clearance from Flint to Rhuddlan, and 700 to 1,000 from Rhuddlan to Deganwy. It was not, however, all-weather road construction.[27]

Edward's Scottish Wars tell us much more about his use of the Roman road system and provide tantalising hints about those parts of the system we do not yet fully understand. Like John, he made use of an east coast route between Newcastle and Berwick that afforded him access to Alnwick and Bamburgh. March of 1296 saw him going north from Newcastle, via Brunton and Bamburgh, only to branch westwards along the Tweed to Wark, before doubling back to Coldstream, Hutton, and finally Berwick, where he laid siege to the town through most of April. Success then drew him further north to Dunbar, via Coldingham, where the castle had been besieged by the English, falling after Edward had reached it and a battle was fought. From Dunbar he headed west to Haddington, then south to Lauder, presumably having cut across to Dere Street (Margary 8) on his way down to Roxburgh. These moves make little sense with the road system as portrayed by Margary, who has Dere Street as the most easterly route in the Scottish Lowlands, but as we shall see later (below, Appendix 5), there is good reason to suspect that there is a Roman basis for these elements of Edward's itinerary.[28]

A curious little addition was then an expedition through Liddesdale to Castleton, but it signified greatly in Roman road circles, for it appeared to exploit an old road, known as the Wheel Causeway, which James MacDonald, supported in print by Francis Haverfield, pronounced to be of some antiquity, but not Roman. Its exclusion from Margary's work indicates he concurred. Haverfield helpfully pointed out its use by Edward and sundry other belligerent expeditions but left aside the issue of its construction. Whether a native track or a Roman road of some form, its existence is beyond doubt.[29]

Edward was not finished yet. It was still only May and he now made for Edinburgh in June, then on to Stirling, Perth, Aberdeen, and beyond in July and August. This is much further north than any known all-weather Roman road, but he was closely following the route indicated by known Roman temporary camps, which, as Edward was to do, reached as far as the Moray Firth during the first century AD northern campaigns of Agricola. We have witnessed the exploitation of native roads and trackways for campaigns before, following the initial Roman invasion (above page 9), and here (as Maxwell has observed) we appear to see Edward doing the same and mimicking Agricola's progress north. Looping round, he returned south, reaching Berwick in the fourth week of August.[30]

Edward was abroad in 1297 but the Earl of Surrey marched north from Berwick to relieve Dundee and was met at Stirling Bridge by the Scottish army under William Wallace and Andrew Murray. The site of the battle was dictated by the fact that this was the lowest bridging point of the Forth and there was a boggy area, Flanders Moss, immediately to the west. These same factors also dictated the course of the Roman road past Stirling (Margary 9).

Inevitably, therefore, the Roman road was an integral part of the battle, if seldom acknowledged as such. After the English defeat, Surrey beat a hasty retreat to Berwick.[31]

Edward's next expedition north in person was in June of 1298 but this time he cut across from Alnwick and travelled north on Dere Street, reaching no further than Stirling, before going south to Peebles on Margary 7 and across to Ayr (presumably on the imperfectly understood Margary 79). He returned to Carlisle in September and remained in the border region until December. This bare account masks Edward's important victory on 22 July at Falkirk. Some discussion of the location of the battlefield has hinged around the proximity of the Edinburgh/Stirling road (Margary 9, although its course is uncertain between Cramond and Camelon) to the two main favoured sites, although it should not be forgotten that the Antonine Wall Military Way (Margary 90) may also have been available.[32]

In 1300, Edward campaigned in the south-west of Scotland. He started out from Durham in June and proceeded via Evenwood, Bowes, Brough, Brougham, and Skelton to Carlisle, which would have involved Margary 8, 820, 82, and 7. From Carlisle he went to Ecclefechan, Applegarth, Tinwald, and Dumfries, a route that involved Margary 7 and 76. His final move was from Dumfries down to Caerlaverock Castle, but there is no road recorded by Margary for this stage. However, the presence of a fortlet (Ward Law) next to Caerlaverock has led to the suggestion of a road running from Dalswinton, through Dumfries, to the end of this peninsula. Returning to Dumfries he next turned west to Kirkcudbright, another area with no known Roman road, but a fortlet at Gatehouse of Fleet and a fort at Glenlochar hint at a road yet to be found which Edward was perhaps using. By 30 August he was at Dornock, east of Annan, and probably about to ford the Solway near Burgh-by-Sands (where later he was to die), as he is found at Drumburgh the next day. He returned to Caerlaverock once more before heading south from Carlisle in November and taking the Stainmore Pass back to Yorkshire.[33]

In 1301, Edward once more ventured into the lowlands, sending his son north from Carlisle whilst himself moving west from Berwick, through Norham, crossing the Tweed at Coldstream and making for Peebles. Margary records no Roman road along the Tweed east of Peebles but it is not unreasonable to expect one at least as far as Newstead and possibly all the way to Tweedmouth (see below, Appendix 5). Fieldwork by members of the Trimontium Trust has been productive in suggesting a route as far as the central lowland fort. Edward headed up to Bothwell Castle and then, via Dunipace, to Linlithgow, where he spent three months before heading south in February 1302. That last move suggests the continued use of the Antonine Wall Military Way (Margary 90).[34]

Edward did not return to Scotland until May 1303, when he followed the familiar east coast route as far as Alnwick, but then moved westwards via Chatton to Roxburgh. He then embarked on another expedition into northern regions, supported by a fleet moving up the east coast, reaching the Moray Firth again, recalling his achievement of 1296 and presumably using much the same routes.[35]

During 1306, we find Edward in the north again and in August he appears to have been moving along the Stanegate, with visits to Corbridge, Hexham, Carlisle, and repeatedly to Newbrough. In September he included Bradley, Henshaw, and Melkridge in his itinerary, but always returning to Newbrough. Finally, in October, he settled at Lanercost, since by this time he was seriously ill. He stayed there until March 1307, when he moved to Carlisle, before leaving for Burgh-by-Sands in July, where he was to die of dysentery before he could lead his army across the border again. Whilst he was at Carlisle, Robert Bruce achieved a significant victory over the English at the Battle of Loudoun Hill in May.[36]

Loudon Hill shows how Roman roads could be exploited tactically. Bruce deployed his army on the road (Margary 79) running past the eponymous Roman fort and limited the available frontage (both because the road ran across boggy ground and he had dug additional obstacles), with disastrous effect for the opposing English force. He repeated this stratagem at Bannockburn in 1314, where this time he occupied the flanks of the road (Margary 9) with pitfalls.[37]

Whilst an itinerary for Edward II has also been reconstructed, it reveals little more about the use of the Roman road system than can be gleaned by studying the movements of his father. For a while, internecine strife amongst the Scots helped him, but soon Bruce had turned to guerilla warfare, much to Edward's frustration. The campaign of 1314 that culminates in Bannockburn is more illuminating. Leaving Berwick on 17/18 June he marched north with his army, accompanied by enough waggons to cover twenty leagues if placed end to end (about 44 km if a Roman *leuga* was intended). Heading for Stirling to relieve the siege there, his army was met and defeated at Bannockburn on 24 June.[38]

There was widespread Scottish raiding in the north of England, reaching as far south as Teesdale, and in 1319 we witness a Scottish raiding party avoiding Edward's forces by returning up the Stainmore Pass (Margary 82) and thence to Gilsland, presumably using the most direct road, the Maiden Way (Margary 84). They returned by the same route the next year, burning Gilsland and ravaging Stainmore as far as Brough, before heading west into Westmorland for more of the same.[39]

Edward's troubles moved south, with the revolt of the barons under Thomas of Lancaster. At the 'Battle' of Burton Bridge, at the beginning of 1322, Lancaster's forces held the bridge there across the Trent, immediately east of Margary 18. Edward, approaching from the south-west (so presumably along that very road) split his force and crossed the Trent only to find he could not get back using a ford (a classic example of why bridges are necessary to an all-weather strategic road network). Fleeing north, without actually engaging the king's forces, Lancaster reached Boroughbridge. Had he continued north on Margary 18, he would have reached the Don at Templeborough; the road network as proposed by Margary and others would have required him to head north-east to Doncaster on Margary 710 in order to continue north-westwards on Margary 28 (50 km), although the most direct route would have been due north to Castleford (35 km), so this may indicate a gap in our knowledge of the Roman network.[40]

Boroughbridge is a very interesting battle from the point of view of Roman roads. Dere Street passed through the Roman town of Aldborough, but in medieval times this had slipped from ascendency, possibly when the Roman bridge over the Ure failed, and a new settlement at Boroughbridge came into existence (although, unlike (Ald)borough, Milby, or Langthorpe, it is not mentioned in the Domesday Book, which may imply that this change had yet to happen in the eleventh century). This meant the Great North Road was now running to the west of Dere Street. Intriguingly, excavation has shown that the likely site was very close to an early Roman fort, at Roecliffe, which seems to have been guarding a road crossing which may have been prehistoric in origin (see above page 7). It may therefore be the case that, when the Roman line of Dere Street past Aldborough went out of use, the more direct prehistoric line was reinstated and became the Great North Road at this point. Whilst a timber bridge at Boroughbridge itself played an important part in the battle, there was a nearby ford that Sir Andrew Harcla took the precaution of guarding with a schiltron of pikemen on 16 March 1322. Many interpretations of the battle assume the ford was near Aldborough (Figure 25) but, despite changes to the Ure around Boroughbridge, local tradition persists that it was fordable at Langthorpe, which is just to the west of Boroughbridge and on the north bank opposite the Roman fort, to the west of the later canalization.[41]

Edward followed up with a less-than-successful invasion of Scotland in August, retreating south through Berwick and Newcastle to Rievaulx Abbey in Yorkshire, but this only led to Bruce crossing the Solway, presumably travelling

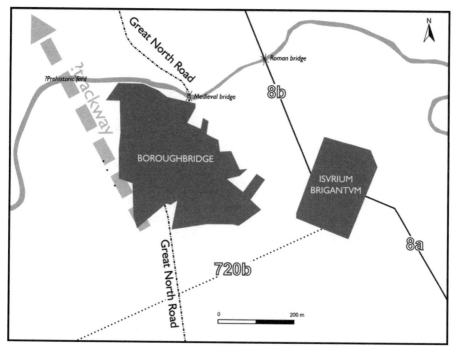

Figure 25: Aldborough, Boroughbridge, and the River Ure crossings.

down the Stainmore Pass, and then confronting Edward's forces in the Battle of Old Byland in October of the same year, which resulted in another defeat for the hapless English king. Although there is no known Roman road in the vicinity, Margary 814 from Malton may have supplied the missing link, since Barbour's poem (and other sources) makes reference to a '*peth*'.[42]

Edward III, crowned 1 February 1327, tended to be more successful in his Scottish adventures, although that same year saw a defeat at the hands of the raiding Moray and Douglas at Stanhope Park. The English, having marched in a single day from Barnard Castle to Haydon Bridge, then lost patience and headed back down to Weardale to intercept the Scots. The subtleties of this manoeuvre are lost on us now, since we only have the fragmentary Margary 821 striding over the moors to the south of Stanhope, which may have linked Corbridge with either Bowes or Greta Bridge, but its proximity to Stanhope Park suggests it played a role, and John of Fordun's comment, that the English army sat at the end of the road waiting for the Scots, indicates that they saw no other way for them to move.[43]

The Battle of Dupplin Moor in 1332 is notable for the prominent role played by the Gask Ridge (Margary 9). Seemingly named as the location of the camp of the Scots' baggage train, the road was still in use in the medieval period, since it survives in large part today. A fortified Flavian road, noted for its chain of signal stations, it allowed access to Perth from the west by means of higher ground to the north of the River Earn. Scots raiding at the beginning of 1333 saw Gilsland being burnt again, but this time from the west, followed by an English incursion. Edward's journey to his triumph at Halidon Hill in 1333, thereby relieving a siege of Berwick by the Scots, revisited previous monarchs' journeys between Newcastle and Tweedmouth.[44]

In 1346, the Battle of Neville's Cross saw the Scots defeated and their king captured. It took place just to the west of Durham, in the angle between two Roman roads, Margary 80 and 83, the latter providing a link between the former and Dere Street (Margary 8). By the time of the battle, it is possible this cross route had fallen from use (it is not shown on Ogilby's 1675 map) but there is no way to be certain of this. On balance, the position of the battle would seem to argue against that.[45]

The Scots were far from finished. Bolstered by a detachment of French troops under Jean de Vienne in 1385, they headed towards Roxburgh from Edinburgh (which indicates the use of Dere Street, Margary 8). Deciding Roxburgh could not be taken, they then moved off down the Tweed towards Berwick, on the way taking Wark, Ford, and Cornhill Castles. The English under Richard II retaliated by raiding into Scotland, travelling up the east coast once more to Berwick, but then venturing along the Tweed to burn Melrose Abbey (near the Roman fort at Newstead). They then continued north to Edinburgh and appear to have been observed on their way, passing up Lauderdale (if Froissart is to be believed), the size of their force obliging the Scots and their allies to avoid the advancing English army and go raiding in the south-west around Carlisle instead. After burning Dunfermline, Perth, and Dundee, Richard intended pursuing the Scotto-French force to the south-west, but was instead persuaded to return the way he came.[46]

Shortly afterwards, a major incursion was mounted into the north of England in 1388 which saw Newcastle besieged by Scottish forces under Douglas, which introduces a new and interesting element to the story of the road system on northern England. The Scots returned home from Newcastle via Ponteland and ended up fighting the English at Otterburn. Although adjacent to Dere Street (Margary 8), so technically yet another battle near a Roman road, the route adopted by the Scots and the pursuing English is not a Margary route and does not appear elsewhere in Anglo-Scottish conflicts, Dere Street and the western route through Carlisle being favoured by the Scots, the east coast by the English.

The possibility of a road linking Newcastle directly with Dere Street has not been considered by scholars but will be examined further below (Appendix 5).[47]

The Welsh revolt against English rule by Owain Glendŵr in 1400 saw the battle of Mynydd Hyddgen in 1401. Although the precise location is unknown, its general vicinity has been suggested. No Roman road is known close by, but an east-to-west route (Margary 64) is pointing towards it.[48]

After that brief interlude, the Scots returned to the fray and, in 1402, a force marched from the Forth towards Newcastle but, upon its return, was intercepted by Hotspur near Wooler at Homildon Hill. This resulted in a major Scottish defeat, supposedly commemorated by the nearby Battle Stone (which is actually a prehistoric standing stone, recalling the association of ancient tracks and roads with such monuments).[49]

Hotspur's unease over his treatment after Homildon was a contributory factor to his rebellion against Henry IV which culminated in his death at the Battle of Shrewsbury in 1403. Hotspur raised an army in Cheshire and then marched south towards Shrewsbury, presumably down Margary 6. Henry was at Burton-on-Trent when he heard of the revolt and moved to intercept Hotspur. Shrewsbury is puzzling as there is no immediately obvious link to the Roman road system, Margary 6 being more than 5 km to the east. A 'campaign' road, towards the Roman vexillation fortress at Rhyn Park, up the valley of the Perry from Wroxeter, has been proposed but even this may have been too far south so there may well be an as-yet-unidentified Roman road in the area, possibly linking Margary 6 and 64, or more likely anticipating the route of Ogilby's road from Shrewsbury to Wrexham.[50]

The existing situation with the Welsh rebellion began to merge with another evolving problem – France – in the year 1405, when a French invasion of Wales occurred in support of Glendŵr. Their force landed at Milford Haven, a port that was to see repeated use in later years for military ventures, united with the Welsh rebels and captured local towns, including Carmarthen, before marching through South Wales, presumably using Margary 60, route 6 up to Hereford, then the incomplete (from our point of view) 63 to get to Worcester for an indecisive confrontation with the English forces under Henry IV.[51]

The rebellion of Henry Percy finally came to an end in 1408 at the Battle of Bramham Moor. This occurred at one of the major intersections of Roman roads in the north of England, where the north-to-south Margary 28 and 280 met the east-to-west routes 72 and 729. The confusion of roads here suggests a palimpsest of different phases in the development of the network.[52]

The Battle of Piperdean took place on the much-travelled east coast road to the north of Berwick-upon-Tweed (1436; see Appendix 5). Hostilities between

England and Scotland resumed in 1448, with the English destroying Dunbar, and the Earl of Salisbury's army Dumfries. The Scottish response was to attack Warkworth and Alnwick, culminating in the Battle of Sark, which was fought near Gretna, just 2 km from Margary 7 and near a presumed route to the west.[53]

The onset of the conflict later known as the Wars of the Roses in 1455 saw a small but significant battle fought at St Albans. Henry VI had marched there with a force of men and taken up position in the town whilst Richard, Duke of York, had marched from the north and set up his standard to the east of the town, the former having the misfortune of ending up captured by the latter. The significance of the Roman road network to this conflict goes without saying, since two major components (Margary 1 to the south-east and north-west of the town) were used to move the armies. The first major battle was Blore Heath in September 1459 which is, unlike most of the conflicts described here, more than 7 km away from the nearest Roman road (Margary 19, to the south-west). A Yorkist force was marching south-westwards, heading for Ludlow from Middleham, and was met by a Lancastrian army on Blore Heath. The Roman villa at Hales lies only 2 km to the south of the battlefield, however, so it might be anticipated that an access road ran from there to Margary 19. By October, the two sides met again at Ludford Bridge, just south of Ludlow Castle and the Roman road from Weston-under-Penyard (Margary 613) is aligned on this crossing of the Teme, although Margary only records it as far as Ashton, 10 km to the south of Ludlow. However, Richard of York retreated from Worcester to Ludlow and no direct Roman road is known for that route so this may well represent another gap in our knowledge of the system.[54]

The next confrontation, in July of the following year, was the Battle of Northampton and it took place to the south of the River Nene at the abbey of St Mary de la Pré. This lay next to the river crossing, towards which Margary 17 seems to have been directed and, like the modern A428, it may have continued to Bedford. Henry VI had come from Coventry, so route 17 was his likely access to the town, whilst Warwick was approaching from London and his most direct route would have been Margary 1. The next battle, in December, occurred near Sandal Castle in what is now West Yorkshire. The Lancastrians, having marched west from Kingston upon Hull to Pontefract, encamped there and awaited the Yorkists. Sandal is some 10 km from Margary 28, but the short stretch of Margary 728 near Swillington points straight towards it.[55]

The Battle of Mortimer's Cross in February of 1461 involved a Roman road (Margary 6), although precisely how is unclear, given the uncertain nature of this battle. The movement of the Lancastrian army, from Wales into England, was intercepted by a Yorkist force. This may have been from south to north along the

Roman road, in which case it was directly involved, or, as has been argued, from west to east along the London to Aberystwyth road recorded by Ogilby, when the presence of the Roman road will have been largely coincidental. A third possibility, an east-to-west interception of a south to north movement is also a possibility. The next engagement occurred at the second Battle of St Albans, in the same month, where a Yorkist force attempted to block the Roman road (Margary 1) north of St Albans to deny the Lancastrians access to London. The preparations for this action saw the attempted tactical use of a road once more, with obstacles being placed to either side of it by the Yorkist force. However, the advancing Lancastrians pre-empted this by changing course and approaching from Dunstable instead and encamping on Bernard's Heath, which implies their use of Margary 21 to avoid the blockaded northern road. March saw the next encounter between the Yorkists and Lancastrians at Ferrybridge, 5 km east of Margary 28 as it passed through Castleford. The Lancastrians held the bridge at Ferrybridge and the Yorkists attacked both from the south and, using the Roman road to outflank them and cross the Aire further west, from the north. The Lancastrians retreated north to Towton, which lay 4.5 km east of Margary 28. From this, it seems clear that what was later to be known as the Great North Road (subsequently the A1), which left the Roman route at Barnsdale Bar, 11 km to the south of the Ferrybridge crossing, already found favour over the original Roman route. It is possible that the more modern road is actually a southern continuation of the Rudgate (Margary 280) or a prehistoric predecessor. Ferrybridge was the site of a henge and may have been a crossing point of some significance long before the Romans arrived.[56]

Three years later, a small Yorkist force under the Marquess of Montagu was sent north from York to escort a Scottish delegation. An attempt to intercept Montagu was made by the Lancastrians at Newcastle and then on Hedgeley Moor, 10 km south-east of Wooler, where they were defeated after venturing out from Alnwick. This was a significant location as it appears to have been a fork in the Roman system between the original course of Devil's Causeway (Margary 87) towards Tweedmouth and a later extension to a higher Tweed crossing at Cornhill (see below, Appendix 5). This location therefore afforded a choice of heading north-westwards to ultimately join Dere Street, whilst the more northerly Devil's Causeway course led to the coastal route often favoured by English armies in the past. The Battle of Hexham was fought in the same year, some 3 km south-west of the point where Dere Street bridged the Tyne west of Corbridge and led to another significant Lancastrian defeat. Codrington noted the possibility of a Roman road running south-westwards from the crossing point towards Whitley Castle. Selkirk, citing additional earlier references, records some physical evidence for its existence; strangely, Margary made no comment on the possibility of the existence of this road, even if only to dismiss it. At least one aerial photograph taken in 2006 shows an ambiguous linear feature south of the Tyne that may be related to the road.[57]

The Battle of Edgecote Moor in 1469 occurred within an area devoid of any Roman roads nearby, but with at least one road (Margary 166) pointing north-westwards towards it, once more serving to underline how incomplete our knowledge is for some areas. We are on more certain ground with the Battle of Losecote Field (Empingham) the following year, for here the Great North Road (Margary 2) was central to the deployment of the Lancastrian forces.[58]

The accepted location for the Battle of Barnet in 1471 lay between two south-east to north-west oriented Roman roads (Margary 167 and 220), just 3 km west of route 220 and near the junction of two roads shown by Ogilby. The same year saw the decisive Battle of Tewkesbury, on the Gloucester to Worcester road (Margary 180). Involving a complex series of move and counter-move around the West Country, the Lancastrian forces, having headed north from Gloucester, were caught up with by the Yorkist army and battle followed. Exhausted, the Lancastrians had been obliged to abandon some of their artillery, highlighting the fact that whatever their inadequacies, Roman roads were of continued importance for the movement of the more cumbersome components of any medieval army.[59]

The Battle of Bosworth Field in 1485 must be one of the most famous English conflicts and the debate over its exact location has been heated and long running. Archaeology has recently suggested that the location of the conflict actually lay adjacent to the Roman road from Leicester to Mancetter (Margary 57), whereas the traditional battlefield site, on Ambion Hill, had long been identified as lying some 1.3 km from the same road.

A prominent role was played by a Roman road in the Battle of Stoke Field in 1487, where the Lancastrian and Yorkist forces deployed between the Fosse Way (Margary 5) and the Trent.[60]

The events that led up to the Battle of Blackheath (or Deptford Bridge) in June 1497, the culmination of the Cornish Rebellion, saw a rebel army march from Wells to Bristol, Salisbury, and then Winchester, before heading to Guildford, finally arriving at Blackheath. Movement from Bristol to Salisbury and then Winchester can comfortably be accomplished with the main network as Margary understood it, but beyond Winchester there is no route known into Surrey. However, medieval Winchester possessed a gate in the north-east (the Durngate) and the east (East Gate) and the Gough Map shows a road running from Winchester to Guildford via Alresford, Alton, and Farnham. Thus it would be surprising if there was no corresponding Roman gate and, indeed, road for at least one and probably both of them. The alignment of Alresford Road certainly looks suggestive of a Roman origin and recent work by the North East Hampshire Historical and Archaeological Society has provided further convincing evidence for the existence of a road between Winchester and Staines using documentary sources and some limited excavation. In September there was a second uprising in Cornwall, with Perkin Warbeck (who claimed to be Richard IV) landing at Whitsand Bay near Plymouth and then marching on Exeter and then Taunton. The inadequacies of our knowledge of the Roman road network in the Cornish peninsula have already been mentioned but this adventure may give some hint of its ultimate extent in the south. At the same time, the castle of the Prince Bishops of Durham at Norham was attacked by James IV, who marched south with an artillery train (which included the bombard, Mons Meg). Unusually, he chose not to use Dere Street or the east coast route, but rather took a road that does not normally feature in Anglo-Scots warfare, from Haddington, across the Lammermuirs, and into the Merse (see Appendix 5). The fact that the route was able to accommodate artillery may indicate a Roman origin for it. [61]

The sixteenth century saw more border warfare in the north, with a minor battle at Milfield in 1512/13 occurring on a possible Roman route (see Appendix 5) before James IV returned to Norham in 1513, this time using the Dere Street route to bring up his artillery (perhaps indicating that the route over the Lammermuirs had proved less than satisfactory). This action was prior to his defeat at Flodden, again near a possible Roman road (see Appendix 5). His captured artillery was briefly stored in Etal Castle before being transported to Berwick.[62]

So passes the great medieval period of Roman road exploitation. This was by no means the end of their role in British history, as will become apparent. The Roman road system, modified and decaying, patched and diverted as it was, was far from finished as an agency of war.

Post-Medieval (AD 1540–1900)

Two long-term wars must dominate any consideration of the post-medieval use of Roman roads: the continued conflict with Scotland, and the English civil wars. This is the era when complaints about the decaying road system became loud and frequent and the authorities had to take action. Ultimately, this resulted in a complete overhaul of the system and the foundation of the turnpike trusts, but this did not happen until long after the end of the civil wars, so the Roman network still provided the skeleton to the flesh of these bloody conflicts.

After Flodden, many of the battles of the northern wars that became known as the Rough Wooing were more like minor skirmishes. The Battle of Haddon Rigg in August of 1542 took place just over 2 km to the south-west of Carham and close to the Tweed valley road (see Appendix 5). Just two months later, an English force made its way back along the Tweed from Berwick to attack Kelso and the surrounding region but had to return after running out of supplies. However it was not until November of that year that a decisive encounter occurred in the Battle of Solway Moss. James V led a force of 18,000 men south on the western side but was taken ill near Lochmaben, suggesting he was using Margary 7 for his attack (perhaps unsurprisingly). After crossing the Esk, the road passed along a low ridge before encountering the Lyne and it was between these two rivers that the small English force caught the much larger attacking Scottish army and the majority of the action took place close to the Roman road, according to Sir Thomas Wharton's account (and thus some way to the south of the present extent of Solway Moss).[63]

The Battle of Ancrum Moor in 1545 saw an English army, which had been raiding in the Borders, defeated by the Scots and once again a Roman road played a (quite literally) central role. Returning to Jedburgh from Melrose, so moving down Dere Street (Margary 8), the English army spotted a Scottish force moving westwards from Penniel Heugh (to the east of the road) and pursued them, the battle itself occurring to the west of the Roman road near Lilliardsedge.[64]

Roman roads may have enjoyed similar significance in the Battle of Pinkie Cleugh in September 1547. The English army, under Somerset, had advanced up the east coast from Berwick with 900 carts and fifteen artillery pieces, accompanied by a fleet with supplies. Camping near Prestonpans, they met the Scots in battle to the east of the Roman fort at Inveresk, which probably lay at the junction of the northern end of Dere Street (Margary 8), the eastern coastal route (see Appendix 5), and Margary 7 (which is aligned on Inveresk for most of its course, even though Margary has it turn towards Cramond). Indeed, Dere Street even appears to be included in an eyewitness sketch of the battle by William Patten. The resultant Scottish rout went in three directions: towards Leith, to Holyrood, and south to Dalkeith, all of those probably along Roman roads in the form of the east coast route, Margary 7, and Margary 8 respectively.[65]

The so-called Prayerbook Rebellion against Edward VI in 1549 saw a number of clashes between the rebels and loyalist forces, largely choreographed around the Roman roads of the region. The aftermath of a skirmish at Crediton (on Margary 493) saw the rebel force split, part going to besiege Exeter, the other part to the east of it at Clyst St Mary (Margary 49). The Battle of Fenny Bridges was then fought at the point where Margary 4 crossed the River Otter, the rebels under Arundell blocking Russell's attempt to march from Honiton to Exeter. Russell's second attempt to relieve Exeter avoided the main road and went south-westwards instead, with an encounter with the rebels at Woodbury Common suggesting a link road between Margary 4 at Honiton and Margary 49, nearer the south coast. Russell continued towards Exeter and the next battle was at Clyst St Mary. The execution of some 900 prisoners by the loyalists led to a renewed rebel attack on Clyst Heath, only for them to be defeated again and Exeter subsequently relieved. The whole sorry affair ended with a final battle where it had all started, at Sampford Courteney, which is situated on Margary 492, less than 3 km from the Roman fort at North Tawton.[66]

The events surrounding Mary Queen of Scots and her ambitions towards the English throne led to the Battle of Carberry Hill in 1567 and her surrender after a day-long stand-off. She had spent the night at Fa'side Castle, which also featured in the Battle of Pinkie Cleugh, lobbing a few desultory rounds at the English forces. As has already been alluded to, the road from Carberry down to Musselburgh is probably the northern end of the Dere Street.[67]

There was one last battle between England and Scotland and that occurred at Carter Bar in 1575 (sometimes known as the 'Raid of the Reidswire'). Surprisingly, this did not take place close to Dere Street (Margary 8), but rather at the headwaters of the Rede, where the modern A68 crosses the border, so it is possible that this, together with the A6088, represents at least in part a link road running over towards Margary 89 in the vicinity of Hawick (a suggestion that may be reinforced by a number of -chesters place-names along the route).[68]

Although the road system had somehow muddled through the medieval and the beginning of the post-medieval periods, the strain was beginning to show and the sixteenth century was the time when complaints about the condition of the roads became most strident. In 1555, the Highways Act placed the burden of upkeep of roads upon the parishes through which they ran. This was renewed and extended in 1563, 1575–6, and then made perpetual in 1587. However, these provisions were still concerned with repair and maintenance, not construction. New roads were still some way away, but something had changed: a number of the battles are indeed fought next to Roman roads, but roads which had been replaced by alternative routes. The Roman version may already have been in decay, either as hedgerows (and thus boundaries) or even ploughed out altogether. As we shall see, ironically, the alternative replacement routes may well have been a reversion to the older routes the Roman roads had supplanted. This was a new dynamic in action and the next stage in the evolution of our road network.[69]

The series of conflicts often simplified as the English Civil War was played out on the evolved network, but the Roman system of roads remained at its core and still had a strategic role to play. That being said, the first battle to be considered here, at Newburn ford, was not on a known Roman road, although only a short distance south of Hadrian's Wall and the accompanying Military Way which was, by all accounts, still a significant road in 1640. The ford, which was almost certainly in use in prehistoric times, to judge from finds of an Iron Age or Roman cart wheel from nearby, was defended by Charles' English forces and attacked by Scottish Covenanters from Newburn, to the north, resulting in an English rout. It serves to underline how the pre-Roman network could still be influential in the post-Roman period.[70]

Two years later, the Battle of Powick Bridge, generally regarded as the first action of the Civil War, was fought near Worcester, just 2 km to the west of Margary 180. Held to be of little account as a battle, it has a few intriguing aspects with regard to the Roman roads of the area. First, the overnight march of Nathaniel Fiennes' Parliamentarians from Alcester to Worcester is indicative of a missing (and surely logical) link in the Roman network. Second, a series of alignments of lanes and footpaths in St John's and Lower Wick, along which Fiennes advanced on the day of the battle, points towards the medieval bridging point and appears to line up with the change in course of the known Roman road from south-westerly to slightly east of south at the southern end of Rainbow Hill. This might indicate the existence of a spur road continuing in that same south-westerly direction, across the bridge, perhaps ultimately intended to link up with Margary 612 around Ross-on-Wye.[71]

The site of the Battle of Edgehill, which was fought a month after Powick Bridge, lies some 7 km from both Margary 5 and Margary 56. Whilst it is conceivable there is an unknown minor road nearby, this confrontation is more important from the point of view of the strategic moves made by the opposing armies as they moved towards it. The king marched his army back towards London from their base in Shrewsbury, naturally using Watling Street (Margary 1), in order to tempt a Parliamentarian attack. Most accounts then go on to say that Essex marched from Worcester and the two armies met at Edgehill, but this is difficult to understand in the context of what we know of the formal Roman network. This is perhaps the first hint at the revival of the use of the informal, pre-Roman network. The Battle of Turnham Green (and the skirmish the day before at Brentford) took place in November, near the junction of Margary 4 and 40.[72]

The Battle of Braddock Down in January of 1643 was fought in Cornwall, more than 30 km beyond the westernmost extent of the Roman road system as recorded by Margary but well to the east of the Cornish milestones from the western extremity of the peninsula, so it is not beyond the bounds of possibility that the A390 has a Roman origin. Two months later, the action at Hopton Heath in Staffordshire, just north-west of Stafford, occurred when a Parliamentarian force with artillery returning from Lichfield was intercepted by the Royalists, and it may indicate the existence of a link road between Wall (which is near Lichfield) and Chesterton. Back in Cornwall, the Battle of Stratton in the May, like Braddock Down, was not fought on or near a known Roman road. However the place-name is suggestive (one of the standard variants derived from *strata*), as is a long alignment of the A39 between Kilkhampton and Helebridge, adhering very closely to a 205/25 degree line. This impression is only reinforced by the brace of isolated milestones further down the north coast, near Tintagel.[73]

In June, the Battle of Adwalton Moor was fought immediately adjacent to Margary 712, although this was to some extent coincidental, with the Parliamentarian marching south-east out of Bradford in order to avoid a Royalist siege and the two forces running into each other at Adwalton.[74]

The Battle of Lansdown Hill in July is a classic example of a conflict fought out over a landscape dictated by the Roman infrastructure. Margary 542 ran north-west out of Bath, over Lansdown Hill and across the battlefield. The A420 to the north is Ogilby's London to Bristol road and may represent a link road between Margary 5 (the Fosse Way) and Margary 54 to Sea Mills and the Severn crossing. Just over a week later the Battle of Roundway Down occurred to the north of Devizes, on that same Bristol to London road recorded by Ogilby and south of Margary 53 which is now only marked by hedgerows along this stretch, so it seems likely that the Ogilby road had already replaced it by 1643. Continuing as the A4361, the alignment of the Roman road takes it to Avebury, so a prehistoric origin is likely: in other words, the prehistoric route was replaced by the Roman road which was in turn replaced by the reinstated prehistoric route![75]

The first Battle of Newbury in September of 1643 occurred when a Parliamentarian army under Essex, marching from Hungerford, was met on the western side of Newbury by the Royalists. This occurred just east of the point where Margary 53 joins route 41. Again, the Roman road is derelict for its whole length between the abandoned Roman town at Mildenhall and that junction with Ermin Street so it is likely it was already out of use by the time of the battle, replaced by the modern A4 following the line recorded by Ogilby.[76]

In January of 1644, the Battle of Nantwich took place immediately next to the line of Margary 700. Once again this may be coincidental, since much of the route of the road is derelict and only short lengths of road still adhere to it. Moreover, the action occurred from north to south, not east to west.[77]

The Battle of Cheriton occurred in March of 1644, near Alresford and to the east of Winchester, situated close to the likely line of a Roman road that was not included by Margary but has recently been investigated. Cropredy Bridge was fought three months later not far from Edgehill, and all the caveats that applied to the latter are associated with the former battle too. Lostwithiel, in June, was fought a little further to the west of Braddock Down and not far from the newly discovered Roman fortlet at Restormel, further pointing to Roman penetration of the peninsula. Marston Moor followed in July of the same year and was located between – and within easy reach of – two Roman roads that continue in use to this day: Dere Street (Margary 8) and the Rudgate (Margary 280).[78]

The Battle of Naseby, in June 1645, did not happen anywhere near an acknowledged Roman road, nor does there appear to be any evidence for any unrecognized examples in the vicinity. Students of the Civil Wars think of it as significant for the major defeat of the Royalist army, so students of Roman roads might be forgiven for thinking this conflict marks the end of the association of Roman roads with British battles, were it not for the motte and bailey castle which, when viewed in the context of the relationship of other such fortifications with Roman roads, may at least give pause to wonder whether the road from Naseby to Sibbertoft and on to Theddingworth may indeed have ancient origins.[79]

The Battle of Langport was fought in Somerset in July 1645, on a ridge of high ground that protrudes into the Somerset Levels. No Roman road has been recognized in the vicinity but a number of important villas are known in the area as well as the important Saxon royal centre of Somerton adjacent to the north-to-south Margary 51, so it is perhaps unsurprising that the road running along the ridge, the B3153, is laid out more-or-less straight, with gentle angular turns, like a Roman road. Rowton Heath in September of the same year was to the west of Chester but some 2 km to the south of Margary 7, near Long Lane which runs for some 22 km down towards Nantwich with some straight alignments that may point to a Roman origin. In the spring of 1646, the Battle of Stow-on-the-Wold was fought on the Fosse Way (Margary 5), although that may be coincidental, as Astley's troops were in fact marching from Worcestershire to Oxford; it may be that he was proceeding along a road of which the only known fragment is Margary 560. The Battle of Worcester in 1651, at the end of the

Civil Wars, revisited the site of Powick Bridge, which of course was fought at the very beginning.[80]

The turnpiking of roads in Britain began in earnest in 1663 with the first Turnpike Act. The system of levying tolls to pay for the upkeep of roads was already well established but was now formalized and extended and, as such, was a qualified success. By and large it is still only maintenance, not new constructions, but these do begin to happen.[81]

In 1685, the Battle of Sedgemoor was a part of the Monmouth Rebellion. The would-be usurper Monmouth led his army out of Bridgwater along the road to Bristol on a circuitous route that was to lead them to the royalist army. Although not recognized as such, there must be a suspicion that the road from Bridgwater to Bristol is Roman in origin. The road south-eastwards along the Polden Hills certainly was Roman and probably a pre-Roman ridgeway, but Monmouth seems to have kept to small lanes and employed a causeway in order to launch a surprise attack on his enemy. The royalists had likewise been approaching Bridgwater from the east, also using a causeway. These causeways were in existence by the fifteenth century and a Roman building nearby at Slape may hint at an even earlier origin for them.[82]

The 1715 and 1745 uprisings saw the last major conflicts on mainland British soil that are relevant to this discussion, and Roman roads still exert an influence on proceedings. Prestonpans, to the east of Edinburgh and west of Haddington, had featured as the camp site of the English prior to the Battle of Pinkie Cleugh, and in 1745 the army of Charles Edward Stuart defeated government forces in the first major confrontation of the Young Pretender's uprising. As before, it occurred next to the main east-coast road between Berwick and Edinburgh (see Appendix 5).[83]

As the Scottish army marched south, an attempt was made to intercept it by the government garrison of Newcastle, under Marshall George Wade, as we have already seen.[84]

As the rebel army marched south, a skirmish with government forces at Clifton Moor in Cumbria took place less than 2 km west of Margary 7 on the successor road running parallel to the Roman route and, as such, sums up the relationship between the Civil Wars battles and the Roman road system: it had evolved but was still influential in events.[85]

Battles and roads

Intriguingly, the association between roads and battles can be a two-edged sword, as the reader will quickly have realized. If a majority of battles are fought on or near Roman roads, then unlocated battles stand a good chance of having also been fought in such circumstances. Hence the plausibility of the suggestion that the Battle of Catraeth (c AD 600) took place at Catterick, or that the Anglian battle with the Picts at Nechtansmere (AD 685) occurred at Dunnichen near the Roman camp at Lunanhead. Moreover, this would suggest that long-sought-after major battles associated with Arthur, like Mons Badonicus or Camlan, may very well also have occurred near a Roman road. The exploitation of the Roman road network by medieval castles can also prove instructive. As an example, the Norman castle at Stafford, and the battle fought nearby (above page 76) may indicate the proximity of a previously unidentified Roman road, in this case perhaps one linking Margary 191 with 793. The association can be even more productive when looking for confirmation of a newly-identified route for a Roman road, so that the battle of Malcolm's Cross (1093) near Alnwick, where the Scottish king Malcolm Canmore was slain by an English army, serves as one of many indicators of a Roman road running from Newcastle upon Tyne to Tweedmouth, subsequently followed by the route of the Great North Road in Northumberland (see Appendix 5).[86]

It is perhaps ironic that the conflicts that litter the British landscape have one thing in common: they are almost inevitably the result of civil strife. The few examples of successful invasions, like the Danes or the Normans, exploited the Roman road system and there can be little doubt that it would have had its role to play had Operation Sea Lion gone ahead in 1940 (particularly given the apparent German lack of appreciation of the minor road system).[87]

Boundaries

Roads were not just routes along which post-Roman military campaigns were conducted, however. They were frequently used to delineate property boundaries, most famously with the Watling Street acting as part of the border between Wessex and the Danelaw (it is even named in the treaty of c AD 886 drawn up between Alfred and Guthrun). The Fosse Way and Icknield Way are both mentioned in early charters, being used as boundaries, and Dere Street as a medieval boundary has already been mentioned (above page 41). This suggests that names had become attached to the old Roman roads fairly early on in the post-Roman period and some of these names were evidently generic: Watling and Ermin(e) Street are certainly still applied to more than one road. Many roads are still coincident with parish boundaries, virtually all of which are Anglo–Saxon in origin (although some may even relate to Roman villa estate boundaries) so this has come to be one of the means of identifying routes once they have fallen out of use.[88]

In a law of 1050, Edward the Confessor supposedly named the roads protected by the King's Peace, these being 'Watling Strete, Fosse, Hikenild Strete, and Erming Strete'. It is now impossible to be sure precisely which roads were intended, the only clue given being that two ran up and down (i.e. north to south) and two across England (east to west), but it is a not unreasonable assumption that these roads can be identified with those we know as Watling Street (Margary 1), the Fosse Way (Margary 5), Ryknild Street (Margary 18, rather than the Icknield Way, Margary 333), and Ermine Street (Margary 2, as opposed to Ermin Street, Margary 41). Similar legislation is enacted by later monarchs, reflecting their continuing importance.[89]

It was not only the roads themselves that were used as boundaries. We have already seen how the Rey Cross, a stone set up on the boundary of the Diocese of Glasgow and said to mark the site of the death of Eric Bloodaxe, may in fact have been on the site of a Roman milestation. There is also a tradition that the London Stone, now situated on the north side of Cannon Street but originally on the south side, at the entrance to what is thought to be the governor's palace, may in fact be a Roman milestone or even a *milliarium*, a central milestone from which measurements along radiating roads were taken. It was certainly acting as a landmark and boundary stone in the ninth century AD, when it is mentioned, and continued to do so into the eighteenth century. As a manuport (it is made of oolitic limestone from the Chilterns) it has certainly been brought to the city, but the truth of its origins may never be known.[90]

Maintenance

Medieval monarchs were sometimes more concerned with the form of a road than they were with the state of its surface. Henry I required that two waggons should be able to pass each other on a highway, and that sixteen knights should be able to ride abreast. As with the Romans, a road was seen not just as the surfaced strip in the middle, but also the margins too. The Statute of Winchester of 1285 saw important provision for the road network of Britain. This required manorial landowners to keep the margins of a road clear to a distance of 200 ft to either side 'so that there may be no ditch, underwood or bushes where one could hide with evil intent'. The upkeep of roads could be funded by pavage, a toll imposed on road users and supposedly intended for the maintenance of the road fabric. In 1353, Edward III decreed pavage for the '*alta via*' westwards out of London, namely The Strand between Temple Bar and Westminster (Margary 40). Although a picture of poor quality roads is often painted for the medieval period, it has been pointed out that the fact that medieval kings could move around the kingdom throughout the year suggests this is perhaps a pessimistic view of the realities of medieval land transport.[91]

Deviations to avoid obstacles are most obvious in any long straight stretch of road which suddenly makes a loop to one side. Although the reason for the detour may no longer be apparent, its effect on traffic often remains with us until today, whilst the old line may often be preserved in boundaries of some kind. Not all such deviations may be recent, however, for part of Stane Street appears to include an original Roman one, where difficult terrain was avoided by a detour (Figure 26).[92]

It is appropriate that Edward I, under whom the Statute of Winchester was enacted, should have travelled and campaigned widely on the Roman road network. Indeed, as will become apparent later (Chapter 5), his itineraries provide one of the aids to identifying previously unsuspected Roman roads.

In 1555, a highways act known as 'the Statute of Phillip and Mary' made parishes, rather than manors, responsible for the upkeep of roads and examples

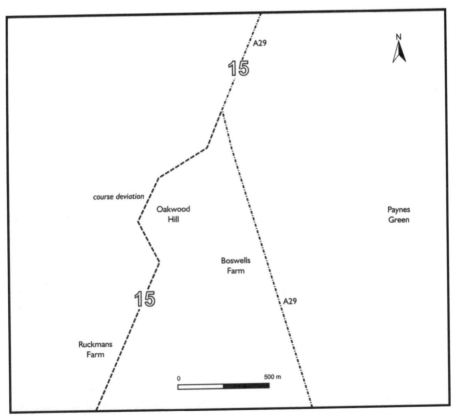

Figure 26: A Roman course deviation on Stane Street.

of individual bequests being made towards the upkeep of the road system are known. Individuals were required to give several days of 'statute duty' for the upkeep of the system, including the provision of waggons and draught animals. Still, however, this is maintenance and not construction. So what was being maintained? The existing system, of course, and that remained largely Roman.[93]

Nodal points and medieval towns

Many Roman military and civil sites were subsequently occupied in the early medieval period, albeit not always in exactly the same location (the Saxon settlements at Corbridge and London being situated next to, rather than on, Roman remains). One of the major attractions of such sites would be their position at nodal points or hubs in the road network. Some sites did not continue beyond the Roman period, however, and one of the reasons for this could well have been roads falling out of use. Two examples of this are Silchester in Berkshire, now a greenfield site with no major roads passing through it, and Mildenhall in Wiltshire, both evidently key nodal points in the Roman and pre-Roman system. Examination of the fossilized remains of the road system in the surrounding modern landscape shows just how effectively they have been removed by comparison with other sites (Figure 27). Sometimes the node in the road system will remain in use but the Roman site be replaced by a nearby medieval settlement, as happened with Wroxeter and Shrewsbury or Corchester and Corbridge. At Mildenhall, the main north-to-south roads (Margary 43 and 44) were diverted to the new medieval town of Marlborough (which was placed slightly further west on the east-to-west Margary 53).[94]

This continued use of large parts of the Roman road network serves to explain why so many prominent English towns and cities have a Roman origin, and equally why some do not. Just as Silchester or Mildenhall fell out of favour, so other settlements may have been located to take advantage of other routes, perhaps even some retained from the prehistoric period. This surely serves to emphasize the reliance upon trade moving along the road system in the medieval and – by implication – in the Roman period too. When populations were less mobile than they are today, it is primarily goods and services (and their purveyors) that would have travelled. Without roads, much of Britain would be deprived of trade.

The enduring importance of communications in medieval Britain is also reflected in the siting of important castles. This is as true of motte-and-bailey castles of the eleventh or twelfth century as it is of stone castles of later times (Figure 28). Indeed, the coincidence of location between castles and

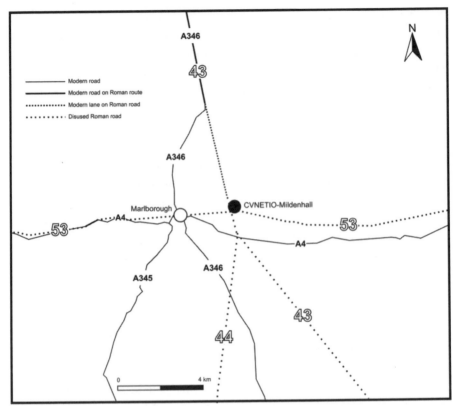

Figure 27: Shifting the population centre from Mildenhall-Cunetio to Marlborough. Did the roads move because of the settlement change or vice versa?

Roman forts is less than accidental: not only do the same strategic and tactical considerations hold true, they oversee the same communications network. In some cases medieval castles actually sit within Roman forts, as at Tomen-y-Mur, Bowes, Brough, Brougham, Cardiff, Portchester, or Newcastle upon Tyne (the former Monkchester) but more often they content themselves with being near neighbours.[95]

The military were not the only element of medieval society with an interest in good communications. The church made widespread use of Roman military sites, with early medieval ecclesiastical centres being established at locations such as Chester-le-Street (where St Cuthbert's mobile remains enjoyed a brief sojourn), Inveresk, and of course in legionary fortresses at Caerleon, Chester, and York (all three of which also attracted a castle for good measure). So it was that *castra* became –*chester* (from the Old English *ceaster*) just as surely as *strata* became –*street* (Old English *straet*). The great monastic centres required good

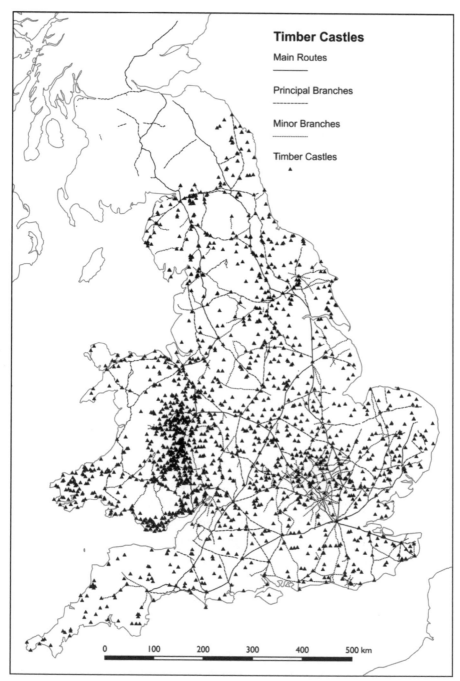

Figure 28: Roman roads and the timber castles of England and Wales (using data from www. gatehouse-gazetteer.info).

lines of communications, particularly to facilitate the gathering of tax and the transportation of their produce and this was one reason why Mastiles Lane continued in use from prehistory, through the Roman period, into the medieval and modern eras. As in the Roman period, much will have gone by river and sea, but a great deal still needed roads.[96]

Whilst part (arguably a major part) of the Roman all-weather road network continued in use into the medieval period – one estimate, using the Gough Map (see below page 111), suggests forty per cent of the 3,000 miles of road depicted – it seems fairly certain that the same must have been true of those parts of the prehistoric network that were never formally adopted by the Romans, but nevertheless continued in use. Many, perhaps even most, of the drove roads of the medieval period may owe their origins to existing tracks. 'Portways', 'portgates', and – most particularly – salt roads will have been adopted and adapted to suit the changing needs of medieval society in Britain, just as seems to have happened to the Roman network. It is therefore very likely that a majority of modern byways, country lanes, minor classified – and unclassified – roads probably have a prehistoric origin. Additionally, Hindle has written of 'roads that made themselves' between settlements, effectively the same phenomenon we saw described when animal tracks became hunting trails, and so on.[97]

The evolution of the Roman road

The most important maintenance a road could receive was, perhaps a little surprisingly, continual use. Lack of use would allow plants to colonise rapidly, especially blackthorn. This would not only break up the metalling but also, once established, tend to render the road impassable fairly rapidly. However, frost and wet would attack those portions that remained in use and lead to potholing and it is for this reason that various legal measures were taken in the medieval period to maintain the system. The fact that such legislation is repeated over the ages suggests an unwillingness to participate in such work, and that may be supported by the common complaints about the state of roads in Britain. However, it has also been suggested that the volume of complaints almost certainly exaggerated the true state of the road network.[98]

Course deviations are frequently visible on Roman roads that have continued in use, usually manifested as a short loop before the original straight line is resumed. In some cases, deviations could be more substantial, as when the A68 runs parallel to, and immediately next to, the Roman Dere Street (Margary 8f), just to the south of Newstead. The way in which this came about could be seen on old twentieth century trans-Sahara routes, where surfaces were, in parts, so degraded that vehicles ran next to, but not on, the original course. In the medieval period, we can also see this on the Stanegate near Hadrian's Wall, where numerous later trackways run alongside the Roman road, or again on Dere Street near Chew Green, forming multiple (or 'braided') trackways.[99]

The absence of Roman roads or inadequacy of existing routes in much of central and western Highland Scotland led to the construction of the military roads of the first half of the eighteenth century to help quell the rebellious Scots. George Wade had encountered considerable difficulties trying to march his army along the Tyne valley during the 1745 uprising, the remains of the Stanegate being largely disused and replaced by the Carelgate (possibly the course of its prehistoric antecedent), which was in a poor state of repair, and that (through Act of Parliament) led directly to the subsequent construction of the Military Road (the B6318/A69) which utilized Hadrian's Wall for long stretches, both as a quarry and – in parts – as a foundation.[100]

After centuries of service, the Roman road network finally began to be enhanced and augmented during the nineteenth century. The advent of turnpike roads, with their system of tolls, finally saw the arrival of something approaching a viable means of funding road construction and repair, although the system did have its problems and in some places did not last very long. Moreover, far from constructing a completely new road system, it largely just upgraded what was already existing: for the most part, Roman roads. Construction techniques even resembled those of their predecessors, but the development of tarmac in the early twentieth century (the adding of coal tar and later asphalt to the 'Macadamized' rammed-gravel surfaces used on the turnpikes) provided a durability the Romans were seldom (but not always) unable to achieve. Engineers gradually became more adventurous, producing cuttings and embankments to ease the gradients of the old system.[101]

One of the few nineteenth century engineers who actually set about building new roads, rather than improving what already existed, was Thomas Telford. His project for an alternative Great North Road sought to link Morpeth, to the north of Newcastle upon Tyne, with the Dere Street, thus providing a more direct link to Edinburgh than already existed. He changed the line taken by the turnpike in many places and, for a time, both his new road (which is now the A697) and the original course ran almost parallel with each other for some distance (Figure 29). It is ironic that, in doing this, he was almost certainly doing exactly what the Romans did when upgrading the existing British network – keeping the general course, and even long sections of the original road, but modifying specific stretches where he thought it necessary. It is even

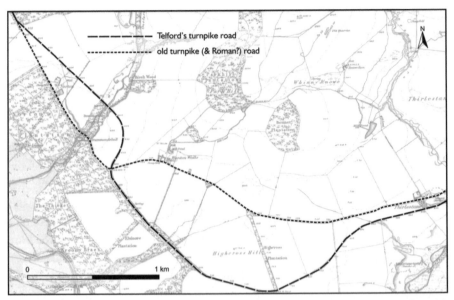

Figure 29: Parallel roads: the old turnpike and Telford's successor at Thirlestane, Scottish Borders.

more ironic that the turnpike road he was replacing may have been Roman in origin.[102]

The first truly new road system to be constructed in Britain after the Romans was in fact the railways, the so-called permanent way. Requiring major engineering (in terms of cuttings, embankments, bridges, and tunnels), because the technology was so sensitive to gradients, the system spread across Britain. Even so, it was still influenced by the Roman road network, for the towns and cities it linked were often located where they were because of that same Roman road system. Moreover, many of the topographical factors that determined the course of a road would have much the same effect on a railway, so that it is not unusual to find a Roman road, railway, modern road, and possibly even a canal forced through a geographical 'pinch-point' such as the Watford Gap.[103]

The popularity of the motor car saw roads improved even further, although this was still only in the form of strengthening and widening (particularly with the conversion of trunk roads into dual carriageways). Finally, the motorway system saw the first serious campaign of genuinely new road construction, with roads designed specifically for the needs of the motor vehicle, using gentle curves and gradients (rather than the sudden turns and hills of earlier roads), often requiring major engineering to modify the landscape to suit the needs of the road. Paradoxically, we seem to have done to the Roman network what the Romans did to the prehistoric system they found: replaced or upgraded the major routes and continued using the rest of it with only the minimum of modification.[104]

Subsequent developments to the road system have in many cases fossilized Roman roads beneath later surfaces. Occasionally, the chance to excavate these occurs, but the practicalities of working on a trunk road often render this difficult. Nevertheless, roads buried in this way are preserved in the condition immediately prior to their being resurfaced and they are protected from the sort of degradation suffered by roads that are no longer in use.

Paradoxically, then, once a road goes out of use, it seldom disappears completely. Nowadays it is rare to find a modern road actually grubbed up once it has ceased to serve its original function, and as trunk roads around Britain have been upgraded, and their awkward parts smoothed out, small sections on the original Roman line may survive, often serving as lay-bys or farmyard access roads, possibly preserving their original surfaces below layers of modern metalling.

Chapter 5

Rediscovery

But though antient ways are soon sunk in grounds formerly woody and soft, and now much improved and inclosed; yet such ways as were laid through this county would probably be well paved; which may so far make it more probable, that *Stane-street* has been antient and *Roman. John Horsley*[1]

Roman roads are still an important constituent element in the modern landscape of Britain, not least through the role they continue to play in the infrastructure. There has always been a kind of tacit understanding of their importance, but it is only when antiquarians like Horsley begin to take a closer look at them that the mechanisms for their survival, and hence the means to study them, would become apparent. Tracing a Roman road requires the accumulation of a series of clues. Each of these, in and of itself, will be no proof of a route, but taken together, they serve to provide a tell-tale body of evidence. Understanding these clues inevitably requires some degree of comprehension of the role they have played in shaping modern Britain.

Traces in the landscape

It is quite unusual for a Roman road to have vanished completely. More often than not it will have left a variety of indications to its existence and students of Roman roads have used these to identify or verify possible routes. Margary outlined his methodology and these principles have been repeated and expanded upon at the same time as remote sensing techniques for archaeology have improved. Indeed, alternative methodologies have developed that are driven by serendipitous observation through aerial photography, geophysical survey, or even the excavation of unexpected roads.[2]

One of the most obvious ways that Roman roads have been identified in the landscape is where they have remained in use and a modern road exhibits the characteristics of its predecessor. Since, for the most part, the Romans laid out their roads in straight stretches with obtuse-angled turns where necessary, they differ markedly from normal sinuous British country roads, or the sweeping, gently curvaceous routes preferred by more recent roads and motorways that have to take account of the higher speeds of modern travel. However, as we have seen (above, page 104), modern roads do not always sit directly on top of a Roman predecessor, since they can undergo lateral 'creep'.[3]

Occasionally roadworks afford the opportunity (albeit on a very small scale) to confirm the existence of an underlying Roman road and such opportunities are one of the few ways in which modern developer-funded archaeology can make a positive contribution to road studies. Even more rarely, major road engineering works will permit some form of larger-scale examination, as has happened in recent years on the Fosse Way in Nottinghamshire, Roman Ridge to the north of Castleford, and Ermin Street through Gloucestershire and Wiltshire. These are very rare, however, but nonetheless valuable for the detailed information they can provide on structural aspects of a particular short stretch of road.[4]

What such developer-funded archaeological work cannot do, however, is provide a synthetic overview of the road system of the sort Margary, and before him Codrington, attempted. This has to rely upon work undertaken by volunteer (one hesitates to use the term 'amateur') fieldworkers who devote time to tracing and, in most instances, excavating trial trenches across Roman roads. Until recently, attempts to consolidate this knowledge have been few and far between, but the Cadw Roman Roads Project in Wales has borne fruit with one report already published for the south-east of the principality. Elsewhere, preliminary work is underway to update the whole of Margary's system by the North East Hampshire Historical and Archaeological Society (see below page 127).[5]

The course of roads that have gone out of use can be preserved in field boundaries, often continuing the route of a modern road where it veers from the Roman route for some reason. This happens for the reasons discussed above in relation to the role of a road as a boundary – even if a road used as a delimiter went out of use, the notional line it marked would usually continue to exist. As such, this has proved to be another valuable tool for road hunters.[6]

There is a wide and much-exercised range of place-names that are indicative of the proximity of a Roman road and they are cited by most of the modern authorities. The most obvious is 'street', derived from the Anglo-Saxon interpretation of the late Roman word for a road, *strata* (see above page 41). This can occur in the name of a town (Chester-le-Street: Margary 80; Stretford: Margary 7; Streatham: Margary 150; Stretham: Margary 23), village (Stretton: Margary 1 and 18), farm (Streatham Farm: Margary 140), route, or other significant landmark. Other common place-names include 'path' or 'peth' in some part and the same is true of 'gate' and 'causeway' (or 'causey'). Another word that it is thought can point to the proximity of a Roman road is 'chester', derived from the Anglo-Saxon *ceaster*, coming directly from the Latin *castra* for a military base of some kind (but in this case interpreted more widely to include native British settlements).[7]

One of the more puzzling associations of names with Roman roads is that of 'coldharbour' and 'caldecot'. Although the meaning of these words (particularly coldharbour) has been much debated, with little sign of a plausible interpretation being reached, it has long seemed fairly clear that there *is* an association between the place-name and the presence of a Roman road nearby. This apparent relationship has been questioned using statistical methods and, whilst objections have also been raised as to the antiquity of the name 'coldharbour', the conviction that this place-name can be a reliable indicator of the proximity of a Roman road persists, not least as any statistical analysis can only ever be based on known roads. Thus the presence of such a name well away from a known Roman road could equally signify the proximity of an as-yet-unidentifed road and thus render the statistical analysis as good as meaningless.[8]

These, then, are the first two major landscape clues to the existence of a Roman road: the right kind of alignments and related place-names.

Documentary evidence

It has been stressed just how important the later use of Roman roads is in affirming their continued existence. We know of such use, particularly military campaigns, through surviving historical accounts and other documentary evidence, such as official records, and these comprise the third set of clues.

Medieval histories frequently record details of military campaigns and, as has already been pointed out, armies prefer (and have always preferred) to use roads for movement wherever possible. The recurrent use of the same route over a long period is usually indicative of a Roman origin for a road. This does not mean that medieval armies *always* used a metalled Roman road and ignored other parts of the network, but rather that it was usual for them to take the most convenient route (which for an army is almost always a metalled road).

Similarly, royal itineraries reconstructing the day-to-day progress of kings around Britain can prove a valuable confirmatory source for the continued use of large sections of the Roman road network. Medieval kings travelled widely around their kingdoms, and detailed records of their movements and the associated accounts were maintained, listing the places visited in each year in order. The nature of such expeditions, invariably accompanied by a large entourage, meant that the best road available was desirable. As with John, superimposing a map of the various surviving and reconstructed itineraries upon one of the Roman road systems as we currently understand it can not only act as a window on some parts of that system which were still in use, but also allow a much more comprehensive composite picture of the whole to be formed. However, it has to be remembered that just because a Roman route was not used by an itinerary, it does not necessarily follow that it was no longer active. Conversely, just because an itinerary uses a route with no known Roman predecessor it does not mean there is not one to be found.[9]

Legal documents can also be useful. The most famous example is probably the treaty drawn up between Alfred the Great and Guthrun, where the Watling Street was used as part of the delimitation of the Danegeld. This also works on a smaller scale, however, where descriptions of Anglo-Saxon parish boundaries incorporated lengths of Roman road. The road up the Greet Valley, near Osmanthorpe in Nottinghamshire, is recorded in this way.[10]

Medieval maps, like those of Matthew Paris (c. 1250) and the so-called Gough map (c. 1360), are other potential sources of valuable information. Of the four versions of Paris' (which is based on an itinerary from Dover to Newcastle), only one actually marks the course of a road. The Gough map contains far more information and provides a number of interesting details, such as an east–west road across south-eastern England – from Canterbury to Southampton via Hythe, Rye, Winchelsea, Battle, Boreham Street, Lewes, Shoreham, Arundel, Chichester, and Havant (Plate 16) – which is only partly attested from known portions of Roman road (Margary 130, 140, and 421). The modern place-name Boreham Street (although only 'Borham' on the map) is of course suggestive of the proximity of a Roman road. This route appears to be confirmed by other 'street' place-name evidence (Ham Street, Brook Street, Reading Street, and Gardiner Street in Herstmonceux), and seems to have hugged the contemporary coastline (now much altered by sea-level change and alluviation). It may also have been employed for at least one royal itinerary, perhaps even providing a highway for William the Conqueror's invading army in 1066 (see above page 76). However, the Gough map is also surprising for some of its omissions. Whilst a road from Canterbury to Southampton is shown, the arguably more important route to London (Margary 2) is not. Similarly, Hadrian's Wall is depicted, but no road accompanies it, despite King John's evident use of the Stanegate. One estimate suggests that forty per cent of the approximately 3,000 miles of road shown on the Gough map were Roman in origin, but it clearly presents a partial (in more than one sense) picture.[11]

At a more local level, tithe maps and their associated documents can sometimes prove invaluable in providing details of field names, some of which can produce place-name evidence for a road, or even reveal a long-lost field boundary, ploughed out during the inevitable enlargement of field systems in recent times.

Bertram and Stukeley

An interesting footnote to Roman roads studies, and one which was to have repercussions into the modern era for the mapping of the road system, concerns what is known as the Bertram Map. The antiquarian Stukeley 'discovered', and encouraged Charles Bertram (an Englishman who had been living in Copenhagen) to publish a rather unusual map he claimed to have found, supposedly compiled from material recorded by a medieval writer, Richard of Westminster (identified by Stukeley with one Richard of Cirencester, who had indeed lived at Westminster). The whole map was subsequently shown to be a collection of data garnered from various sources, but interestingly it still has a habit of being able to 'predict' the course of undiscovered roads. A rational explanation for this might be that the hoaxer, Bertram, used contemporary roads to fill in the gaps in his other sources, thus – given the nature of the contemporary road network – most of his major roads were bound to be Roman in origin. It is therefore more by luck than judgement that he may have included as-yet-unrecorded stretches of Roman road.[12]

Fieldwork

One of the attractions of the study of Roman roads has been that the tools are readily available to any who take an interest, even the lone fieldworker. Unlike major archaeological projects, which nowadays require vast amounts of money and a huge army of specialists, the pursuit of a road need not be expensive nor particularly labour-intensive. Such research can indeed be carried out by the determined individual, Ivan Margary's preferred way of working, but ultimately, the back-up of a small team, such as many archaeological societies can provide, has proved invaluable, and this was what lay behind the group known as the Viatores (see page 121). Whilst research can piece together many of the clues outlined above to show the likely course of a Roman road (and examples of alignments, place-names, and accounts of medieval armies using a road are pretty compelling circumstantial evidence), final proof requires some sort of archaeological investigation. This process can best be summed up as research, exploration, and examination. Even the last of these can, however, lead to less than satisfactory conclusions. Roads can often look Roman when in fact they were not. A number of routes excavated by Raymond Selkirk and claimed as previously unknown components of the Roman network have been disputed by other researchers, but the most famous contentious 'Roman' road has to be the paved section at Blackstone Edge. This last is certainly on or near a genuine Roman road (Margary 720), but the point at issue is whether that particular surface is Roman or later. It is salutary to recall for how long Roman roads have been used and repaired.[13]

Research

Researchers looking for Roman roads in Britain usually begin by examining maps. Even the modern 1:50,000 Ordnance Survey Landranger series can be of some use for this, but by far the best place to start is the First Edition Ordnance Survey six-inch (1:10,560) series, most of which date to just after the middle of the nineteenth century (although in Scotland William Roy's maps of the 1749–55 Military Survey can be enlightening). The OS six-inch maps are of a large enough scale to enable details such as field boundaries and settlement names to be included, yet sufficiently small to allow something of an overview of a likely road course in relation to the topography and place it in the context of other monuments in a given area. Conveniently, all of these are now accessible online.[14]

One needs to be aware of the shortcomings of the Ordnance Survey's recording of monuments in the past with particular respect to Roman roads. A marked tendency can be detected to 'join the dots' between possible sightings of a road on the First Edition six-inch series and Margary is occasionally dismissive of some of the Survey's more idiosyncratic identifications (although not averse to using the same technique himself at times!). This inevitably leads to misrecording and misunderstanding of the course of a road, and many a vain attempt at exploration has resulted from a misplaced reliance on the clairvoyant capabilities of the Ordnance Survey.[15]

Copies of old Ordnance Survey record cards exist for most monuments recorded on their maps and these are usually available in the respective National Monuments Records (NMR) for England, Scotland, and Wales. These can be compared with the information on the OS maps, and the three NMRs integrate this data, together with other material, on their base maps for any given area and this is all now generally accessible online. The heritage environment records (HERs, formerly sites and monuments records or SMRs) for any county or regional council have their own records. These will often overlap with the appropriate NMR, but each will usually contain at least some material that the other does not have. Such national and regional databases include large numbers of aerial photographs from a variety of sources, and to these have to be added the coverage that used to be held by the Cambridge University Committee for Aerial Photography (CUCAP). An ever-increasing number of HERs and SMRs are also accessible online.[16]

Aerial photography is vital in understanding Roman roads. Coverage, both vertical and oblique, increased dramatically during the Second World War and, once its value had been recognized, has continued to expand in breadth and depth. The largest single campaign after the war was undertaken to mark the turn of the millennium in 2000 by Getmapping plc, producing what they called the Millennium Map. Starting with England, they have subsequently expanded their coverage to the whole of Britain. Aerial photographic surveys like this, combined with high-resolution satellite imagery, form the basis of virtual globe software such as *Google Earth*. Indeed, the advent of internet access to large-scale aerial and satellite coverage has revolutionized archaeological research and given rise to the tabloid use of the cliché 'armchair archaeology'. Neogeographical tools (like *Google Earth*) provide the means to survey routes and compare more than one set of coverage, where available. Some areas of Britain are even covered by black and white photography from the Second World War in this way, all mapped onto the modern base provided by Google. To illustrate the potential of this visual data, a file containing Margary's map of the road network plotted onto *Google Earth* is available on the accompanying website (see Chapter 7).[17]

Aerial photographs not only permit an overview of a section of road, in much the same way as maps do, but also provide evidence for previously-unknown roads. Crop or soil marks will sometimes reveal the line of a road in this way. A good example of this is a previously unknown minor road on the eastern coastal plain of Scotland, not far from the legionary fortress at Inchtuthil (Plate 17). Now under agricultural land, the road shows as a pale line flanked by its dark drainage ditches but also accompanied by what appear to be quarry pits on either side, beyond the ditches. Since the road is at this point crossing a river floodplain, the purpose of these was almost certainly to provide sand and gravel for the construction of the road. This road, for whatever reasons, is not indicated by any other form of evidence except for aerial photographs and is a clear demonstration of the value of aerial photography. Another road (Margary 64), near Trefeglwys (Powys), shows up well in an oblique aerial view (Plate 18), its course indicated in turn by a hedgerow, parch marks, and then a matching modern road alignment.

Lidar (Light Detection And Ranging) is a comparatively new archaeological technique that uses airborne laser survey of the ground surface to produce extremely accurate maps of the topography and has the potential to identify features that might otherwise go unnoticed, even in the field. It has the useful

1. The popular view of Roman roads arriving in Britain. *(courtesy Rupert Besley)*

2. The Ridgeway, looking north–east towards Uffington Castle hillfort. *(photo: M.C. Bishop)*

3. Mastiles Lane confined by eighteenth century enclosure, near Malham Camp. *(photo: N. Sheridan)*

4. The Vindolanda milestations. *(photo: M.C. Bishop)*

5. Wade's Causeway
on Wheeldale Moor.
(photo: M.C. Bishop)

5. Wade's Causeway on Wheeldale Moor. *(photo: M.C. Bishop)*

6. Road foundation in the *vicus* at Brough-on-Noe. *(photo: M.C. Bishop)*

7. Milestones from Crindledykes. *(photo: M.C. Bishop)*

8. Milestation XXI on the Via Nova Traiana in Jordan with multiple milestones. *(photo: © M.C. Bishop)*

9. Painted milestone inscription from Jordan. *(photo: D. Graf)*

10. Milestone (from the Military Way?) reused as a gatepost near Great Chesters. *(photo: M.C. Bishop)*

11. The *agger* of Margary 54 just visible as a linear mound on Durdham Down in Bristol. *(photo: M.C. Bishop)*

12. The truncated *agger* on Dere Street (Margary 8) north of Corbridge. *(photo: M.C. Bishop)*

13. The Stanegate (Margary 85) at Haltwhistle Burn. *(photo: M.C. Bishop)*

14. Pack and draught animals on Trajan's Column. *(photo: M.C. Bishop)*

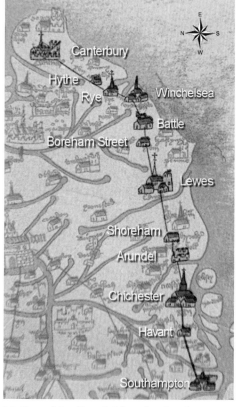

15. A tarmac single-track road surface decaying. *(photo: M.C. Bishop)*

16. Part of the Gough Map, showing the Canterbury to Southampton route – a missing Roman road?

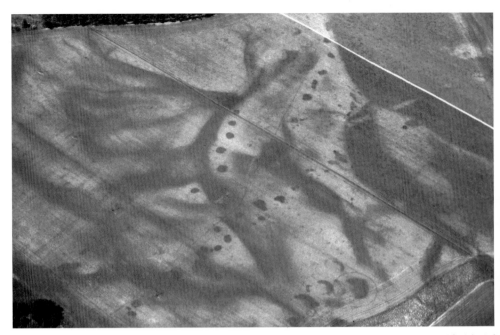

17. A road near Inchtuthil (unknown to Margary) found from the air. *(photo: © RCAHMS (Aerial Photography Collection); licensor www.rcahms.gov.uk)*

18. A road (Margary 64) indicated by a hedgerow, parch marks, and modern road alignment near Trefeglwys (Powys). *(photo: © Crown copyright: RCAHMW)*

capability of being able to penetrate the canopy in wooded areas in order to reveal the underlying terrain. Most such mapping in Britain was initially done for the Environment Agency to assist in flood prediction and that can be archaeologically useful. Increasingly, however, bespoke surveys are being undertaken to examine archaeological landscapes.[18]

Exploration

A route suggested by the study of maps would next be checked on the ground. However good maps or aerial photographs might be, it is always deemed essential that a road be explored on the ground. Some roads may even first suggest themselves by being driven along. Nevertheless, there are plenty of 'Roman' roads that are in fact straightened modern sections of older roads, although these should always be apparent by comparison of old maps with newer editions. More importantly, the observation of an *agger* on the suspected line can only truly be appreciated from the ground, although modern methods of lidar survey can pick out extremely subtle micro-earthworks. At Charthouse-on-Mendip, archaeological lidar survey has demonstrated the continuation of the Roman road (Margary 45) on the alignment described by Margary.[19]

There are many ways of exploring a Roman road within its landscape. A lucky few will be able to overfly a suspected road, but even this might not produce the same insights into the lie of the land or lines of sight provided by travelling along the surface of a road. This can be accomplished in a number of ways.

Whilst it might be thought that a car provides a useful means of transport for a survey of a fairly long stretch of road, in fact it has distinct disadvantages (besides the obvious environmental ones), not least that – should it prove desirable to inspect part in greater detail – it can be difficult to park safely (or even legally in the case of some roads). Walking is probably the most straightforward way of exploring a Roman road that has been employed, but is of course very slow and, where following a course along a modern trunk road in the countryside, can be positively dangerous. The ideal compromise might be to use a bicycle or (and this is admittedly rare) ride a horse. Slower than a car, but faster than walking, such methods permit an overview of fairly large sections of a road, while still at the same time allowing the researcher to stop virtually anywhere they wish. There is also the added advantage of unhindered access to routes that have been reduced to the status of bridleways (as often happens with Roman roads).

Examination

The only way to prove the existence of a road conclusively is by some sort of physical intervention or 'ground truthing', but there are other techniques that can provide qualitative data about the nature of a supposed road. All will require the cooperation of landowners and, in certain circumstances, some (probing, geophysical survey, and trenching) may even necessitate applications for scheduled monument consent.

Simple fieldwalking, with the permission of the landowner, has long been used to provide evidence of, and crude dimensions for, ploughed-out road surfaces. In most cases where this happens, however, such roads will be visible without even needing to enter a field, especially from the air.[20]

Probing is quick and simple and supplies simple binary data about a road, since it either makes contact with a hard surface or it does not. Of course, frequent strikes on hard material need not necessarily be caused by the remains of a road, but if it is on the line of a road that has been suspected for other reasons, then it may well be another indication of the promising nature of the investigation. This will obviously only work on roads that have gone out of use, and probably in a rural area. Note that probing is illegal on a scheduled monument without having first obtained scheduled monument consent. The outlines of scheduled areas are accessible online using Defra's MAGIC mapping facility (see Chapter 7).[21]

Some researchers have had success with archaeological dowsing, although there is as yet no objective assessment of the efficacy of the technique in relation to Roman roads, nor even any indication of how widespread its use might be. If there is uncertainty over how dowsing works, there seems little doubt that it *can* work, under the right circumstances (and the writer knows of at least one dowser who enjoys a measure of success in using the technique as part of his armoury of methods for tracing Roman roads). Nevertheless, it should be pointed out that any results supported *only* by dowsing are almost invariably going to be the object of academic criticism.[22]

Geophysical survey (and related forms of remote sensing) provide more sophisticated data about extent, course, and features of a road, but there is still much that it cannot provide (except indirectly), such as dating evidence. In this respect, resistivity survey is perhaps the most useful in road prospection, since roads normally provide high-resistance readings, side ditches low ones. It is, however, labour intensive for large scale survey.[23]

Far and away the best way to test the existence and nature of a Roman road is to excavate a section through it. Unfortunately, it is also the most costly and time-consuming method. A sondage will provide details of the materials and methods of construction, show the precise width and depth of the road at the chosen location, and how many (if any) resurfacings or repairs were made, as well as placing the road in the context of any flanking ditches or quarry pits, provided that trenches are made sufficiently long to encounter such items.[24]

What others have done before

The study of the roads of Roman Britain has always been the province of amateur scholars, by and large, and none of the major scholars who might be named were tenured academics. Fortunately, this does not mean the quality of their scholarship is in any way inferior to that of their colleagues whose interests lie elsewhere, but is rather a sad reflection of the lack of attention most scholars pay to the road system in Britain.

Comments on the Roman road network in Britain can be found in many antiquarians. Roger Gale's *Essay Towards the Recovery of the Courses of the Four Great Roman Ways* was appended to the sixth volume of Leland's *Itinerary* in 1764, so it is unsurprising that Horsley's *Britannia Romana* of 1732 contains much on the subject of Roman roads, since Horsley originally undertook his journey in 1725 in the company of Gale. Equally, during his travels around Britain, Daniel Defoe noted the importance of Roman roads and even examined the structure of some examples. However, Thomas Codrington was arguably the first of the great amateur scholars to produce a detailed survey of the road network and Margary was quick to acknowledge his influence in his own work. An engineer by training, Codrington is otherwise best known for his volume *The Maintenance of Macadamised Roads* (perhaps less so for his *Report on the Destruction of Town Refuse*), so the precise nature of his background – and the likely reasons for his interest in Roman roads – is not hard to find. His work, *Roman Roads in Britain*, first published in 1903 when he was seventy-six years old and revised twice before his death in 1918, provided an overview of the road system of Roman Britain. In his review of the third edition of the work, Francis Haverfield, doyen of Romano-British studies, noted acerbically 'as so often happens, the surveyor has excluded the geographer' and 'Mr Codrington cares little for what others have done before him'. Haverfield characteristically did not 'get' the cataloguing instinct betrayed by most students of roads and always sought the big picture. Codrington's work remains worthy of examination, however, not least for those roads he saw fit to include but Margary chose to exclude (often without comment). A good example of this is Codrington's route 17, north of Ilkley, one branch heading north towards Hayshaw (where two pigs of lead had been found in the eighteenth century) and another north-eastwards towards Aldborough. Margary includes the latter (as 720b) but ignores the former. [25]

Best known for his 'ley line' theories, subsequently transmogrified into something resembling a minor cult, it is often overlooked that Alfred Watkins was an ardent proponent of the existence of a prehistoric road network, even if his proposed routes were impossibly straight. What is significant is Watkins' acknowledgement that pre-Roman peoples had the wit and ability to have and indeed use a road network, an attitude that has not always been shared by his more traditional successors.[26]

Few prehistorians – and probably even fewer Roman scholars – have heard of Hippisley Cox. Whilst Alfred Watkins' *Old Straight Track* has attracted much attention, and a fair measure of opprobrium, for his 'ley line' theories, a quieter voice was proposing an extensive system of prehistoric trackways running across southern England. Hippisley Cox noted the association between prehistoric monuments and his 'green roads', most of which were ridgeways, and for this he is important. Completely straight routes of the type proposed by Watkins may look good on paper and even work in very flat areas, but they are completely impractical in the British Isles: one only has to look at more recent examples to see how roads have always been moulded to the landscape. The same was true of railways and only modern air corridors come anywhere near approaching Watkins' ideal.[27]

One of the most-studied roads has always been Stane Street, running between Chichester and London (Margary 15). A monograph by Hillaire Belloc was followed by a 'critical review' by Capt W.A. Grant, which contained the memorable put-down 'Mr Belloc has not feared to rush in where others have feared to tread'. These were followed by S.E. Winbolt's masterful *With a Spade on Stane Street*, which – concentrating on the archaeology and, by and large, avoiding personal abuse – has set the tone for countless subsequent road reports.[28]

These were the predecessors to Margary and – unlike Codrington, if Haverfield is to be believed – he was only too aware of their contribution to his labours. Ivan D. Margary began his interest in Roman roads purely locally, publishing *Roman Ways in the Weald* in 1948, but soon expanded his compass to include all of the roads of Britain. He produced what was then the definitive account of the Roman network in *The Roman Roads of Britain* in 1955, and this went through two further editions before he died. The second was a major reorganization into one volume, but the third enjoyed just a few pages of addenda at the end. Despite much new work, this magnum opus, long out of print, has never been superseded and is still much sought after. Margary, like Codrington, was unusual in his willingness to tackle the subject on a nationwide basis, a much more difficult task than writing about a particular region known to a scholar, since the writer inevitably becomes more dependent on other researchers in a way that is less true of regional studies. The scale of his contribution to the study of Roman roads in Britain can be gauged by comparing his map of the system with that of Codrington, separated by only five decades of study (Figure 30).[29]

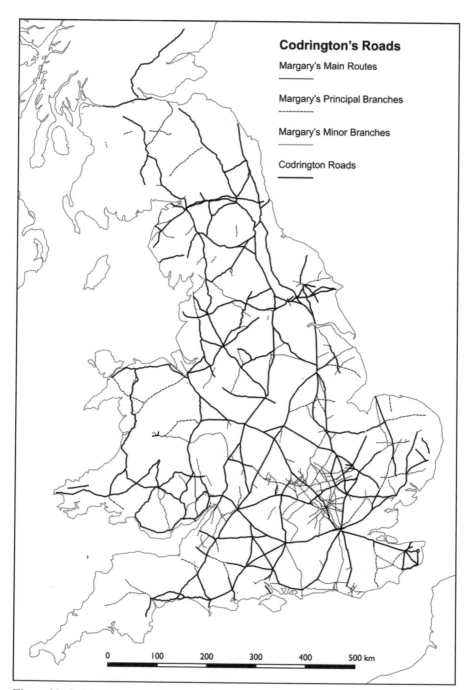

Figure 30: Codrington's network (1918) compared to that of Margary's (1973).

There are, however, a number of problems with the road system as defined by Margary.

First, and most obviously, the hierarchy he employs (Main Routes, Principal Branches, and Minor Branches) is his definition and may not have been shared by the Romans (if, indeed, they even viewed their roads in such a hierarchical way). It is a simple matter (but no more valid) to take his overall network and re-assign priorities, whether it be based on nodal points or the routes themselves as they appear on a map, a manifestation which, we must remember, was denied the Romans in anything more than the most rudimentary form. An excellent example of this would be the road between the legionary fortresses of Chester and York, which one might expect to have been of some importance (it was certainly fortified in the first and second centuries AD). In Margary's system, this consists of 7a (Main Route), 712 (Minor Branch), and 28b and 28c (Principal Branch).

Second, the system is quite obviously incomplete. Fragments of roads float in the middle of nowhere (Margary 164, 731, or 821, for instance), whilst others head determinedly cross-country only to terminate abruptly (Margary 31, 151, or 713). Two stubs may point suggestively at each other (Margary 55 and 183) only to be given differing classifications (a Principal Branch and a Minor Branch in that instance). In some cases strategically logical links between nodal points – the pre-Hadrianic forts at Templeborough and Castleford, for example – are completely absent. Codrington at least considered two candidates for a northern road from Templeborough, even if he was uncertain about them; Margary ignored them. Other, more recent, fieldworkers have added considerably to our knowledge for a particular area, but there is no official coordinated attempt to do the same for the whole of Britain (nor does there appear to be any interest in one, but there is at least now an unofficial project to remedy this: see below page 127). Similarly, South-West Scotland is poorly served by known Roman roads, despite a number of Roman military sites and a number of what may be indicative medieval battlefield sites. Attempts to address this imbalance point up the inadequacy of the research undertaken on the region until Wilson's comparatively recent studies.[30]

Third (and this may be seen as nit-picking for a work of such a great sweep), and at the opposite end from Haverfield's criticism of Codrington for his lack of overview, Margary could be less than precise in his descriptions of roads, misspelling of place-names, and the almost complete absence of Ordnance Survey grid references.

The incompleteness factor is one of the major obstacles to any attempt to draw scientifically acceptable conclusions about Margary's network: as with the coldharbour study, statistics derived from an incomplete dataset are always going to be of questionable value. The other such obstacle is that Margary's network is not necessarily that used by the Romans (which may have included native trackways to a greater or lesser degree). Furthermore, it might be argued that insufficient allowance was made for the fact that what we see now may well be a palimpsest, incapable of taking into account the possibility that roads came into and went out of use over time, so that there was (and still is) in effect an ever-evolving network.

Setting aside his idiosyncrasies (such as the frequent misspelling of place-names), a final problem lay in Margary's own methodology. He was a southerner and the leading expert on the road network of Kent and Sussex. He worked closely with the Viatores, who covered the Midlands, but the further his subject matter moved from his own familiar territory, the more he became dependent upon other authorities. Not all of these were of the same standard as his own endeavours and one occasionally senses him questioning (if very politely) conclusions that have been drawn by fieldworkers elsewhere. He certainly attempted to visit many of the roads in his book, but there is little doubt that he did not know the whole system as well as the region with which he was familiar; nobody could.[31]

Therefore it is important to distinguish the entity that is Margary's Roman Roads from what might be termed the Original Roman Road Network, the former being very closely defined for us, but the latter an ideal, the extent of which is currently unknowable beyond the bald statement that it was not the same as the former. It turns out that these are, however, only two of many possible networks.

After Margary, prominent researchers have mainly remained regional in their interests. Key amongst these was a loose association of enthusiasts who called themselves, rather romantically, 'The Viatores' (a Latin term meaning 'road surveyors'). Working on the assumption that they would make more progress by cooperating than by pursuing their own individual courses (both real and metaphorical), they worked closely with Margary and concentrated on the south-east Midlands of England. The results of their labours can be seen by comparing their map with that portion of Margary's from just nine years earlier that covers the same area (Figure 31). The Viatores employed a more detailed method of publication than Margary, however, including detailed descriptions of routes, Ordnance Survey grid references and, doubtless at great expense, two-colour map sections showing annotated routes overlain on the two-and-a-half-inch OS map base, together with drawn sections wherever they had been dug. This approach left little doubt about their suggested routes, even though

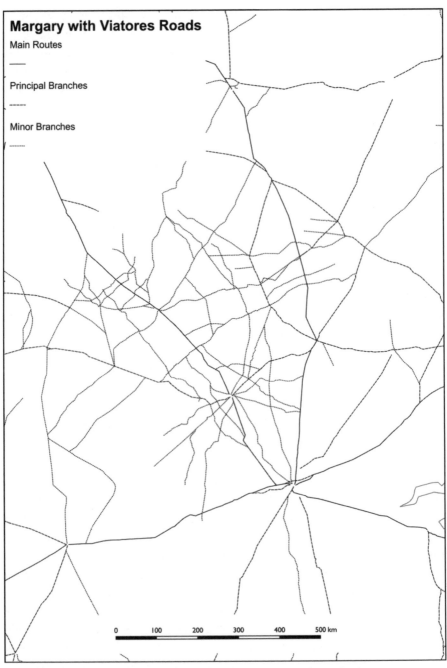

Figure 31: Margary's network (1973) with The Viatores' (1964) contributions.

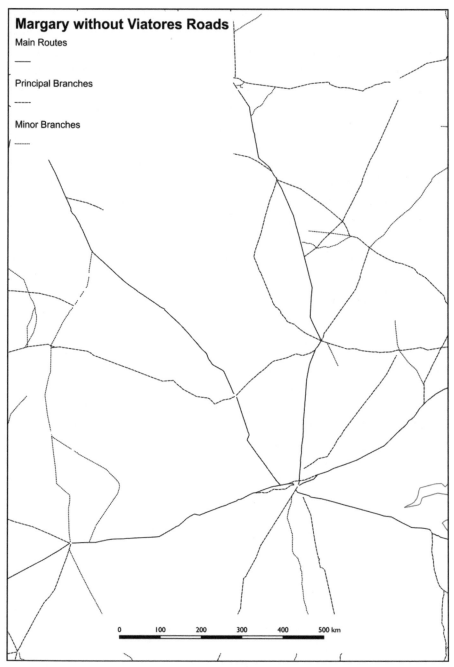

Margary without Viatores Roads

Main Routes

———

Principal Branches

- - - - -

Minor Branches

- - - - - -

Margary's network without the Viatores' contributions.

some of them may be open to question in specifics. One of the most crucial observations that could be made about their work was the density of Roman (and Romanized) roads that could be found using diligent research followed up by fieldwork. Indeed, the comparison in Figure 31 appears to supply a salutary lesson in what may await discovery in the rest of Britain. At the same time, their methodology can be (and indeed has been) criticized, and it seems their findings need to be taken with a pinch of salt in many cases.[32]

The Viatores were quite unusual in their approach and road chasing tends to be a solitary pursuit, by and large. Norman Field specialized in the roads of Dorset, particularly those he thought were connected with the early conquest period. In more recent years, whilst in North Wales, Edmund Waddelove has produced detailed accounts of his elucidation of the road network in that area. Martin Allan has undertaken similar work in the Lake District, tracing the roads from Brougham to Moresby and Hardknott to Ravenglass. Attempts are now being made to coordinate much of this 'amateur' research (with the ultimate aim of producing an update to Margary's last edition of his catalogue of roads), whilst new examples are still occasionally found by excavation (as on my own sites at Roecliffe and Melton) or by aerial and geophysical survey.[33]

One individual who combined many of these approaches, often controversially, was Raymond Selkirk. Often mischievously anti-establishment in his books, with provocatively teasing blurbs on their dust jackets, Selkirk was sometimes criticized for his more extreme suggestions, usually at the risk of overlooking his many genuine observations of value. Nevertheless, some of his proposed routes have been shown to be, at the very least, questionable. Whatever else he might have been, Selkirk was an acute and accomplished observer (something perhaps attributable to his maritime and aviation background), and this quality of observation tends to be evident in the work of all students of the Roman roads of Britain.[34]

What is ironic is that the 'establishment' against which Selkirk and others rail is arguably profoundly disinterested in the study of the road network, finding it far less sexy than frontiers or Roman and native interaction. This may help to explain why the great road scholars in Britain – Codrington, Margary, Field and their ilk – were amateurs (in the sense that they were not paid to do what they did) and enthusiasts, and there were no professional archaeologists interested in doing what they did. This is not universally true of Roman road studies, with the likes of Chevallier writing on the roads of France or Graf and Kennedy on those of Arabia, and it appears to be a curiously British trait. Now, perhaps more than ever before, when archaeology is being increasingly 'professionalized' and some object that there is no room left in it for amateurs, it is a good time to remember that the steady increase in our knowledge of the Roman roads of Britain is almost exclusively due to the labours of amateur scholars. The one academic project in this field – the Birmingham Roman Roads Project – is run by the extramural department at the University of Birmingham; traditional university archaeology departments seem reluctant to engage in this field. Nevertheless, there may be hope in the rise of community archaeology, with one such project hoping to trace the route of the Stanegate (Margary 85) between Corbridge and the North Tyne.[35]

One of the by-products of regionalism in interest in roads is that some areas invariably get left out of the system. Whilst some areas of Margary's maps seem to lack much detail, others appear completely barren. Cornwall, for instance, has produced a number of milestones (Figure 9), but seemingly no roads west of Devon. It is extremely unlikely that these stones have all been transported a long way from a known Roman road, whilst place-name evidence, such as Stratton (a 'strata' place-name), provides hints that what appears to be a blank on the map may well have had its share of Roman roads that will, at some point, repay investigation.

Using documentary sources and a limited amount of field observation, it is still possible to find likely new roads that merit further investigation. The success of the Viatores in filling in the gaps in the northern Home Counties shows how this is possible and further examples are offered below in Appendix 5.

So it is that the factors governing any notional map of the Roman road network are more than just dependent upon geographical and historical factors, but must also allow for the presence or absence of research into a given area. So, as with any archaeological distribution map, a map of the Roman roads of Britain such as Margary's is as much a record of archaeological endeavours as it is one of Roman strategic thinking or infrastructure planning. It will doubtless continue to change in the years to come.

Mapping Roman roads

The reader might expect the mapping of the Roman road system in Britain to have improved considerably in recent years. Unfortunately, this is not the case, at least so far as the published information is concerned.

The Ordnance Survey produced a succession of *Roman Britain* maps, arguably reaching an apogee with the fourth edition of 1978 at a scale of 1:625,000. Subsequently, the project lost its way somewhat, the nadir coming with the much-criticized fifth edition of 1989. For various reasons the Survey moved away from serious academic mapping of Roman Britain completely, the most recent edition (the sixth) being aimed solely at schoolchildren: in this it appears to be returning to the territory of old-fashioned educational wallcharts and, sadly, abandoning any academic aspirations (with some sensitive design, the two, of course, need not be mutually exclusive).[36]

Their criteria for the inclusion of roads, or their categorization as known or suspected, have (inevitably) been open to criticism, and some lengths of road varied in status between editions, often seemingly at the whim of the cartographers. This all seems most curious, when it is recalled that Margary's work was undertaken with the close cooperation of the Ordnance Survey, whose maps had, since their first editions of the nineteenth century, recorded the known and suspected courses of Roman roads.

Between the fourth and fifth editions of the Ordnance Survey *Roman Britain* maps, students of the road system were encouraged by the appearance in 1983 and 1987 of two British sheets of the *Tabula Imperii Romani* at a scale of 1:1,000,000, albeit on a different projection to that used by the Ordnance Survey. The *TIR* was (and apparently still is) a project to produce maps of a consistent quality for the entire Roman empire. The pace of new discoveries soon left the maps looking out of date, however, and there does not seem to be a policy of regularly updating the series. Ultimately, all paper-based maps and atlases are now at a disadvantage in comparison to digital mapping.[37]

The problems inherent in studying the road system of Roman Britain can be summed up eloquently in one simple question: which road system? The differences between the various mapping schemes, their varying (and not always transparent) criteria, and the inevitable distance of the researcher from most of the primary evidence mean that an element of scepticism is always advisable before accepting a suggested course as a fact. This sentiment will be familiar to any professional archaeologist sent to a remote location on a watching brief because the Ordnance Survey records the likely course of a Roman road at that point, only to find their speculation overly optimistic.

By way of illustration, it may be worth reviewing one simple example, the Roman road from Bath to Sea Mills (Figure 32). The first edition of the six-inch (1:10,560) Ordnance Survey 'county' maps records its course (even naming it the Via Julia, after the spurious antiquarian tradition). By the time of the third edition of the *Roman Britain* map in 1956, its route is recorded as certain between Bath and just west of Bitton, and assumed until Sea Mills. The fourth edition is more specific, recording it as unknown immediately west of Bath, known to the east and west of Bitton, and uncertain as far as Sea Mills. This situation is repeated on the 'revised' fourth edition. However, the relevant *TIR* sheet chooses to ignore the road completely. This despite the

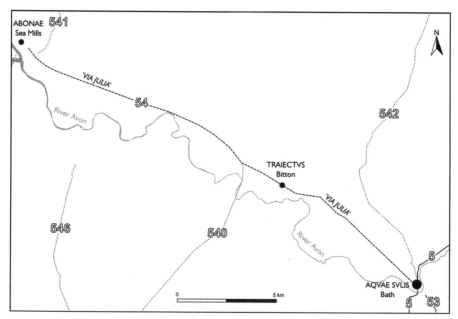

Figure 32: The so-called Via Julia between Bath-Aquae Sulis and Sea Mills-Abonae.

fact that, in the first edition of his book, Margary gave a detailed account of its course (including references to at least one place where the road was tested by excavation), supposedly working in consultation with the Ordnance Survey. Admittedly, the OS convention for an uncertain course could look alarmingly similar to interrupted sections of certain road course, but the same excuse does not exist for the *TIR* omission. It is difficult to see how the various lengths of *agger*, excavated sections, and numerous alignments of this road can translate into a non-existent road on the *TIR* sheet.[38]

All this means that students of the Roman road system (and of Roman Britain in general) effectively lack a modern interpretation of the available evidence, despite the huge advances in modern technology. Steps are now being made to redress this state of affairs, with an attempt by the North East Hampshire Historical and Archaeological Society to coordinate work on the road system in their region since Margary, with a view to updating his corpus, and a useful listing of criteria for the identification of a new Roman road produced. These are detailed on their website as follows:

5* Major Roman Road where the course on the ground is exactly known for most of its route. Applies to routes like the Devil's Highway [sic] or Foss Way, and not many more are likely to be found.

4* Margary's criteria for establishing a Roman Road: cumulative evidence upon an alignment, with excavation in at least one place on most alignments. While the line across country is established, it does not mean that each piece of evidence must be shown to come from Roman origins, nor that the Road's exact position is known on the ground except at excavation sites or possibly at terrace sites.

3* Accumulative evidence upon the alignments, but without the excavation evidence. Quite a lot of the Margary entries are of this class. Individual pieces of evidence may be coincidence, but the whole gains credibility the more alignment evidence is gathered, until it becomes quite probable that the alignments are Roman.

2* Projects based on sound documentary theory, but without the full standard of accumulated field evidence upon alignments. May be becoming probable. Some Margary entries of this class.

1* Sound documentary theory of long lines of parish, field & property boundaries, paths, place names, Saxon Charter and other historical documents, air photos, but without significant field evidence. A few Margary entries of this class.

0* Some documentary or field evidence, but not enough to assign any probability. May be worth expanding research from evidence available. Margary entries in this class exist.[39]

Whilst it is possible to quibble over details (even excavation of a road surface may not provide absolute proof of a road's Roman date), this star-rating system provides an interesting alternative way of viewing the road system as currently perceived. Margary chose to grade his network subjectively upon his view of the significance of a given length of road, but the NEHHAS scheme plots them by the quality of evidence, thereby avoiding the assumptions of importance implicit in Margary's method. Neither, of course, is (or can be) complete, but both hint at the potential for future research on the road system in Britain. The work of the Society to date is accessible on their website, together with summaries of work that has been submitted to them.[40]

Where to next?

So, what is the future of Roman road studies in Britain? With the most recent edition of Margary (1973) now badly in need of updating, no serious themed mapping being published by the Ordnance Survey, and apparently no plans to update the *TIR* for Britain, the situation does not look too promising. Moreover, with site-specific developer funding providing the lion's share of archaeological finance, and no sign of a major campaign of research being mounted by any of the national archaeological bodies, the study of the road system remains firmly in the hands of amateur scholars. The question is, how can it progress?

The answer must lie in the sort of initiative mounted by The Viatores in the 1950s and 1960s, where local researchers cooperated to draw a larger picture. Attempts are already in hand to update Margary's work, as we have just seen, but clearly what is really needed is an open source map using GIS techniques, contributed to and accessible by all researchers, but free of any debt of copyright to any body other than that allowed by a licence similar to the GPL, perhaps the Open Content License (OCL). The internet renders such a project feasible and, obviously, desirable, in the face of indifference in most quarters. Whether it will come to pass or not is a different matter. There may also be hope in any future change in the funding basis for British archaeology that might one day occur: as an example, RESCUE (the charitable trust for British archaeology) have proposed a general development tax that would to some extent alleviate the close ties of current developer-funded project research to very limited goals and perhaps even permit wider funding to broader projects like the study and mapping of Roman roads, a task with which bodies such as English Heritage and the Royal Commissions for Ancient and Historic Monuments of Scotland and Wales would be well-equipped to assist.[41]

Much remains to be done at even the most basic level in terms of mapping the road network – the work of The Viatores, Allan, Field, and Waddelove shows just how much can be achieved and there are still huge gaps in the system that urgently require filling, with roads that seemingly go nowhere: Brough-by-Bainbridge has two known roads running to it, but these are not connected to anything; Margary 720b from Ilkley to Aldborough obviously needs completing, as does the trio of roads (Margary 17, 170, and 222) to the east of Northampton which appear to be heading for a junction. Some major Romano-British towns have known or probable gates and no known roads running from them, Winchester (Venta Belgarum) being an example, on its east side. Similarly, Aldborough (Isurium Brigantum) is defined by only one known road (Margary 8) passing through it, yet has more than two gates. These lacunae are poignant reminders of the gaps in our knowledge. Indeed, wherever there are roads in

Roman Britain, there are loose ends: at least 500 km (311 miles) of them, at a conservative estimate, in a system of approximately 11,938 km (8,067 miles) of roads identified by Margary. New roads are found all the time (for example at Melton), by no means all of them expected, and the basic groundwork (in terms of research and fieldwork) in tying together the known network remains to be done.[42]

Chapter 6

Conclusions

Here then, sitting upon this Roman road I considered the nature of such men, and when I had thought out carefully where the nearest Don might be at that moment, I decided that he was at least twenty-three miles away, and I was very glad: for it permitted me to contemplate the road with common sense and with Faith, which is Common Sense transfigured; and I could see the Legionaries climbing the hill. I remembered also what a sight there was upon the down above, and I got upon my horse again to go and see it. *Hilaire Belloc*[1]

The road system of Roman Britain cannot be viewed in isolation. In many ways, it could be argued that it is not only a metaphor for the Roman occupation as a whole, but also for our approach to the study of the period. Far from being an isolated incident which quickly passed, the Roman occupation latched onto an existing, receptive environment, and in turn left behind a framework that enabled the development of medieval society into the post-medieval world. It is difficult not to see continuity there and, at its heart, thoroughly integrated, that brief, often despised interlude of the Roman presence. Our secret history of the Roman roads of Britain can thus be summarized as a series of 'secrets' that have been overlooked or underplayed, rather than suppressed: the wise reader should always be suspicious of any book that claims archaeologists have indulged in a conspiracy.

We have seen how wheeled traffic, and the roads which it required in order to be of use, existed long before the Romans came and probably evolved out of the tracks made first by animals and then by the hunters pursuing them. The invading Roman army certainly revolutionized the road network, there is no doubt about that, but they did not invent it. What we perceive as the Roman network also seems not to be the whole story, not just because research has yet to reveal all of the formalized roads in use, but also because much of the prehistoric network appears to have continued in use at the same time. *So our first 'secret' is that the Romans did not give us a new road network, they merely adapted an existing one.*

Once the army had arrived on the shores of the south coast of England, they needed to move inland rapidly to achieve their goals. The existence of a prehistoric system of roads made this possible during the campaigning season, whereas constructing the necessary backbone for an advance *de novo* was outwith even their renowned engineering capabilities. So it is that the formalized network so familiar from maps of Roman Britain was a consolidation of what was already there, improved upon and prioritized where necessary in order to meet a new set of criteria. For, once the Roman army no longer needed to retain a large field army in one place, they were obliged to spread it out and supply it, providing a series of garrison points for this very purpose. This network of strong points provided the troops to secure the supply chain, along with safe havens for overnight stops. Were they doing this because they feared an invading enemy army or merely as a precaution against low intensity insurgency, a technique of warfare to which the Britons had all too readily adapted themselves in the decades immediately after the invasion? We can certainly see the same approach being used from the earliest stages of the occupation right through to the end of Roman rule, although in the aftermath of the initial advance, when Roman towns were being encouraged, an alternative to military fortifications became available. The Roman army seems to have been ubiquitous, linked together by a communications network that was focused along roads. Moreover, many 'frontier systems' actually seem to have been no more than fortified roads. *Thus our second 'secret' is that, rather than staring forlornly across frontiers, the Romans looked along their roads.*

'What have the Romans ever done for us?' is by now a familiar refrain, the joke deriving from the long accompanying list of benefits of Roman rule. However, it could be argued that the Romans never intended their road network for anybody but themselves, but that the Law of Unintended Consequences ensured that it went on to facilitate civilian movement and trade, just as the military roads of the Highlands were to do in the eighteenth century. This helped bolster the status of some settlements so much that, when Roman rule ended, many of them continued to be of consequence up until modern times. *Our third secret, then, is that the provision of an all-weather road network for military purposes, when combined with the existing pre-Roman network of tracks and roads, had unexpected benefits for the inhabitants of Britannia.*

A road network is not a monolithic entity, however, and the system in Roman Britain not only changed with the arrival and departure of the Roman administration, but continued to evolve during the Roman period. This is hardly surprising: after all, the equipment of the soldiers tramping along those routes changed over the four centuries of their presence in the island and it would be truly remarkable if the road network did not also undergo a subtle yet potent evolution. Many factors could dictate why a road should start to be used more or to fall from favour. Perhaps a new shrine might be constructed, or an old one closed; equally, a long-established garrison might move on and not be replaced, or a new fort be constructed. *This brings us to our fourth secret: the road network as it is (admittedly imperfectly) reconstructed is a palimpsest, an accumulation of many different networks, perhaps even an expression of the changing identity of Roman Britain.*

The Romans left an important legacy for their successors and it is one that was exploited in full measure. Of course, this was not only the formalized all-weather system of roads, but also the prehistoric system they had in turn inherited. However, those toughened military roads were always going to be attractive for armies on the move, so it was inevitable that opposing forces would meet on or near Roman roads in times of conflict. In the immediate post-Roman period, this was probably occurring on an almost exclusively Roman system but, as time went on, it became more of a Roman-influenced network, particularly once turnpiking began in earnest. Nevertheless, Roman roads and the settlements they established lay at the heart of medieval England, both in times of conflict when armies used the network, and in peace when kings exploited it for their itinerant perambulations around the island. *Our fifth secret is therefore that the Roman system definitely had a profound effect on medieval life, both martial and peaceful, and that it probably still exerted some influence in the later periods, to the point where most of the post-Roman battles in England and Wales (and a good few in Scotland too) were fought on or next to a Roman road.*

This leads directly to consideration of a rather useful by-product of this continued use of the old Roman road system. Since it provided a ready-made infrastructure for army movements, it was bound to be exploited by armies in the post-Roman period. This doubtless decreased with time, but since even the newly minted turnpike network of the seventeenth century and later made bold use of its Roman predecessor, it continued to exert an influence on post-medieval army movements. *The sixth secret is that our knowledge of the Roman road network can be a valuable tool in assessing the location of unknown or poorly attested battle sites.* This is a two-edged sword, since well-known battle sites might indicate previously unsuspected Roman roads.

The study of the Roman roads of Britain is dominated by Ivan Margary and his magisterial book. His approach was not without its faults for, just as his predecessor Thomas Codrington had been criticized by Haverfield for not getting the 'big picture', so Margary provided a reasoned catalogue prefaced by a methodology which now seems outdated and almost trite. It would be churlish, however, not to acknowledge the vast contribution his work has made to the subject, not least in the way it dominates the sites and monuments/ heritage environment records of counties and regions, as well as the various national monuments records. It is significant (if a little depressing) that there has been no successor to Margary, particularly now that the tools for the study of the road network have so drastically improved. Digital mapping, sub-metre-accuracy lidar survey, a wide range of geophysical survey techniques, and readily available neogeographical tools like virtual globes and geographical information systems all make his achievement that much more remarkable, equipped as he was only with paper maps, cameras, and a car. *And so our seventh and final secret is that the study of the Roman road network in Britain is patently incomplete, but rests upon a solid foundation provided by a number of scholars, both professional and (like Margary) amateur, so there is much that can and should be accomplished.* The works of Field, Waddelove, Davies, and Poulter hint at the ways in which this might develop in years to come.

The secret history of the Roman roads of Britain does not really contain any secrets at all, in all honesty. Many have been quietly uttering most of what appears in this book for many years, but it has generally been ignored. However, if a thing is worth repeating, it should be repeated. So next time you see traffic roaring along a modern road, die-straight on top of its Roman predecessor, give some thought to its meandering origins, long before an all-weather surface was laid down on this carefully surveyed course, and to those that came after and whose continued use of it ensured it would survive until today as a vital part of the nation's infrastructure. Only then should you ponder what the transport network will look like in 2,000 years' time.

Chapter 7

Further Reading

Books

Until recently, there have been no really good, current books on Roman roads in Britain. The standard work by **Margary** (first edition in two volumes in 1955 and 1957; second edition 1967; third edition 1973) is now out-of-date and in need of revision; nevertheless it is still an invaluable work of reference and is occasionally available in one of its three editions on the secondhand market. The third edition route descriptions have been used as the basis of the website accompanying this book (see below).

The most succinct and readily-available study of the subject of Roman Roads in Britain is the Shire Archaeology volume by **Davies** (2009), replacing the dated volume by **Bagshawe** (1979). Both are useful as an introduction. **Davies** has also produced a more detailed study of Roman Roads in Britain (2002) and a diachronic study (2006) of British roads, ranging from prehistory to the modern day. For a refreshing alternative view on the surveying and layout of Roman roads, see **Poulter** (2010).

There are considerably more accounts of the roads of individual regions, usually the results of the labours of individuals. Noteworthy here are the following studies of Roman roads in Dorset by **Field** (1992), the northern Lake District by **Allan** (1994), and North Wales by **Waddelove** (1999).

A medieval perspective on the road system of Britain can be found in another Shire Archaeology volume, this time by **Hindle** (1998), whilst a useful diachronic regional study is that of **Dodd and Dodd** (1980), examining the roads of the Peak District from prehistory to modern times.

An invaluable comparative study of military road building is that of **Taylor** (1996) which explores the work of Wade, Caulfeild, and their colleagues.

Maps

Two main strands of mapping are of use for the study of the known (or strongly suspected) Roman roads of Britain. Access to a good library will be necessary to consult these.

Arguably the most important are the First through Fourth editions of the Ordnance Survey's *Roman Britain* maps, now out of print (the 6th edition is, unfortunately, markedly inferior to these and best avoided for serious study of Roman roads).

Then there are the two volumes of the *Tabula Imperii Romani* (TIR 1983; 1987), one each for the north and south of Britain, also now out of print.

Multimedia

Ironically, the work of Margary's predecessor, **Codrington** (1918), is now more accessible than his illustrious successor, thanks to the text of his book being available on the World Wide Web as both a scan and a transcription. The transcription, undertaken by Bill Thayer, will be linked to maps of the roads, thus making it an extremely dynamic resource: http://tinyurl.com/Codrington-Roman-Roads

A scan in the form of a PDF and computer OCR transcription is also available: https://archive.org/details/romanroadsinbrit00codruoft

A further useful website is that of the Birmingham Roman Roads Project which details the progress of its members in increasing knowledge of the road system in the West Midlands: http://www.brrp.bham.ac.uk

The NEHHAS website devoted to their Roman road project is accessible at: http://www.hants.org.uk/nehhas/RRAbstracts.html

A particularly useful resource is the complete coverage of mainland Britain by six-inch First Edition Ordnance Survey maps provided by British History Online: http://www.british-history.ac.uk/map.aspx?pubid=270

Less useful at the time of writing is the Old Maps website which provides the same thing but in a more constrained (and somewhat clunky) interface: http://www.old-maps.co.uk

Both of these are of inferior quality (they use the same, rather dated, monochrome scan) by comparison with the greyscale coverage of Scotland provided by the National Library of Scotland's Map Library Digital Map resource: http://maps.nls.uk

Finally, details of scheduled ancient monuments (including lengths of Roman road) are accessible on an OS map base by means of Defra's MAGIC website: http://www.magic.gov.uk/

Secret History of Roman Roads Website

A website accompanies this book and provides access to Google Earth and Google Maps files which provide representations of Margary's interpretation of the Roman road network in Britain. It includes additional detail, such as overlays for Codrington's roads, other more recently identified and suggested routes, as well as the locations of post-Roman battlefields, castles, and religious houses which may owe their locations to Roman roads.

The website can be found at http://romanroadsinbritain.info

Margary's road numbers

Despite appearances, Margary's numbering system is not strictly numerical. Instead, his *Main Routes* have single digits (e.g. 1), *Principal Branches* double digits (e.g. 10), and then *Minor Branches* triple digits (e.g. 100). For the sake of simplicity, however, his routes (together with those of the Viatores, who adopted his system) are listed here in strict numerical order. The roads listed by the Viatores and included by Margary are enclosed in square brackets, e.g. [167 St Albans/Mill Hill].[1]

Margary	Between	Traditional name
Main Routes		
1a	Dover/Canterbury	Watling Street
1b	Canterbury/Rochester	Watling Street
1c	Rochester/London	Watling Street
1d	London/St Albans	Watling Street
1e	St Albans/Towcester	Watling Street
1f	Towcester/High Cross	Watling Street
1g	High Cross/Wall	Watling Street
1h	Wall/Wroxeter	Watling Street
2a	London/Braughing	Ermine Street
2b	Braughing/Chesterton	Ermine Street
2c	Chesterton/Lincoln	Ermine Street
2d	Lincoln/The Humber	Ermine Street
2e	Brough on Humber/York	–
3a	London/Chelmsford	The Great Road
3b	Chelmsford/Colchester	The Great Road
3c	Colchester/Baylham	–
3d	Baylham/Caistor St Edmund	The Pye Road
4a	London/Silchester	–
4b	Silchester/Old Sarum	Port Way

Margary	Between	Traditional name
4c	Old Sarum/Badbury Rings	–
4d	Badbury Rings/Poole Harbour	–
4e	Badbury Rings/Dorchester	–
4f	Dorchester/Exeter	–
5a	Axmouth/Ilchester	Fosse Way
5b	Ilchester/Bath	Fosse Way
5c	Bath/Cirencester	Fosse Way
5d	Cirencester/High Cross	Fosse Way
5e	High Cross/Leicester	Fosse Way
5f	Leicester/Lincoln	Fosse Way
6a	Chester/Wroxeter	Watling Street (West)
6b	Wroxeter/Leintwardine	Watling Street (West)
6c	Leintwardine/Monmouth	Watling Street (West)
6d	Monmouth/Chepstow	–
7a	Chester/Manchester	–
7b	Manchester/Ribchester	–
7c	Ribchester/Low Borrow Bridge	–
7d	Low Borrow Bridge/Brougham	–
7e	Brougham/Carlisle	–
7f	Carlisle/Crawford	–
7g	Crawford/Cramond	–
8a	York/Aldborough	Dere Street
8b	Aldborough/Catterick Bridge	Dere Street
8c	Catterick Bridge/Binchester	Dere Street
8d	Binchester/Corbridge	Dere Street
8e	Corbridge/High Rochester	Dere Street
8f	High Rochester/Newstead	Dere Street
8g	Newstead/Dalkeith	Dere Street
9a	Camelon/Strageath	–
9b	Strageath/Kirriemuir	–

Principal Branches

10	Canterbury/Richborough	–
11	Canterbury/Upstreet	–
12	Canterbury/Lympne	Stone Street

Margary	Between	Traditional name
13	Rochester/Hastings	–
14	London/Lewes	–
15	London/Chichester	Stane Street
16a	St Albans/Alchester	Akeman Street
16b	Alchester/Cirencester	Akeman Street
17	Norton/Northampton (Duston)	–
18a	Bourton on the Water/Alcester	Ryknild Street
18b	Alcester/Wall	Ryknild Street
18c	Wall/Derby (Little Chester)	Ryknild Street
18d	Derby (Little Chester)/Chesterfield	Ryknild Street
18e	Chesterfield/Rotherham	Ryknild Street
18ee	New Whittington/Rotherham	–
19	Stretton/Whitchurch	–
21a	St Albans/Braughing	–
21b	Braughing/Worsted Lodge	–
22	Braughing/Godmanchester	–
23a	Arrington (Wimpole Lodge)/Cambridge	–
23b	Cambridge/Littleport	Akeman Street
24	Godmanchester/Sible Hedingham	Via Devana
25	Upton/Denver	The Fen Road
26	Ailsworth/Ancaster	King Street
27	Lincoln/Burgh-le-Marsh	–
28a	Lincoln/Doncaster	–
28b	Doncaster/Tadcaster	Roman Ridge
28c	Tadcaster/York	–
29	South Newbould/Malton	–
30	London (Clapton)/Great Dunmow	–
31	Bradwell on Sea	–
32	Braughing/Colchester	Stane Street
33a	Chelmsford/Ixworth	–
33b	Ixworth/Holme next the Sea	Peddars Way
34a	Wixoe/Baylham	–
34b	Baylham/Peasenhall	–
35	Pulham St Mary/Peasenhall	–

Margary	Between	Traditional name
36	Halesworth/Woodton	Stone Street
37	Bunwell/Thetford	–
38	Smallburgh/Denver	–
39	Toftrees/Holkham (Dale Hole)	–
41a	Silchester/Speen	Ermin Street
41b	Speen/Cirencester	Ermin Street
41c	Cirencester/Gloucester	Ermin Street
42a	Silchester/Winchester	–
42b	Winchester/Bitterne	–
43	Winchester/Wanborough	–
44	Old Sarum/Mildenhall	–
45a	Winchester/Old Sarum	–
45b	Old/Sarum/Mendip Hills (Charterhouse)	–
46	Badbury Rings/Kingston Deverell	–
47	Dorchester/Ilchester	–
48	Dorchester/Weymouth (Radipole)	–
49	Charmouth/Exeter	–
51	Ilchester/Puriton	–
52	Bath/Frome	–
53	Speen (Wickham)/Bath (Batheaston)	–
54	Bath/Sea Mills	–
55	Cirencester/Hailes	White Way & Salt Way
56a	Eatington/Finmere	–
56aa	Epwell/Neithrop (Banbury)	–
56b	Eatington/Droitwich	–
57a	Huntingdon/Leicester	–
57b	Leicester/Mancetter	–
58a	Six Hills/Grantham (Saltersford)	–
58b	Grantham (Saltersford)/Donington	–
60a	Newnham/Caerleon	–
60aa	Crick/Sudbrook Spur	–
60b	Caerleon/Cardiff	–
60c	Cardiff/Neath	–
60d	Neath/Carmarthen	–

Margary	Between	Traditional name
61	Gloucester/Mitcheldean	–
62a	Caerleon/Brecon	–
62aa	Spur road at Brecon	–
62b	Brecon/Llandovery	–
62c	Llandovery/Llanfair Clydogau	Sarn Helen (East)
63a	Stretton Grandison/Kenchester	–
63b	Kenchester/Brecon	–
64	Wroxeter/Trefeglwys	–
66a	Chester/Caer Gai	–
66b	Caer Gai/Dolgelly	–
67a	Chester/St Asaph	–
67aa	Balderton/Holywell	–
67b	St Asaph/Caerhun	–
67c	Caerhun/Caernarvon	–
68	Caernarvon/Caer Gai	–
69a	Caerhun/Tomen y Mur	Sarn Helen
69aa	Trefriw/Dolwyddelan	–
69b	Tomen y Mur/Pennal	Sarn Helen
69c	Pennal/Llanio	Sarn Helen
69d	Llanio/Carmarthen	Sarn Helen
70a	Sandbach/Warrington (Wilderspool)	King Street
70b	Warrington/Wigan	–
70c	Wigan/Preston	–
70d	Preston/Lancaster	–
71a	Derby (Little Chester)/Buxton	–
71b	Buxton/Manchester	–
72a	Ribchester/Ilkley	–
72b	Ilkley/Tadcaster	–
73	Ingleton/Brough by Bainbridge	–
74	Brougham/Troutbeck	High Street
75	Carlisle/Egremont	–
76	Lockerbie/Lochmaben	–
77	Crawford/Dalswinton	Well Path
78a	Roberton/Castledykes	–

Margary	Between	Traditional name
78b	Castledykes/Glasgow	–
79a	Peebles/Castledykes	–
79b	Castledykes/Loudoun Hill	–
80a	Barmby/Durham	–
80b	Durham/Newcastle on Tyne	–
81a	York/Malton	–
81b	Malton/Whitby	Wade's Causeway
82	Scotch Corner/Brougham	–
83	Willington/Durham	–
84	Kirkby Thore/Carvoran	Maiden Way
85a	Corbridge/Carvoran	Stanegate
85b	Carvoran/Carlisle	Stanegate
86a	Wallsend/Portgate	Military Way
86b	Portgate/Carvoran	Military Way
86c	Carvoran/Carlisle	Military Way
86d	Carlisle/Bowness on Solway	Military Way
87	Bewclay/Tweedmouth	Devil's Causeway
88	High Rochester/Whittingam	–
89	Lockerbie/Newstead	–
90	Bridgeness/Old Kilpatrick	The Military Way
Minor Branches		
100	Richborough/Dover	–
101	Woodnesborough/Sandwich	–
110	Sturry/Reculver	–
130	Benenden/Canterbury	–
131	Maidstone/Dover	–
140	Barcombe Mills/Hardham	–
141	Newhaven/The Dicker	–
142	Pevensey/Glynde	–
143	Stone Cross/Jevington	–
144	Seaford/Ripe	–
145	Heighton Street/Lewes	–
146	Ripe (land settlement)	–
147	South Malling	–

Margary	Between	Traditional name
150	London/Brighton	–
151	Rowhook/Winterfold Heath	–
152	Codmore Hill/Marehill (Pulborough)	–
153	Chichester/Brighton	–
154	Clayton Wickham/Portslade	–
155	Chichester/Silchester	–
156	Chichester/Sidlesham	–
160a	Towcester/Alchester	–
160b	Alchester/Dorchester-on-Thames	–
160c	Dorchester-on-Thames/Silchester	–
160cc	Dorchester-on-Thames/Fair Cross	–
161	Kirtlington/Fritwell	Ash Bank
161A	Kirtlington/Hanwell	Port Way
162	Fleet Marston/Lillington Dayrell	–
162A	East Claydon/Fulwell	–
163	St Albans/Hedsor Wharf	–
[163A	Nash Mills/Flaunden	]
[163B	Chorleywood/Langley Park	]
164	Oxford (North Hinksey)/Wantage	–
[165	St Albans/Laleham	]
166	Fenny Stratford/Wormleighton	–
[166A	Little Brickhill/Bletchley	]
[167	St Albans/Mill Hill	]
168a	Great Chesterford/Tring	Icknield Way
168b	Aston Clinton/Pyrton	Lower Icknield Way
[169	Eaton Bray/Elstree	]
[169Aa	Pitstone/Boxmoor	]
[169Ab	Pitstone/Leckhampstead	]
[169B	Ivinghoe Beacon/St Albans	]
[169C	Nash Mills/Edgware	]
170	Irchester South/Dungee Corner	–
[170a	Irchester/Kempston	]
[170b	Marston Mortaine/Limbury	]
[171	Water Stratford/Olney	]

Margary	Between	Traditional name
[172	Woughton on the Green/Spinney Lodge	]
[172A	Spinney Lodge/Piddington	]
[172B	Spinney Lodge/Ashton (Park Farm)	]
[173a	Fleet Marston/Dorchester-on-Thames	]
[173b	Little Brickhill/Fleet Marston	]
[173c	Little Brickhill/Bedford	]
[173d	Bedford/Alconbury	]
[174	Thornborough/Stoke Goldington	]
[175	Fenny Stratford/Dungee Corner	]
[175A	Willen/Little Horwood	]
[176	Little Brickhill/Arrington Bridge	]
[177	Tilsworth/Hexton (Mortgrove)	]
180	Birmingham/Gloucester	–
181	Derby (Little Chester)/Stoke on Trent	–
182	Derby (Little Chester)/Sawley	–
183	Bidford on Avon/South Littleton	–
189	Catcliffe/Oldcoates	–
190	Water Eaton/Featherstone	–
191	Water Eaton/Pendeford Hall	–
192	Greensforge/Droitwich	–
193	Greensforge/Newtown	–
[210a	Ickleford/St Albans	]
[210b	Ickleford/Dungee Corner	]
[211	Ayotbury/Friarswash	]
212	St Albans/Cheshunt	–
213	Dunstable/Cheshunt	–
[214	Ware/St Albans	]
220	London/Stevenage	–
221	Baldock/Coleman Green	–
222	Biggleswade/Old Warden	–
[223	Shefford/Cople	]
[224	Bedford/Wimpole (Coomb Grove)	]
[225	Sandy/Sharnbrook	]
230	Newnham/Thriplow	Ashwell Street

Margary	Between	Traditional name
[231	Cambridge/Bolnhurst	]
240	Cambridge (Red Cross)/Mare Way	–
241	Cambridge (Red Cross)/Barton	–
250/1	Branch roads at Castor	–
252	Road at Farcet	–
260	Bourne/Lincoln	Mareham Lane
261	Baston/Pepper Hill Farm South	Baston Outgang
262	Sleaford/Lincoln (Bracebridge Heath)	–
263	Stainfield/Burton Coggles	–
270	Horncastle/South Ferriby	High Street
271	Caistor/North Kelsey	–
272	Bullington/Grainthorpe	–
273	Stixwould/Saltfleetby	–
274	Owmby Cliff/Usselby	–
280	Tadcaster/Whixley	Rudgate
281	Cantley spur road	–
300	Chelmsford (Little Waltham)/Great Chesterford	–
320	Easthorpe/Colchester	–
321	Colchester/Shrub End	–
322	Colchester/Long Melford	–
329	Braughing (Horse Cross)/Perry Green	–
330	Bildeston/Ixworth	–
331	Coney Weston/Attleborough	–
332	Roudham Heath/Hockwold	–
333	Babraham (Worsted Lodge)/Hunstanton	Icknield Way
340	Barham/Wickham Market	–
360	Arminghall/Kirby Bedon	–
370	New Buckenham/Morley	–
420	Winchester/Wickham	–
421	Chichester/Bitterne	–
422	Otterbourne/New Forest (Stoney Cross)	–
423	Dibden/Lepe	–
424	Stoney Cross/Fritham	–
470	Stinsford/Stratton	–

Margary	Between	Traditional name
490	Exeter/Topsham	–
491	Exeter/Teignbridge	–
492a	Exeter/Launceston	–
492b	Launceston/Redruth	–
493	Crediton/Burrington Moor	–
510	Polden Hills/Kingweston	–
511	The Street Causeway	–
540	Mendip Hills (Compton Martin)/Bitton	–
541	Sea Mills/Gloucester	–
541a	Berkeley Road/Iron Acton (Engine Common)	–
542	Bath/Chavenage Green	–
543	Easton Grey/Arlingham	–
544	Cirencester/Kingscote Park	–
545	Flax Bourton (Gatcombe)/Abbots Leigh	–
546	Bedminster/Farrington Gurney	–
560	Moreton in Marsh (Dorn)/Little Compton	–
561	Swalcliffe/Warmington	–
562	South Newington/Hanwell	–
569	Hanbury/Stoke Heath	–
570	Water Newton/Irchester	–
571	Ailsworth/King's Cliffe	–
572	Leicester/Lutterworth	–
580	Greetham/Three Queens	Sewstern Lane
590	South Collingham bridge	–
610	Dymock/Stretton Grandison	–
611	Huntley (Bordwood)/Weston under Penyard	–
612a	Weston under Penyard/Monmouth	–
612b	Monmouth/Usk	–
613	Weston under Penyard/Ashton	–
614	Weston under Penyard/Lydney	The Dean Road
615	Weston under Penyard/Hope Mansell	–
620	Brecon/Taf Fechan	–
621	Llandrindod Wells/Cardiff	–

Margary	Between	Traditional name
622	Brecon/Neath	–
623	Carmarthen/Llandrindod Wells	–
630	Tillington/Abergavenny	–
631	Abbey Dore/Newton	–
642	Caersws/New House	–
643	Caersws/Carno	–
660	Road at Holt	–
670	Chester/The Wirral (Raby)	–
700	Nantwich/Peover	–
701	Chester/Warrington (Wilderspool)	–
702	Manchester/Wigan	–
703	Ribchester/Poulton le Fylde	–
704	Ribchester/Lancaster	–
705	Lancaster/Overborrow	–
706	Whittington/Lupton	–
707	Low Borrow Bridge/Kendal	–
710a	Buxton/Brough on Noe	Batham Gate
710b	Brough on Noe/Templeborough	Long Causeway
710c	Templeborough/Doncaster	–
711	Brough on Noe/Glossop	Doctor's Gate
712	Manchester/Thorner	–
713	Buxton/Leek	–
720a	Littleborough/Ilkley	–
720aa	Ripponden/Rastrick	–
720b	Ilkley/Aldborough	–
721	Bradford/Elslack	–
722	Skipton/Ingleton	–
728	Austhorpe/Woodlesford	Street Lane
729	Scarcroft/Hazlewood	–
730	Brough by Bainbridge/Buckden	–
731	Sedburgh/Kirkby Stephen	–
740	Ambleside/Ravenglass	–
741	Castlesteads/Keswick	–
750	Silloth/Workington	Coastal Route

Margary	Between	Traditional name
751	Maryport/Papcastle	–
752	Papcastle/Moresby	–
753	Papcastle/Keswick	–
754	Old Carlisle/Maryport	–
780	Lurg Moor/Largs	–
790	Carnell/Mauchline	–
800	York/Stockton on the Forest	–
801	York/Clifton	–
809	Wreckenton/South Shields	Wreckendyke
810	Stamford Bridge/Bridlington	–
811	Fridaythorpe/Bridlington	–
812	Malton/Lutton	–
813	Malton/Bainton	–
814	Malton/Hovingham	–
815	Malton/Bulmer	–
816	Malton/Filey	–
817	Sherburn/Seamer Beacon	–
820	Bowes/Bishop Auckland	–
821	Stanhope/Eggleston	–
865	Birdoswald/Bewcastle	–
868	Longtown/Netherby	–
869	Drumburgh/Kirkbride	–
905	Castlecary/Crowbank	–

Appendix 2

Early Medieval Battlefields and Roman Roads

* Roads indicated with an asterisk were not included within Margary's original numbering scheme

Date	Name	Margary No.
455	Aegelsthrep (Aylesford?)	13?
465	Wippedes fleot	?
456–7	Creacanford/Crecgan ford (Crayford)	1?
485	Mearcraedes burna	?
491	Andredes cester (Pevensey)	142
508	Natanleaga (Netley Marsh)	422
514	Cerdices ora	?
517	Badon (Mons Badonicus)	?
519	Cerdicesford (Charford?)	424?
530	Wihtgaraesburh (Isle of Wight)	?
537	Camlann	7, 84, 85, 86?
542	Glen Water	?
552	Searoburh	4, 44, 45
556	Beranburh	43
568	Wibbandun	?
571	Bedcanford	?
573	Arderydd/Armterid/Atterith (Arthuret)	7
577	Deorham (Dyrham)	542
577	Metcaud	–
6th Century	Argoed Llwyfain	?
584	Fethanleag (Stoke Lyne)	160
590	Leithreid	?
593	Woddesbeorg/Wodnesbeorg (Adam's Grave)	53
593–600	Catraeth (Catterick?)	8?
596	Ratho	?
605/6 or 613/16	Cair Legion (Chester)	6/7/66/670/701

Date	Name	Margary No.
614	Beandun (Bindon?)	49
617	River Idle	28?
628	Cirencester	5/16/41/55
633	Haethfelth (Heavenfield)	8, 86
634	York	2/8/28/800/801
634	Heavenfield/Denisesburna	8/86
642	Strathcarron	9, 90
652	Bradenforda (Bradford-on-Avon?)	?
655	Winwidfeld (Garforth?)	28, 728
658	Peonnan (Penselwood?)	?
661	Posentesburh	492
665	Badon (Mons Badonicus)	?
675	Biedanheafod (Bedwyn?)	43, 53
676	Rochester	1, 13
679	Trent (Littleborough?)	28, 189
685	Dunnichen Moss/Nechtanesmere	?
710	Lining (between Tamar and Lynher)	?
710	Between Rivers Haefe and Caere (Falkirk?)	90?
715	Woddesbeorg/Wodnesbeorg (Adam's Grave)	53
722	Hehil (R Hayle?)	?
722	Taunton	?
727-9	Monacrib/Crei	9
733	Somerton	51
752	Beorgfeord (Burford)	16
757	Merantun (Marden?)	?
760	Hereford	6
776	Otford	?
779	Benson	160
796	Rhuddlan	67
798	Whalley	72
802	Kempsford	41
822	Deganwy	?
825	Galford	492
825	Ellandun	43

Date	Name	Margary No.
836	Carhampton	?
838	Hingston Down	?
840	Southampton	421
840	Portland	48?
843	Carhampton	?
848	River Parrett	51
851	Canterbury & London	1
851	Aclea (Oakley)	101?
853	Thanet	?
860	Winchester	42, 43, 45, 420
866	York	2, 8, 28, 800, 801
867	York	2, 8, 28, 800, 801
869	Thetford	37, 333
870	Englefield	160
871	Reading	160
871	Ashdown	160
871	Basing	155
871	Meretun/Merantun	?
871	Wilton	45?
874	Repton (poss)	18
876	Wareham	?
877	Anglesey	?
878	Cynwit	?
878	Ethandun (Edington)	?
881	Conway (mouth of)	?
885	Rochester	1, 13
886	London	1, 2, 3, 15, 40, 167, 220
893	Farnham	?
893	Bleamfleote	?
893	Buttington on Severn	64
893	Chester	6, 7, 66, 670, 701
894	Chichester	15, 155, 156, 421
895	River Lea	3?, 20?
904	Forteviot (Strathearn)	9

Date	Name	Margary No.
904?	Scone	9
910	Tettenhall	191
914/918	Corbridge	8, 85
914/16	Hook Norton	561?
914/16	Luton	168, 213
915/17	Archenfield (Weston-under-Penyard?)	611, 612, 614, 615
916	Brecenanmere (Llangorse Lake?)	62
917	Derby	18, 181, 182
920	Between Tempsford & Bedford	225
920	Wigingamere (Newport)	?
920	Tempsford	225
920	Colchester	3, 321, 322
920	Maldon	*119j
920	Davenport	71
923	York	2, 8, 28, 800, 801
937	Brunanburh	7?, 18?, 710?, 670?
943	Tamworth	1
948	Castleford	28
950	Nant Carno	643
950–4	Fetteresso	?
954	near Llanrwst	69
954/5	Stainmore	82
971	Maldon	31?, *119j
973	Luncarty	9
980	Thanet	?
980/1	Southampton	421
981	Padstow	?
982	Portland	48?
987	Anglesey	?
987/8	Watchet	?
988	Maldon	31?, *119j
991	Maldon	31?, *119j
993	Bamburgh	*Appendix 5 J
994	London	1, 2, 3, 15, 40, 167, 220

Date	Name	Margary No.
997	Lydford	5
997	Watchet	?
997	Rathinveramon (Cramond?)	7
999	St David's	?
999	Rochester	1, 13
1001	Aethelingadene (Alton?)	155
1001	Pinhoe	4
1004	Thetford	37, 333
1004/5	Monnivaird (Monzievaird)	?
1006	East Kennet	53
1006	Durham	80
1010	Ringmere	33, 37, 337
1010	Mortlach	?
1010	St Bride	?
1013	London	1, 2, 3, 15, 40, 167, 220
1016	Penselwood	?
1016	Sherston	5, 543
1016	Brentford	4
1016	Otford	?
1016	Assandun	*119r
1016	Coldstream	*Appendix 5 G
1018	Carham on Tweed	*Appendix 5 C
1022	Abergwili	623
1039	Rhyd y Groes/Crosford	64
1052	Porlock	?
1053	Hereford	6, 63
1057	Dunsinane Hill	9?
1056	Glasbury on Wye	63
1057	Lumphanan	?

Appendix 3

Medieval Battlefields and Roman Roads

Date	Name	Margary No.
1066	Gate Fulford	800
1066	Stamford Bridge	80, 810
1066	Hastings	13
1066	London	1, 2, 3, 15, 40, 167, 220
1069	Stafford	?
1081	Mynydd Carn	?
1093	Alnwick	*Appendix 5 A
1098	Menai Straits	67
1130	Inchbare	9?
1136	Swansea	?
1136	Carlisle	7, 75
1138	Clitheroe	72
1138	'Battle of the Standard', Northallerton	80
1141	Lincoln	2, 27
1141	Winchester	42, 43, 45, 420
1143	Wilton	4, 45
1153	Tutbury	?
1164	Renfrew	78?, 780?
1174	Alnwick	*Appendix 5 A
1194	Conway	?
1199	Mold	?
1217	Lincoln	2, 27
1257	Y Cymerau (Aberglasney)	623
1262	Maelienydd (Cefnllys)	?
1263	Blorenge Mountain	62
1263	Largs	780?
1264	Lewes	14, 145

Date	Name	Margary No.
1265	Evesham	63?, 180
1271	Caerphilly	621
1282	Llandeilo Fawr	623
1282	Menai Straits	67
1282	Orewin Bridge	621
1283	Castell y Bere	?
1259	Maes Moydog	?
1296	Loudon Hill	79?
1296	Berwick	*Appendix 5 B
1296	Dunbar	*Appendix 5 B
1296	Stracathro	9?
1297	Sanquhar	?
1297	Dalswinton	77
1297	Lochmaben	76
1297	Stirling Bridge	9
1298	Falkirk	9, 90
1300	Cree	?
1303	Roslin	?
1303	Stirling	9
1304	Happrew	79
1306	Methven Park	9
1306	Dalry	?
1307	Turnberry	?
1307	Glentrool	?
1307	Sanquhar	?
1307	Loudon Hill	?79
1307	Ayr	?
1307	Fail	?
1307	Barra Hill	?
1311	Corbridge	8, 85
1311	Berwick	*Appendix 5 B
1311	Linlithgow	?
1312	Hexham	*Codrington (Erming Street North 13a)
1312	Durham	80

Date	Name	Margary No.
1312	Hartlepool	?
1313	Edinburgh	7, 8?, *Appendix 5 B?
1313	Perth	9
1314	Edinburgh	7, 8?, *Appendix 5 B?
1314	Bannockburn	9
1315	Fordell	?
1316	Skaithmuir	?
1317	Lintalee/Linthaughlee	?
1317	near Berwick	*Appendix 5 B
1317/18	Donibristle	?
1318	Berwick	*Appendix 5 B
1319	Mytton (Myton in Swaledale)	8, 720?
1319	Gasklune (Glasclune?)	?
1322	Burton Bridge	18
1322	Boroughbridge	8
1322	Byland	814?
1327	Stanhope Park	821?
1332	Dupplin Moor	9
1333	Halidon Hill	*Appendix 5 B
1335	Borough Muir	7
1335	Kilblene (Culblean)	?
1346	Neville's Cross	83
1355	Nisbet on Teviot	8
1370	Carham on Tweed	*Appendix 5 C
1380	Solway	7
1381	North Walsham	*Norfolk 97
1387	Radcot Bridge	?
1388	Otterburn/Chevy Chase	8
1392	Glasclune	?
1400	Cockburnspath	*Appendix 5 B
1401	Hyddgen	64?
1402	Ruthin	?
1402	Pilleth/Bryn Glas	?
1402	Nesbit Moor	8

Date	Name	Margary No.
1402	Homildon Hill	*Appendix 5 F
1403	Shrewsbury	?
1403	Caernarfon	67, 68, *Waddelove XII, XV
1404	Beaumaris	?
1404	Aberystwyth	69
1404	Harlech	*Waddelove XVI
1404	Campstone Hill	630
1405	Grosmont	630
1405	Craig-y-Dorth	6
1405	Pwll Melyn	62, 612
1405	Skipton Moor	72
1405	Worcester/Woodbury Hill	63
1405	Haverfordwest	?
1405	Tenby	?
1405	Carmarthen	60, 69
1408	Bramham Moor	28, 280, 72, 729
1436	Piper Dene	* Appendix 5 B
1448	Gretna/River Sark	7
1455	Arkinholm	?
1455	St Albans	16, 163, 21, 210, 212
1459	Blore Heath	?
1459	Ludford Bridge	613?
1460	Northampton	17?
1460	Wakefield	?
1461	Mortimer's Cross	6
1461	St Albans	1, 21?
1461	Ferrybridge	280?
1461	Towton	280?
1464	Hedgeley Moor	87
1464	Hexham	*Codrington (Erming Street North 13a)
1469	Edgecote	166?
1470	Losecoat Field	2
1471	Leicester	5, 57
1471	Barnet	167, 220

Date	Name	Margary No.
1471	Tewkesbury	180
1485	Bosworth Field	57
1487	Stoke Field	5
1488	Talla Moss	?
1488	Sauchieburn	?
1497	Blackheath	1
1497	Norham	*Appendix 5 C
1497	Exeter	49, 490, 491, 493
1512/3	Milfield	*Appendix 5 F
1513	Norham	*Appendix 5 C
1513	Flodden	*Appendix 5 F
1514	Hornshole	?

Appendix 4

Post-Medieval Battlefields and Roman Roads

Date	Name	Margary No.
1542	Haddon Rigg	*Appendix 5 C
1542	Solway Moss	7
1545	Ancrum Moor	8
1547	St Andrews	?
1547	Pinkie Cleugh	7?, 8?
1549	Fenny Bridges	4
1549	Dussindale	* Norfolk 34, 62j
1549	Sampford Courtenay	492
1554	Cooling Castle	?
1554	Wrotham	? [Pilgrim's Way]
1562	Skirmish Hill, Melrose	?
1562/5	Corrichie Hill	?
1567	Carberry Hill	8?
1568	Langside	78?
1575	Carter Bar ('Raid of the Reidswire')	?
1593	Dryfe Sands	7, 76
1600	Perth	9
1639	Megray Hill	?
1639	Brig o'Dee	?
1640	Newburn	?
1642	Powick Bridge	180
1642	Edgehill	?
1642	Turnham Green	4, 40
1642	Tadcaster	28
1643	Braddock Down	?
1643	Hopton Heath	?
1643	Highnam	61

Date	Name	Margary No.
1643	Seacroft Moor	712?
1643	Launceston	492
1643	Reading	?
1643	Grantham	2, 58
1643	Stratton	?
1643	Sleaford	260, 262
1643	Chalgrove	?
1643	Atherton/Adwalton Moor	712
1643	Lansdown	542
1643	Roundway Down	53
1643	Bristol	54
1643	Gainsborough	?
1643	Newbury	41, 53
1643	Winceby	?
1643	Alton	155
1644	Nantwich	700
1644	Newark	5
1644	Bradford	721
1644	Cheriton Wood	?
1644	Selby	?
1644	Cropredy Bridge	?
1644	Marston Moor	8, 280
1644	Lostwithiel	?
1644	Tippermuir (Tibbermore)	9
1644	between Lostwithiel/Fowey	?
1644	Justice Mills, Aberdeen	?
1644	Montgomery	64
1644	Newbury	41
1645	Dundee	?
1645	Leicester	5, 57
1645	Naseby	?
1645	Alford	?
1645	Langport	?
1645	Dunkeld	?

Date	Name	Margary No.
1645	Colby Moor	?
1645	Kilsyth	90
1645	Bristol	54
1645	Philiphaugh	?
1645	Rowton Heath	7
1645	Denbigh	?
1646	Stow-on-the-Wold	5
1648	St Fagans	?
1648	Maidstone	13
1648	Y Dalar Hir	67
1648	Mauchline Moor	790?
1648	Colchester	3, 321, 322
1648	Ribbleton Moor (Preston)	703
1650	Edinburgh	7, 8?, *Appendix 5 B?
1650	Dunbar	*Appendix 5 B
1651	Pitreavie	?
1651	Dundee	?
1651	Worcester	180
1655	Dalnaspidal	?
1659	Winnington Bridge	?
1664	Fyvie	?
1666	Rullion Green ('Battle of the Pentlands')	7
1679	Drumclog	79?
1679	Bothwell Bridge (Hamilton Moor)	78
1680	Airds Moss	?
1685	Keynsham	540
1685	Philips Norton	52
1686	Sedgemoor	?
1689	Dunkeld	?
1715	Preston	70
1715	Sherriffmuir	9
1745	Prestonpans	*Appendix 5 B
1745	Clifton	7
1746	Falkirk	90

Possible Roman Roads in North-East England and South-East Scotland

The Roman road system is fractal: the more closely it is examined, the greater the detail that can be seen. This is what the Viatores, Waddelove, and Allan have all found and the same principle can probably be applied to any area of Britain occupied by the Romans. As a convenient case study, the likely prehistoric, Roman, and medieval network north of Hadrian's Wall and east of Dere Street as outlined here is both an indicator of the potential of even the most cursory of such studies, but also serves to show how much remains to be done just for this one small region.

None of these roads are proven to the degree of five stars outlined by the NEHHAS guidelines listed above (page 128). Most only qualify for a three-star rating, but then, as has been pointed out, the same is true of much of Margary's network.

All of the following roads saw use by medieval armies so were clearly medieval roads. Some may well be prehistoric in origin, retained as an informal part of the Roman network outlined by Margary. Additionally, some – perhaps all – may be Roman in origin, in the sense that they were newly surveyed and laid out on courses that approximated to prehistoric routes, rather than just a resurfacing of an existing prehistoric track or road (a process Margary tended to refer to by calling a route 'Romanized'). The evidence is set out in summary form below to illustrate how the demonstrable use of Roman roads in medieval and post-medieval warfare can be used to suggest previously unidentified ancient routes. It is intended that all will be published in detail elsewhere.[1]

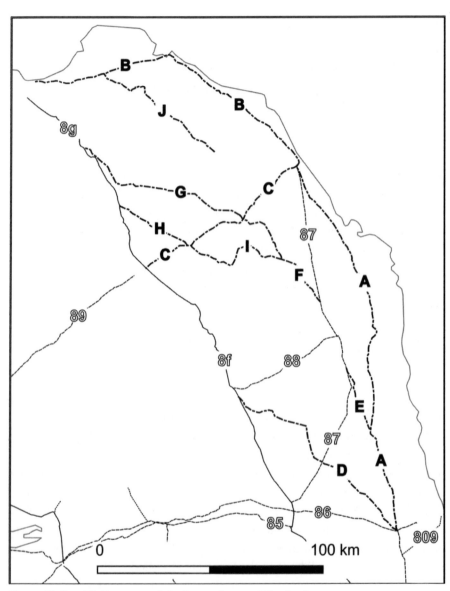

Figure 33: Possible Roman roads in the south–east of Scotland.

Route A: Newcastle to Tweedmouth (Figure 33, A)

Summary

This route links the northern end of the Pons Aelius (the bridge across the Tyne) at Newcastle with the northern end of the Devil's Causeway at Tweedmouth.

Introduction

The course of the Great North Road between Newcastle and Berwick shows sufficiently convincing signs of alignment and place-name evidence to suggest that it too was part of the system. The first part of this route, between Newcastle and Morpeth, was accepted by Codrington, ignored by Margary, but subsequently reinstated by Hafemann, although viewed sceptically by Bidwell and Holbrook, who judged Margary 80 to have been an unimportant route in the Roman period. However, Codrington thought it veered across north-westwards from Morpeth to join the Devil's Causeway, effectively following the line of the present A697 where it diverges from the A1. If, on the other hand, the route is projected northwards, it would have provided a direct link between the Antonine fort at Newcastle and the Tweed crossing, and ultimately to Inveresk and Cramond, also Antonine foundations. Since it would then form a northern extension of Margary 80, these roads would provide a direct route between York and the eastern flank of the Antonine Wall. As such, this is the route surveyed by Ogilby.[2]

Historical role

There were two medieval battles at Alnwick, both with unfortunate results for Scottish kings. The first (1093) led to the death of Malcolm III 'Canmore', whilst the second (1174) saw the capture of William I 'the Lion'. This route can also be matched with the movement of armies and the royal itineraries of Edward I in 1296, 1298, and 1299 as well as on numerous other occasions up to the preparations that culminated in the battle of Pinkie Cleugh in 1547.[3]

Place-name evidence

There are several *chester* place-names along the route, as well as a *coldharbour* and a *causey* (causeway), and two *-peth* names at Morpeth and Hemelspeth.[4]

Brief description

The route approximates closely with that surveyed by Ogilby. Having crossed the Tyne somewhere in the vicinity of the swing bridge, the road probably headed up Pilgrim Street and thence onto Town Moor where a straight alignment took it through Gosforth, North Brunton, Wide Open, Seaton Burn, then Seven Mile House Farm, before crossing the Blythe near Stannington Bridge, and on through Stannington. The course through Morpeth itself is unclear but the alignment continues to the north of it through Helm, where the Ogilby line probably departs from it but the alignment is still marked by field boundaries between Helm and Eshott airfield. Felton, Newton, Alnwick, Charlton, Wainford, Belford, Buckton, Haggerston, Scremerston, and so to Tweedmouth. The modern A1 veers off the Ogilby line just south of Helm and does not rejoin it until near Shilbottle, having been straightened over this section (and in some places looking more Roman than the likely Roman alignment). Other bypasses occur around Alnwick and Belford.[5]

Table of key locations

Point	OS Grid ref
Newcastle	NZ 252 638
Town Moor	NZ 248 656
Gosforth	NZ 243 684
North Brunton	NZ 241 712
Wide Open	NZ 241 726
Seaton Burn	NZ 237 741
Seven Mile House Farm	NZ 229 751
Stannington Bridge	NZ 216 783
Stannington	NZ 213 794
Morpeth	NZ 198 860
Helm	NZ 189 962
Felton	NU 184 006
Newton	NU 172 053
Alnwick	NU 195 126
North Charlton	NU 170 227
Warenford	NU 136 285
Belford	NU 108 341
Buckton	NU 083 384
Haggerston	NU 039 435
Scremerston	NU 006 491
Tweedmouth	NT 995 516

Route B: Berwick to Inveresk (Figure 33, B)

Summary
This route links the northern end of the Devil's Causeway and the Newcastle/
Tweedmouth route, via Dunbar, to Dere Street at Inveresk.

Introduction
Cul-de-sacs are unusual in the Roman road system, and one of the most
prominent is the Devil's Causeway (Margary 87) which runs from just north of
Hadrian's Wall to Tweedmouth. A limited number of first century AD Roman
sites are known along it, including Longshaws and Learchild, whilst finds from
Wooperton may indicate the proximity of another such site. However, it is a
road with no purpose: no major site has as yet been identified at Tweedmouth
and, as was noted earlier in relation to Bewcastle, roads that appear to be dead-
ends may in fact have continued in antiquity. Because of the supposed absence
of Roman roads in the south-east of Scotland (north of the Tweed, south of
the Forth, and east of Dere Street), that region has often been thought of as an
ally of Rome which did not require pacification, but is the lack of roads real or
illusory?[6]

Much of the course of this route has already been identified and published,
albeit without recognizing its significance as part of the Roman road network.
If this road is Roman in origin or at least use then the Devil's Causeway ceases
to be a cul-de-sac and starts to make sense as part of a communication system
running up through the eastern lowlands.[7]

Historical role
Historically, the movements of a saint and of kings and their armies have already
been alluded to as significant indicators of a route between Newcastle upon Tyne
and Tweedmouth and, north of the Tweed, between Berwick-upon-Tweed and
Dunbar and then west towards Edinburgh. The first indications come from the
perambulations of St Cuthbert's corpse, first withdrawn west and then south
to avoid Viking incursions in AD 875, and then taken north to avoid William's
harrying of the north, before ultimately ending up in Durham. Athelstan's
campaign into Scotland, accompanied by a fleet, suggests he will have kept to
an east coast route. King John's journey up to Norham extends the route whilst
the itinerary of Edward I confirms that and extends it north of the Tweed to
Dunbar and then west to Edinburgh. Edward I's siege of Berwick-upon-Tweed
and battle at Dunbar are of note, as of course is Edward III's victory over the
Scots at Halidon Hill, just west of Berwick. The Battle of Piperdean occurred

to the north of Coldingham, where our putative road would cross the moor, whilst the seventeenth century Battle of Pinkie and eighteenth century Battle of Prestonpans ocurred on the route.

The suggested location of Tweedmouth castle may also have been the site of a Roman fort and was well-placed to supervise the southern terminus of a crossing of the Tweed.[8]

Brief description

The most likely Roman bridging point would have coincided with the lowest ford of the Tweed, between Tweedmouth church and Sandgate in Berwick. The subsequent medieval and post-medieval bridges were moved slightly upstream, but the prominence of the route through Sandgate, Hide Hill, Church Street, Wallace Green and Low Greens (the line now partly obliterated by both the medieval and Elizabethan defences but evident on Speed's map of the town) to rejoin the Great North Road near Bede Avenue must be more than coincidental.[9]

Archaeologically, an appropriate route of some antiquity has long been identified to the north of Berwick that not only pre-dates the construction of the new Berwick to Dunbar post road, opened around 1810 but seems to be earlier than the turnpike trusts in this area. The road runs from Berwick, up to Lamberton, past the nineteenth century Ayton Castle (which displaced the original village of Ayton, through which the road ran) and onto Coldingham Moor. It leaves the higher ground, crosses the Piperdean Burn at Head Chester, near Cockburnspath, and its course is then rejoined by the replacement post road (which has instead avoided the higher ground by following the line of the Eye Water). It next has to negotiate the Pease Burn before it proceeds via Skateraw to Dunbar in straight stretches, and thence westwards towards Inveresk.[10]

In terms of its alignment, it resembles other known and proven Roman roads in that it utilizes straight lengths of road where possible. There is also a limited amount of place-name evidence to support the identification, including Chester Hill fort (NT 952 601), Chesterdale Plantation (NT 937 604), The Chesters (NT 800 675), and – as has just been mentioned – Head Chester on the Piperdean Burn (NT 816 693).

This route passes standing stones at Kirklandhill (near Dunbar) and Pencraig Hill (East Linton), and a hoard of Roman-period metalwork was found near to it on Lamberton Moor. The Coldingham Moor section was replaced as the principal post road from Berwick to Edinburgh by the new mail road in 1810, the course of which was for many years reflected by the A1 and stretches of which are still shadowed by the A1(M) between Dunbar and Tranent.[11]

Table of key locations

Point	OS Grid ref
Berwick	NT 998 526
Lamberton	NT 966 571
Ayton	NT 927 613
Cairncross	NT 891 635
Old Cambus	NT 805 695
Bilsdean	NT 764 726
Skateraw	NT 736 750
Broxburn	NT 692 773
Dunbar	NT 678 788
East Linton	NT 589 770
Haddington	NT 508 744
Gladsmuir	NT 457 732
Macmerry	NT 431 723
Tranent	NT 402 728
Musselburgh	NT 345 728

Route C: Tweedmouth to Maxton via Cornhill (Figure 33, C)

Summary

This road forms a direct link along the Tweed from the northern end of both the Devil's Causeway and the Newcastle/Tweedmouth route to Dere Street at Newstead.

Introduction

The likelihood that there was at the very least a prehistoric route up the south side of the Tweed valley is betrayed by a series of Roman camps, including Norham, East Learmouth, Mindrum, Carham, Wooden House Farm, and (assuming it does not relate to Dere Street and is indeed a camp) Maxton. The turnpike road, followed now by the course of the A698, shows every sign of being an aligned Roman successor which met Margary 8 south of Maxton and was probably contiguous with Margary 89. The latter road had its own series of associated camps at Milrighall, Oakwood, Eastcote, and Cavers Mains. A separate series of camps continued up the Tweed beyond Newstead, at Innerleithen and Eshiels, linking with Lyne.[12]

Historical role

The Battle of Carham in 1018 between the Scots and Northumbrians may show a use of this road, but without any information about army movements, it can really only be noted. Carham is 2.5 km from Wark, with its important ford of the Tweed, so the armies' movements could have been east–west or north–south. An important sequence of medieval fortifications lay along the Tweed which, for part of its length, formed the border between England and Scotland, as a direct result of that 1018 Scots' victory. These included Tweedmouth, Norham, Twizell, Cornhill, Wark, and Roxburgh, and most of them either guarded fords or bridges across the river and some were equipped with both. The value of these sites is demonstrated by repeated Scottish attacks on them and typified by the Franco-Scottish foray along the Tweed in 1385 and the English use of the route that culminated in the Battle of Haddon Rigg (near Carham) in 1542 and the attack on Kelso shortly after.[13]

Brief description
The road leaves Tweedmouth near the putative site of the medieval castle and its route is marked first by field boundaries before being taken up by the turnpike road through East Ord and continuing towards Thornton Park. Crossing the Till at Twizel, it proceeded through Donaldson's Lodge on its way to Cornhill and a junction with route F. Passing next through Wark, Carham, and Sprouston, it must have arrived at Maxwellheugh prior to crossing the Teviot somewhere near Roxburgh castle. It probably continued past Trows and Rutherford, ultimately joining Margary 8 (Dere Street). A further continuation to the west seems likely to join Margary 89, traced to just 3.6 km to the south-west of the main road.

Like other Roman roads, it makes use of straight lengths of road where possible and there is some place-name evidence to support its identification as Roman, including Holy Chesters near Donaldson's Lodge.[14]

This route passes within 3 km of a stone circle at Duddo but this seems unlikely to be significant unless it relates to the earlier prehistoric route exploited by the Roman camps along the Tweed (East Learmouth camp is a similar distance south of the proposed Roman route).[15]

Table of key locations

Point	OS Grid ref
Tweedmouth	NT 994 520
East Ord	NT 978 515
Thornton Park	NT 942 484
Donaldson's Lodge	NT 873 416
Cornhill on Tweed	NT 861 394
Wark	NT 825 385
Carham	NT 799 384

Sprouston	NT 757 355
Maxwellheugh	NT 731 331
Roxburgh Newtown	NT 674 313
Muirhouselaw	NT 627 288

Route D: Newcastle to Otterburn (Figure 33, D)

Summary
This road forms a direct link from Newcastle to the southern middle section of Dere Street.

Introduction
Given the certainty of a Tyne crossing at Newcastle, this forms a convenient and logical link to join with Margary 8 (Dere Street), close to the site of the Battle of Otterburn. The proximity of the battle site to the better-known road means this route could be dismissed, were it not for its use by both the Scots and English, moving north-westwards from Newcastle.[16]

Historical role
The route only really features in that one major conflict, which comprised the Scots' withdrawal from Newcastle and their pursuit by the English, culminating in the Battle of Otterburn in 1388. Initially, the Scots mustered for their raid at Southdean (near Hawick) then attacked Prudhoe, demonstrating the use of Dere Street on their way south, but chose to use a different route back – via Ponteland – which was more direct. This may have had something to do with the fact that the Duke of Northumberland was occupying Alnwick and thereby blocking the east coast route (A).[17]

Brief description
The route would presumably have passed through Hadrian's Wall by means of the same gateway as route A, but then headed north-westwards along what is now the A189, the B6918 (formerly the A696) to Ponteland, and then the A696 proper. It then passes through Belsay and Cambo before turning onto a more easterly course, crosses the line of the Devil's Causeway (Margary 87) near a (tentatively dated) Roman-period rectangular earthwork at Edgehouse (NZ 053 806), just south of Ferney Chesters farm. On through Kirkharle, Kirkwhelpington, and Knowesgate, it passes the significantly named Raechester before reaching Otterburn and a junction with the Dere Street (Margary 8).

There is some place-name evidence that seems to support the case for the route, including Ferney Chesters and Raechester.[18]

Table of key locations

Point	OS Grid ref
Newcastle	NZ 239 646
Ponteland	NZ 170 727
Belsay	NZ 111 785
Bradford	NZ 068 800
Kirkharle	NZ 020 825
Kirkwhelpington	NY 993 848
Knowesgate	NY 988 857
Otterburn	NY 891 928

Route E: Morpeth to Longhorsley (Figure 33, E)

Summary
This road provides a link from the east coast route (A) to the Devil's Causeway (Margary 87) and is now followed by the southern portion of the A697.

Introduction
As with the first part of the Newcastle to Berwick route, this road was included by Codrington, ignored by Margary, but subsequently reinstated.[19]

Historical role
The Scottish raid that culminated in the Battle of Homildon Hill in 1402 involved a return march from Newcastle which was intercepted by Hotspur near Wooler, so the Morpeth to Longhorsley spur would have been used for that. Similarly, when the Marquis of Montagu led his Yorkist force north from Newcastle in 1484 to arrive at Hedgeley Moor on their way to Norham, he would have taken this road.[20]

Brief description
The road forks from the Great North Road (Route A) at Warrener's House, to the north-west of Morpeth. It then continues to Longhorsley and on to cross the Coquet near Weldon (the modern road has been artificially straightened now so that it resembles a Roman road but the true alignment lay obliquely to it). It continues through Low Town to Longframlington to join the Devil's Causeway just to the north of the village near Besom Barn.

No appropriate place-name evidence is recorded.

Table of key locations

Point	OS Grid ref
Warrener's House	NZ 182 886
Longhorsley	NZ 149 944
Weldon	NZ 137 984
Low Town	NU 138 000
Longframlington	NU 131 010
Besom Barn	NU 121 025

Route F: Percy's Cross to Cornhill (Figure 33, F)

Summary

This road, together with the Coldstream to Carfraemill section, is a part of a link from the Devil's Causeway to the northern middle section of Dere Street.

Introduction

The modern A697 road, still on Telford's line, diverges from the Devil's Causeway at Hedgeley Moor and a possible Roman course can be detected for much of its length towards Cornhill.[21]

Historical role

The battles of Homildon Hill, Hedgeley Moor, Flodden, and Yeavering all took place close to the course of this route and most depended upon its existence.

The location of Cornhill Castle (possibly only ever a timber fortification, being replaced after 1385 by a stone tower in Cornhill itself) downstream on the Tweed now seems slightly incongruous, given the location of the eighteenth century bridge over the river at Coldstream, but makes more sense when it is understood to have been placed to control an older crossing point (the other medieval castles along the Tweed are all placed at crossing points, either by bridge or ford).[22]

Brief description

From the junction at Percy's Cross on Hedgeley Moor, the route heads through Wooperton and on to Wooler where it changes to a more easterly course. Passing Humbleton it reaches Akeld and changes back to a more northerly course again, although the continuation of a branch road through Kirknewton and Kirk Yetholm may be indicated by its use by Edward I in August 1304 on his way from Jedburgh to Bolton in Northumberland. The main road continues in a north-westerly direction through Milfield, after which it continues to

Cornhill, perhaps by the modern route of the A697, although a more direct north-easterly route passing to the south of Branxton and avoiding that dog-leg is also a possibility. As it nears Cornhill it continues on to cross the Tweed near Cornhill Castle.

There is a Bowchester place-name near Humbleton, whilst the so-called Battle Stone near Homildon Hill is prehistoric and may indicate an early route.[23]

Table of key locations

Point	OS Grid ref
Hedgeley Moor	NU 053 194
Wooperton	NU 043 205
Wooler	NT 992 284
Humbleton	NT 975 290
Akeld	NT 956 296
Milfield	NT 935 338
Cornhill Castle	NT 852 403

Route G: Coldstream to Carfraemill (Figure 33, G)

Summary
This road, together with the Percy's Cross to Cornhill section, is a part of a link from the Devil's Causeway to the middle section of Dere Street.

Introduction
For the most part, this road coincides with Telford's alternative to the Great North Road, now the A697.[24]

Historical role
Although the bridge at Coldstream is eighteenth century in date, there have long been at least two crossings of the Tweed in the vicinity and, as has already been discussed, one probably lay close to Cornhill Castle, where there was a ford to Lennel. Just north-west of Coldstream, the road passes close to the site of the motte and bailey castle of The Mount, near The Hirsel, clearly demonstrating the importance of the route in the medieval period.[25]

Brief description
From a crossing point near Lennel on the modern Scottish side, the road may have passed to the north of the Hirsel, to join the route of the A697 near Hatchednize, proceeding through Orange Lane to Greenlaw, to pass through Whiteburn and Thirlestane but turn northwards before reaching Lauder.

Place-name evidence includes Darnchester and Belchester near The Hirsel and Rowchester just south of – and Chesters north-east of – Greenlaw.[26]

Table of key locations

Point	OS Grid ref
Lennel	NT 851 404
The Mount	NT 814 415
Hatchednize	NT 805 415
Orange Lane	NT 775 426
Greenlaw	NT 708 459
Whiteburn	NT 590 475
Thirlestane	NT 568 479
Carfraemill	NT 508 533

Routes H to J are much harder to define than the other routes with few characteristic straight sections to give them away (and in the Scottish Borders, straight road lengths were frequently a by-product of enclosure and estate formation). Nevertheless, their historical use suggests that something approximating to the following routes existed.

Route H: Birkenside to Springhill (Figure 33, H)

Summary
This road, together with the Maxwellheugh to Akeld section, is a part of a link from the Devil's Causeway to the southern middle section of Dere Street.

Introduction
This road may have approximated to the course of the modern B6397 from Earlston to Kelso.[27]

Historical role
Edward I passed from Lauder to Roxburgh in 1296 and a French force under Jean de Vienne may have used the same route in 1385.[28]

Brief description
The route forked from Dere Street somewhere in the region of Nether Blainslie and Birkenside, passing Smailholm on its way down to the well-attested Tweed crossing near Floors Castle that gave access to the strategically significant Roxburgh Castle.

There are no characteristic straight sections of road and no place-name evidence to support the suggested route.

Table of key locations

Point	OS Grid ref
Birkenside	NT 564 421
Smailholm	NT 652 367
Floors	NT 712 341

Route I: Maxwellheugh to Akeld (Figure 33, I)

Summary
This route, together with the Birkenside to Springhill section, is a part of a link from the Devil's Causeway to the southern middle section of Dere Street.

Introduction
There are few very obviously straight stretches here so this may well just have been a prehistoric track that continued in use as a convenient shortcut through the Cheviots.

Historical role
As mentioned above, Edward I's route from Jedburgh to Bolton in 1304 must have used this route.[29]

Brief description
This route continues the line of Route F from Akeld and probably passed through Kirknewton, Kilham, Kirk Yetholm, Blakelaw and finally Maxwellheugh.
There is no place-name evidence to assist in the identification of the course, but the generalities of the route seem likely.

Table of key locations

Point	OS Grid ref
Akeld	NT 956 296
Kirknewton	NT 915 301
Kilham	NT 885 325
Kirk Yetholm	NT 830 280
Blakelaw	NT 769 308
Maxwellheugh	NT 732 328

Route J: Haddington to the Whiteadder (Figure 33, J)

Summary
This route would link the east coast route to a possible Tweed crossing, perhaps at Wark (where the castle guarded a ford). It evidently began at Haddington and crossed the Lammermuirs to descend into the Merse somewhere near Duns, possibly making for the ford at Lennel.

Introduction
The fact that it is only used twice that we know of, and by the same monarch, suggests it did not enjoy the popularity (and familiarity) of the east coast and central routes, but a Roman origin is nevertheless rendered likely by its use to haul artillery on both occasions. The modern (and turnpiked) road followed the river valleys, but – in the central portion at least – an earlier cross-country route can be discerned.[30]

Historical role
The route was used by James IV first for hauling his artillery to attack Norham Castle in 1497 and next when he mustered his forces at Ellemford.[31]

Brief description
The route evidently began at Haddington and crossed the Lammermuirs via Ellemford and Duns, probably leading down to a crossing of the Tweed near Coldstream. Between Haddington and Ellemford the route is very unclear, but may have passed Garvald before crossing the moors north-west of Ellemford. A Whitchester place-name to the south-east of Ellemford is of interest, as is Chesters near Whitelaw Hill, as well as Stoneypath to the east of Garvald.[32]

Table of key locations

Point	OS Grid ref
Haddington	NT 516 739
Garvald	NT 584 707
Ellemford	NT 727 601
Duns	NT 790 547
Lennel	NT 852 404

Conclusion

It can be seen, therefore, that sufficient evidence, in terms of discernible alignments, place-names, and (most notably) frequent use by armies in the medieval and post-medieval period, is available to suggest that a network of Roman roads existed north of Hadrian's Wall and east of Dere Street. This notion finds some support in the list of military movements and especially battles – including the battles of Dunbar (1296, 1650), Halidon Hill (1333), Piperdene (1436), Pinkie (1547), the siege of Haddington (1548–9), and the Battle of Prestonpans (1745) and part at least even appears on the fraudulent Bertram map (probably more a matter of coincidence or clairvoyance than accurate reportage: see page 112). From an archaeological point of view, there is at the very least a good case for further investigation.

There is however more to this than meets the eye, for the network described here is clearly phased and each component can be seen to have had a specific purpose. The Roman preference for the east coast route to Newcastle (Margary 80) during the Antonine period is indicated by the provision of new forts at both Chester-le-Street and Newcastle at this time. It is possible that the bridge over the Tyne, the Pons Aelius, may also date to this period but in the absence of any physical verifiable remains until now, incapable of proof.[33]

The proposed network north of the Tyne would thus have overcome one of the major weaknesses of the established Dere Street route into Scotland: its all-weather failings. At two points, in the hills south of the Tyne valley and at Soutra, Dere Street was (and still is) vulnerable to closure by snow during the winter months. Margary 80 south of the Tyne and the network described here would have worked around these shortcomings to provide better access to the north at such times, whilst tying the new alternative routes into the existing system in as many places as possible.

Notes

Preface and Introduction
1. Quiller-Couch (1918) 15–16.

Chapter 1: The Prehistory of Roman Roads
1. Viatores (1964) 50.
2. Collingwood and Richmond (1969) 4.
3. Sharpstone Hill: Malim and Hayes (2011). New book: Robb (2013). Roads before the Romans: Forbes and Burmester (1904) 26–39; Margary (1973) 18; Cox (1944). Old Straight Track: Watkins (1925). Akeman Street: Copeland (2009).
4. Armies and roads: Jones (2011) 112. Plautius' landing place: Hind (1989); Frere and Fulford (2001).
5. Pilgrim's Way: Hindle (1998) 13. Chaucer: Littlehales (1896). Thames crossing: Webster (1980) 98.
6. Prehistoric trackways: Taylor (1979) 1–39; Muir (1985) 260–3. Ridgeways: Davies (2006) 29–32; Taylor (1979) 19–20. Somerset Levels: Coles and Coles (1986). Native predecessor to Roman system: Belloc (1924), cf. Davies (2006) 28–9; Margary (1973) 18; Viatores (1964) 49–51. Early wheeled vehicles: Coles and Coles (1986) 180. Earliest wooden wheel: Sheridan (1996) 189.
7. Viatores (1964) 49 citing Fox (1923).
8. Corlea: Raftery (1991) 110. Eton: Allen and Welsh (1996). Vauxhall: Anonymous (1999).
9. Holne Moor: Fleming (1988) 70, Fig 34. Melton: Bishop (1999). Mount Pleasant: NAA (2005). Ley lines: Watkins (1925).
10. Ridgeways: Taylor (1979) 19–20; Rackham (1986) 251; Davies (2006) 29–32.
11. Peak District trackways: Dodd and Dodd (1980) 10–18.
12. Roecliffe: Bishop (1995). Devil's Arrows: Castleden (1992) 249. Thornborough henges: Thomas (1955).
13. Corbridge: Bishop and Dore (1989).
14. Badbury: Frere and St Joseph (1983) 10–11, plate 5. Other hillforts: Field (1992) 154. Burgundy: Madry and Crumley (1990). Roman forts and hillforts: Maxfield (1987) 19. *Oppida*: Witcher (1998) 66–7.
15. Tweed camps: Welfare and Swan (1995) 72–134, 181. Road to Cardean: Margary (1973) 495. Northern camps: Maxwell (1989) 38–67. Edward I: Maxwell (1986).
16. Monastic route: Hindle (1998) 14. Malham camp: Welfare and Swan (1995) 143–5.
17. Roads in the American West: Gregory (1931) 10–11.
18. Avebury: Burl (2002) 212–13. Arbor Low: Dodd and Dodd (1980) 10–12. Via Sacra: Smith (2000) 29. Spartacus: Appian, *Histories* 120.
19. Roads help armies: Barrett (1896) 427. Cart terminology: Stevenson (1983) 49. Britons opposing Caesar: Caesar, *Gallic Wars* 4.33. Mons Graupius: Tacitus, *Agricola* 36. Chariots of the Parisi: Ramm (1978) 13, 21. Edinburgh chariot: Carter and Hunter (2008). Boudica: Tacitus, *Annals* 14.34. *Tropaeum Traiani*: Florescu (1959) Fig 219.

20. Drove roads: Hindle (2001) 56–76; Forster (1888) 99–101. Stagshaw Fair: ibid. 63–70. Transhumance routes: Muir (1985) 206–7; Hindle (2001) 56. Knag Burn gateway: Bishop (2011) 21.
21. Tumuli: Cox (1944) 4. High Rochester: Wilson (2004). Great Chesters: Breeze (2006) 274. Coney Hills: Marwood (1995). Corpse roads: Hindle (2001) 44–6. Mardle Green: ibid. 46.
22. Burgundy network: Madry and Crumley (1990). Beacon Hill: Cox (1944) 33–4.
23. Maen Madoc: Westwood (1856) 407. Bwlch y Ddeufaen: Muir (1985) 263–4. Gelligaer: RCAHMW (1976) 36.
24. Arbor Low: Dodd and Dodd (1980) 10–12. Y Pigwyn: Burl (2005) 184. Silbury settlement: Linford (2208–9).
25. Prehistoric origins: Rackham (1986) 250.
26. Outpost forts: Breeze (2006) 97–102. Bewcastle road: Hodgson (2009) 170.

Chapter 2: Conquest and Construction
1. Viatores (1964) 15.
2. Advance detachments: Josephus, *Jewish War* 3.118. Opening up: Isaac (1988) 126. Teutoburg Forest: Dio Cassius, *Roman History* 56.18–20. Caravan route: Kennedy and Riley (1990) 77.
3. Germanicus: Tacitus, *Annals* 1.56.
4. Assault roads: Peddie (1987) 188–90.
5. Sherman: Barrett (1996) 35.
6. Germanicus: Tacitus, *Annals* 1.56.
7. Campaign roads in Arabia: Kennedy (1982) 169. Proto Dere Street: Bishop (2000) 218. Rey Cross: Richmond and McIntyre (1934).
8. Idleness: Vegetius, *Epitoma Rei Militari* 3.4. Summer season: Taylor (1996) 33. Dere Street: Bishop and Dore (1989) 140.
9. Scaftworth: Noort and Ellis (1997) 447–9; Noort and Lillie (1997). Southwark: Merrifield (1983) 27–32. Ambleside: Armitt (1916) 13.
10. Statius: *Silvae* 4.3.
11. Wall construction: Hill (2004); Graafstal (2012). Stints: Hill (2004) 110–28. Order of construction: ibid. 37–8; cf. Graafstal (2012) 160. Variations: ibid. 129–44. Direction: Poulter (2010) 25–32.
12. Military roads of Scotland: Taylor (1996) 35–6. 1½ yards per man per day: Taylor (1996) 34. Royal Engineers' figures: Peddie (1987) 188–90.
13. Hadrian's Wall: Hill (2006) 146. Cf. Graafstal (2012). Wade's teams: Taylor (1996) 33. Caulfeild's teams: ibid. 26–8. *Manipuli*: Tacitus, *Annals* 1.20.
14. *Mensores*: Vegetius, *Epitoma Rei Militaris* 2.7. Roads, bridges, and tunnels: Austin and Rankov (1995) 114; *CIL* 8.2728. Equipment: Dilke (1985) 88–9; Lewis (2009).
15. Surveying teams: Taylor (1996) 33. The Newcastle to Carlisle Military Road: Lawson (1966). Civil companies: Lawson (1973).
16. Straightness of roads: Poulter (2010) 13.
17. Haltwhistle Burn: Frere and St Joseph (1983) 61 Plate 31.
18. Stane Street: Bagshawe (1979) 14. Ptolemy's coordinates: Dilke (1985) 75–86.
19. London: Johnston (1979) 38.
20. Roman maps: Davies (2002) 44–52; cf. Dilke (1985).
21. Davies (2002).
22. Poulter (2010).
23. Arc: *De Munitionibus Castrorum* 54. Gregory (1989) 170–1.
24. The foot: Jones (2000) 72. Regional measurements: Walthew (1978). Arabia: Kennedy (1982) 150.

25. Crindledykes: *RIB* 2299–2305. Corbridge: Forster and Knowles (1912) 141–2; *RIB* 2296–7.
26. Three Spital milestones: *RIB* 2280–1. Old Spital: *RIB* 2282. Rey Cross camp: Richmond and McIntyre (1934) 50–8; Robinson in Vyner (2001), 76–86. Eric Bloodaxe and the Diocese of Glasgow: Bailey in Vyner (2001), 120. The Rey Cross: Vyner (2001) 118–21.
27. Hodometer: Lewis (2009) 134–42. Scribal errors: Rivet (1970) 39. Turnpike milestones: OS six-inch county series (1857) Yorkshire sheet 11, measured using *Google Earth*. 1743: Albert (1972) 39. 1593: 35 Eliz cap 6.
28. Celtic mile: Black (1995) 98–107.
29. Construction: Codrington (1918) 11–15; Margary (1973) 18–22, 500–1, 503–6; Bagshawe (1979) 15; Davies (2002) 53–66; Davies (2010) 32–42. Statius, *Silvae* 4.3.20–4; 27–37; 40–55. Opinions of Statius: 'more concerned with flattering Domitian than with precise description' – Codrington (1918) – 'succinct and plausible' – Davies (2002) 56. Roman Ridge: Roberts (1998) 5. Inveresk: Bishop (2004), 11.
30. Eighteenth-century corduroys: Taylor (1996) 35–6.
31. Surfaces questioned: Davies (2002) 81–2; Hart (1984) 92.
32. Iron-making debris: Margary (1973) 61, 330.
33. Stane Street: Winbolt (1936) 210. Doctor's Gate: Dodd and Dodd (1980) 40. Axle width: Crow (1995) 33–4.
34. Encroachment of vegetation: Rackham (1986) 257.
35. Wheeldale Moor: Hayes and Rutter (1964); cf. Poulter (2010) 69. Brough-on-Noe: Dearne (1993) 44. Inveresk: Bishop (2004) 10–11, 17, 18.
36. Brough-on-Noe: Dearne (1993) 42. Roecliffe: Bishop (2005) 158.
37. Dere Street's original course: Soffe in Bishop and Dore (1989) 9 and 12. Stanegate eastern extension: Simpson (1972).
38. Corbridge drains: Forster and Knowles (1912) 139–41.
39. Stone spine: Margary (1973) 404. Via Nova Traiana: Kennedy (1982) 144.
40. Corbridge junction: Forster and Knowles (1912) 139. Wade's Causeway: Hayes et al. (1964). Inveresk: Bishop (2004) 21. Roecliffe: Bishop (2005) 150.
41. Vindolanda: Margary (1973) 446. Temple Sowerby: Sedgley (1975) 41–2. Stinsford: Margary (1973) 109. Re-used milestone: e.g. *RIB* 3519. Single milestone: e.g. *RIB* 2310. Group of milestones: e.g. *RIB* 2280–1 or 2290–2. Crindledykes: Bruce (1886); *RIB* 2299–305. Smith's Shield milestone: *RIB* 2308.
42. Jordanian milestation: Kennedy (1982) 146. Gallows Hill: *RIB* 2290–2. Crindledykes: Bruce (1886); *RIB* 2299–305. Date of Stanegate: Poulter (2010) 112–14.
43. Painted milestones: Graf (1995a). Brough milestone: *RIB* 2243. Crindledykes milestone: *RIB* 2299.
44. Margary's network: Margary (1973).
45. Corbridge junction: Forster and Knowles (1912) 139.
46. Shrines, crossroads, and suicides: Lay and Vance 1992, 52.
47. Burial law: Cicero, *De Legibus* 2.23.58. Early London burial grounds: Merrifield (1983) 154. High Rochester: Wilson (2004). Great Chesters: Breeze (2006) 274.
48. Bridges on Highland roads: Taylor (1996) 44–5. Temporary ones: suggested by J.S. Poulter (pers comm). Unacceptable: Tacitus, *Annals* 1.56. Fording: Vegetius, *Epitoma Rei Militaris* 3.7.
49. Trajan's Danube Bridge: Lepper and Frere (1988) 148–51. Caesar's Rhine bridge: *Gallic Wars* 4.17. Pontoon bridges: Lepper and Frere (1988) 50–3. Severus' Tay bridge: Birley (1988) 181.
50. Alfoldean bridge: Winbolt (1936) 97–9. Rossington Bridge: Magilton (1977) 63.
51. Aldwincle bridge: Jackson and Ambrose (1976).
52. Roman London Bridge: Milne (1982).

53. Scaftworth causeway: Van de Noort and Lillie (1997). Bridge: Van de Noort (2001) 168–9. Rossington Bridge: Magilton (1977) 63.
54. Newcastle bridge: Bidwell and Holbrook (1989) 99–103.
55. Hadrian's Wall bridges: Bidwell and Holbrook (1989).
56. Corbridge bridge: Craster (1914) 64–5. Chollerford bridge: Bidwell and Holbrook (1989) 32.
57. *Agger*: Margary (1973) 19–21. The *agger* as an accumulation: Davies (2002) 35–6.
58. Haltwhistle Burn: Gibson and Simpson (1909). Pesco Montano: Coarelli (1982) 325.
59. Tramlines: Cüppers (1990) 312 (Bacharach) Drack and Fellmann (1988) 419 (Langenbruck).

Chapter 3: Development and Use
1. *Reports of Commissioners for Highland Roads and Bridges* 1,22, cited in Taylor (1996) 119.
2. Corbridge: Bishop and Dore (1989) 140. Beaufront Red House: Hanson et al (1979). Stratigraphy: Harris (1979). *TAQ* and *TPQ*: ibid. 97.
3. Deorestrete at Gainford: Curle (1911) 9–10. Watling Street: Keynes and Lapidge (1983) 171–2.
4. Via Julia: Codrington (1918) 277. Sallustius Lucullus: Suetonius, *Life of Domitian* 10.3. Arabian roads: Kennedy and Riley (1990) 77.
5. Baylham House: Frere and St Joseph (1985) 94.
6. Centuriation: Dilke (1985) 88–100; Campbell (2000) 278–316. Colchester: Haverfield (1918) 293–6. Gloucester: Berry (1949). Sussex: Margary (1973) 73; Peterson (2002). Imperial estate: Salway (1981) 637. Orange cadaster: Dilke (1985) 108–10. Aerial photographs: Deuel (1969) 112, 137–8. Northern home counties: Peterson (1990). Middlesex: Sharpe (1918); Peterson (2006). Weald: Peterson (2002).
7. Army and engineering: Goldsworthy (2003) 146–8. Indigenous rights: Churchill (2002) 98–9.
8. Town councils: Chevallier (1997) 32; Frend 1956; Mitchell (1976).
9. Inveresk: Bishop (2004) 18. Milestones: Collingwood and Wright (1965) 691–727; Tomlin et al. (2009) 465–79.
10. Highlands: Taylor (1996) 43. Rutting and flooding: Jackman (1916) 98.
11. *Cursus publicus*: Black (1995). *Mansiones*: Chevallier (1997) 281–91.
12. Pottery: Fulford (1973); cost comparison: Greene (1986) 164–5.
13. Palmyrene Tax Law: Matthews (1984). Customs posts: Sartre (2005) 256–7. *Beneficiarius* posts: Ott (1995) 85–113; Nelis-Clément (2000) 133–210. Brigandage: Grünewald (2004).
14. Peutinger's Table: Margary (1973) 27–8; Rivet and Smith (1979) 149–50; Dilke (1985) 113–20; Talbert (2010).
15. Maps and itineraria: Broderson (2002); Laurence (2002); Salway (2002). Antonine Itinerary: Margary (1973) 27; Rivet and Smith (1979) 150–4; Dilke (1985) 125–8.
16. Caracalla and Severus: Black (1984) later rejected in Black (1995) 106.
17. Luttwak (1976) 127–90, followed by Burnham and Johnson (1979), but then critiqued by Mann (1979) and Isaac (1992).
18. Strategic view of Hadrian's Wall: Luttwak (1976) 66. Abhorrence of wall-top fighting: Hingley (2012) 296. David Divine (1969). Outpost forts: Moffatt (2008) 149. Signalling: Woolliscroft (2001). Protecting friendly peoples: Breeze and Dobson (2000) 46.
19. Number of milecastles and turrets: Bishop (2011) 16 and 18. Milecastle garrisons: Breeze and Dobson (2000) 41. *Exploratores*: Austin and Rankov (1995), 193–4.
20. *Pridianum*: Bowman and Thomas (1994) 90–8.
21. Brigandage: Grünewald (2004).
22. Phasing the network: Webster (1980; 1981); Breeze and Dobson (1985); Bidwell and Hodgson (2009) 7–29.
23. *Vigiles*: Coulston (2000) 89. *Numerus vigilum*: Bishop (1993) 67. *Beneficiarii*: Rankov (1999); Nelis-Clément (2000) 211–68. Regionary centurions: Fuhrman (2012) 222–3.

24. Cavalry unshod: Hyland (1990) 123; army marching order: Gilliver (1999) 32–62.
25. Abuse of system: Tacitus, *Agricola* 19.
26. Vegetius, *Epitoma Rei Militaris* 3.8.
27. Logistics and fort distribution: Bishop (1999b) 111–14.
28. Vegetius and Frontinus: Schenk (1932) 88.
29. Finds from towns and the 'military zone': Bishop (1991).
30. Bozeman: Ward (1996) 226–30. Myos Hormos: Jackson (2002) 98–105.
31. Allied troops' pay: Tacitus, *Histories* 1.67. Shipment of pigs: Elkington (1976) 187–8. By water: Grinsell (1958) 240–2.
32. Lead pigs: Elkington (1976) 192–5; Gardiner (2001).
33. Lead pig weight: Frere et al. (1990) 38–66. Capacity of a mule: Marcy (1861) 109 suggests 125 lbs (57 kg); Engels (1978) 14 cites 200 lbs (91 kg).
34. Vindolanda tablet: *Tab. Vind.* 2, No.343.21; cf. Poulter (2010) 45–6.
35. Native attitude to roads: Witcher (1997); Highlanders' reaction: Taylor (1996) 117. Imperialist ambitions: Witcher (1998).
36. Waterways: Selkirk (1983); balanced view: e.g. Anderson (1992).
37. Tiberius' ride: Speidel (1994) 19.
38. Roman military pace: Vegetius, *Epitoma Rei Militari* 1.9.
39. Cart speeds: Anderson (1992) 12. Mule speeds: Roth (1998) 206–7.
40. *Edict on Prices*: Leake (1826). Inclines: Selkirk (1995) 61. Actual loads: Anderson (1992) 13. Des Noëttes and draft harness: Weller (1999), notably www.humanist.de/rome/rts/load.html. Trajan's Column: Coulston (2001) 109–10.
41. Water transport: Selkirk (1995) 189–264. Selkirk's views challenged: Anderson (1992).
42. Proof: Walters (1999).

Chapter 4: After the Romans

1. Gregory (1931) 91.
2. Decay: Stenton (1936) 1–3. Continuity: Rackham (1986) 257; Poulter (2010) 51–3, 78.
3. Codrington (1879). Blackthorn: Rackham (1986) 257.
4. Trevelyan (1945) 45–6.
5. Battles and roads: Higham (1993) 122. Medieval armies needed roads: Beeler (1956) 290 n.52. Medieval road building: Stenton (1936); Bland (1957); Hindle (1998) 6. Yarmouth to Winterton: Hindle (1998) 20. Road at Corbridge: Craster (1914) 65. Chester to the River Conwy: Colyer (1984) 60. Surviving Roman bridges: Troyano (2003), 100–9. Cromwell Lock: Crompton and Brooke (1885); Salisbury (1995). Ford at Corbridge: Craster (1914) 65. *Et Corabrige*: ibid. 14.
6. Battles: Kinross (1998); Battlefields Trust (2012). Romans: Barrett (1896) 426–7.
7. Roads making themselves: Hindle (1998) 6. *Wealas*: Partridge (1966) 218 cf. Flanders para 5.
8. Natanleaga: Giles (1914) 9. Cerdicesford: Reno (2000) 220. Searoburh: ibid. 10. Beranburh: ibid.
9. Mons Badonicus: Alcock (1971) 68–71. *Obsessio*: Gildas, *De Excidio Britanniae* 26.1.
10. Camlann: Alcock (1971) 67; Reno (1996) 179–201.
11. Catraeth/Catterick: Jackson (1989) 83. Cirencester: Giles (1914) 16.
12. Heavenfield: Giles (1914) 16. Deniseburn: Bede, *Ecclesiastical History* 3.1.
13. Repton: Wood (2010) 79–82. Crayke: Simeon, *History of the Church of Durham* 21; 28.
14. Battle(s) of Corbridge: South (2002) 105–6. *Via regia*: Curle (1911) 14.
15. Simeon, *Libellus de Exordio* 33. Bromborough: Foot (2008) 136–7. Burnswark: Neilson (1910). Brinsworth: Wood (1999) 320.
16. Maldon: Kinross (1998) 12–13.

17. Carham: Duncan (1976). Dunsinane Hill: Marren (1990) 53–4. Lumphanan: ibid. 54. Camps: Jones (2011) 102–3.
18. Statute of Winchester: 13 Edward I. Importance of Roman roads: Steane (1984) 104–5. 'Self-made roads': Hindle (2001) 80 for the concept, 34 described.
19. Fulford in general: Jones (2011). On the possible red herring of the 'Gate' place-name element: ibid. 106. Heslington to Pool Farm: Margary (1973) 427. Stamford Bridge: Kinross (1998) 14–16. Norman invasion: Gravett (1992); Morillo (1996); Morris (2012).
20. Timings: Gravett (1992) 44; Morillo (1996) 181. Roman army speed: Vegetius, *Epitoma Rei Militaris* 1.9. Camp Toccoa to Fort Benning: Ambrose (2001) 28–9. All forced marches over distance, whether Roman, Saxon, or American, include time for sleep and this is incorporated in the above averages. Condition: Morillo (1996) 181.
21. Hastings fought near a Roman road: Gravett (1992) 59. Battle of London: Mills (1996).
22. Battle of Stafford: Forester (1854) 26–7. Cuthbert's route: Stevenson (1855) 687. William's marches: Forester (1854) 29–30; cf. Morris (2012) 234. Malcolm's Cross: Anderson (1908) 110–14.
23. Invasion of 1136: Stevenson (1856) 4:1, 5–6, 39. 1138: ibid, 7. Clitheroe: ibid, 8–9. Battle of the Standard: ibid, 46–51; Kinross (1998) 20–1.
24. Renfrew: Andreson (1908) 243. Whitemoss, Lurg Moor, and Outerwards: Newall (1976). Syleham: Barber (2003) 180; Copinger (1904) 154–6.
25. Treasure: Forster (1881) 28. 1201, 1208, 1212: Hardy (1835).
26. Norham: Church (2003) 256; Hardy (1835). Barons' route: Giles (1849) 391–8. Simon de Montfort at Fletching: Halliwell (1840) 27. Movements prior to Evesham: ibid. 57–60; Kinross (1998) 24. Kempsey milestone: *RIB* 2249. Palmer's Cross: Purton (1901). Haxey: Prestwich (1988) 55.
27. Clearing a road: Morris (1901) 130. Rhuddlan: ibid. 131. Deganwy: ibid. 134. Woodmen: ibid. 139.
28. 1296: Gough (1900) 139–45.
29. Liddesdale: Gough (1900) 141. Wheel Causeway: Haverfield (1899–1900).
30. May to August: Gough (1900) 141–4. Edward I and the Romans: Maxwell (1986).
31. Stirling Bridge: Kinross (1998) 27–9; Paterson (1996) 18–19; Foard (2005b).
32. 1298: Gough (1900) 166–72. Falkirk: Paterson (1996) 22–4. Battlefield site: Foard (2005a).
33. 1300: Gough (1900) 190–2. Caerlaverock road: St Joseph (1952). Gatehouse of Fleet: St Joseph (1983). Glenlochar: Frere and St Joseph (1983) 127–9.
34. 1301: Gough (1900) 203–6. Road to Newstead: Graham and Richmond (1952–3); Anon. (1995) 23.
35. 1303: Gough (1900) 225–32; Paterson (1996) 33–5.
36. 1306: Gough (1900) 264–8. Ailing: Paterson (1996) 44. 1307: Gough (1900) 269–75. Death: Paterson (1996) 48.
37. Decaying roads: cf. Gregory (1931) 94. Loudon Hill: Paterson (1996) 47. Bannockburn: ibid. 63–4.
38. Itinerary: Hartshorne (1861). Frustration: Paterson (1996) 59. Waggons: Childs (2005) 89. Bannockburn: Foard (2006).
39. Stainmore and Gilsland: Maxwell (1913) 227–8.
40. Burton Bridge: Glover (1865) 340–1.
41. Aldborough: Bishop (1996) 1–2. Great North Road: Hindle (1998) 43–5 with Fig. 33. Domesday Book: Morris (1975–1992) 1Y18; domesdaymap.co.uk/place/SE4066/aldborough/ accessed 8.12.12. Battle: Kinross (1998) 36–7; Foard (2003). Roecliffe: Bishop (2005). Ford: Foard (2003) 18; www.biffvernon.freeserve.co.uk/boroughbridge.htm accessed 8.12.12.

42. Solway: Haines (2003) 271. Old Byland: Paterson (1996) 81–2. Barbour: Mackenzie (1909) 476.
43. Stanhope Park: Paterson (1996) 87–8; Maxwell (1913) 257. Fordun: Skene (1872) 344.
44. Gask Ridge: Woolliscroft and Hoffmann (2006).
45. Neville's Cross: Kinross (1998) 40–1. Route: Ogilby (1675) Plate 99.
46. Froissart: Johnes (1901) 1:288–94. Froissart's description of the Scots showing the French the advancing English from a high mountain perfectly describes the terrain south of Soutra. Pluscarden has Richard's invasion the following year and is unclear on the route – Skene (1877) 247.
47. 1388: White (1857); Armstrong (2006). Via Ponteland: Johnes (1901) 2:37.
48. Mynydd Hyddgen: Morgan (1851) 30–2.
49. Homildon Hill: Skene (1877) 259–60; Kinross (1998) 44–5.
50. Battle: Harrison (2002), 42–3. Campaign road: White and Barker (1998) 39 with Fig. 15. Shrewsbury to Wrexham: Ogilby (1675) Plate 98.
51. Worcester: Thomas (1822) 136–43; Wylie (1894) 296–315.
52. Bramham Moor: Wylie (1896) 146–59.
53. Piperdean: Bower, *Scotichronicon* 16.25.16–24. Sark (Lochmaben Stone): Thomson (1819) 18 and 40.
54. St Albans: Anon. (1815) 63–6; Harrison (2002), 46–7. Blore Heath: Twemlow (1912); Kinross (1998) 52–3; Harrison (2002), 48–9. Hales villa: Goodyear (1974).
55. Northampton: Harrison (2002), 50–1.
56. Mortimer's Cross: Kinross (1998) 58–9; Battlefields Trust www.battlefieldstrust.com/resource-centre/warsoftheroses/battleview.asp?BattleFieldId=25 accessed 9.12.12. Ogilby: (1675) Plate 3. St Albans: Anon. (1815) 66–8. Ferrybridge: Gravett (2003) 32–9. Towton: Kinross (1998), 60–1. Harrison (2002) 54–5; Gravett (2003) 40–78.
57. Hedgeley Moor: Kinross (1998) 62–3. Road leading south-west from Corbridge: Codrington (1918) 151–2. Earlier references: Maclauchlan (1851) 20; Forster (1881) 10. Selkirk (1995) 120–5. Aerial photo: NMR NY 9863/26 (20559/50) taken 13.7.06.
58. Edgecote Moor: Kinross (1998) 64–5. Losecote Field: Ellis (1844) 126–8.
59. Barnet: Kinross (1998) 66–9. Tewkesbury: Kinross (1998) 70–1.
60. Bosworth Field (traditional): Kinross (1998) 72–4. New site: Foard (2010). Stoke Field: Kinross (1998) 75–6.
61. Road east from Winchester: Millea (2007) 85; NEHHAS (2011). Warbeck: Macmullen (1858) 90–1. James IV: Graham (1959–60) 224–6.
62. Milfield: Jones (1869) 21–2. Flodden: Kinross (1998) 77–8; Barr (2001). Etal and Berwick: ibid. 117.
63. Haddon Rigg: Lindsay (1728) 169–70. Sir Thomas Wharton's account: Gairdner (1900) 624–5.
64. Ancrum Moor: Kinross (1998) 79–80.
65. Pinkie: Pollard (1903) 79–157. Northern end of Dere Street: Bishop (2004) 175–7. Eyewitness sketch: Pollard (1903) 114–15.
66. Crediton: Sturt (1987) 21. Fenny Bridges: ibid. 75. Exeter: ibid. 51–68. Clyst Heath: ibid. 83. Sampford Courtenay: ibid. 98.
67. Carberry Hill: Colville (1825) 12.
68. Carter Bar: Brown (1911) 128.
69. Highways Acts: Albert (1972) 14–15.
70. Newburn ford: Kinross (1998) 85–6. Condition of Military Way: Hingley (2012) 129–30. Cart wheel: *Piggott (1949)*.
71. Bund (1905) 38–44.

72. Edgehill: Kinross (1998) 87–90. Turnham Green and Brentford: Marsh (2005; 2008).
73. Braddock Down: Foard and Partida (2005). Stratton: Kinross (1998) 91–2. Place-name: Margary (1973) 26.
74. Adwalton Moor: Kinross (1998) 95–6.
75. Lansdown Hill: Kinross (1998) 97–8. Ogilby's road: Ogilby (1675) Plate 11.
76. Newbury: Kinross (1998) 101–3, 123–5.
77. Battle of Nantwich: Kinross (1998) 106–7.
78. Battle of Cheriton: Kinross (1998) 111–12. Winchester to London road: www.nehhas.org.uk/dig.htm accessed 14.12.12. Cropredy Bridge: ibid. 113–15. Lostwithiel: ibid. 120–2. Marston Moor: ibid. 116–19.
79. Naseby: ibid. 128–30.
80. Langport: ibid. 133–4. Villas and roads: Branigan (1976) 14–15. Rowton Heath: Kinross (1998) 139–41. Stow-on-the-Wold: Gardiner (1893) 79–80. Battle of Worcester: Kinross (1998) 147–9.
81. First Turnpike Act: Albert (1972) 17.
82. Sedgemoor: Kinross (1998) 152–5. Causeways: Foard (2003b) 34–5; Baggs and Siraut (1992).
83. Prestonpans: Kinross (1998) 163–5.
84. Wade and the Military Road: Lawson (1966). Carelgate: Ogilby (1675) Plate 86.
85. Clifton Moor: Kinross (1998) 166–8.
86. Dunnichen: Fraser (2002).
87. Danes: Fleming (1985) 253–4. Sea Lion: Fleming (2011) 255.
88. Roads as boundaries: Poulter (2010) 53. Watling Street and the Danelaw: Davis (1982). Fosse Way and Icknield Way: Hooke (2009) 92. Parish boundaries: Pounds (2000), 67–9. Villa estate boundaries: Johnston (2004) 58.
89. Edward the Confessor: Collins (1916) 34–53. Later monarchs: Blair (2003) 256.
90. London stone: Pennant (1813) 4–5; Merrifield (1983) 75–7; Ackroyd (2000) 18–19.
91. Henry: Stenton (1936) 3. Statute of Winchester: Bland (1957) 7–8. Pavage: Cooper (2006) 127. Strand: Pennant (1813) 187. Pessimistic view countered: Hindle (2001) 41.
92. Stane Street: Hindle (2001) 22, Fig. 17.
93. Statute of Phillip and Mary: Byrne (1961) 106.
94. Marlborough and Silchester: Grinsell (1958) 301.
95. Castles and Roman roads: Beeler (1956) 540. Tomen-y-Mur: Nash-Williams (1969) 112. Bowes: Clark (1884) 263. Brough: ibid. 286–8. Brougham: ibid. 294. Cardiff: Nash-Williams (1969) 71. Portchester: Munby (1990) 35–6. Newcastle upon Tyne: Snape and Bidwell (2002) 5.
96. Chester-le-Street: Cambridge (1989) 367. Inveresk: Carrick (1894) 37. Caerleon: Boon (1992). Chester: Mason (2001) 212. York: Carver (1995). Mastiles Lane: Hindle (2001) 47–8.
97. Gough map: Colyer (1984) 60. Portways etc: Hindle (2001) 11–12, 35. Roads that made themselves: Flower (1923) xvi.
98. Blackthorn: Rackham (1986) 257. Complaints: Hindle (2001) 49. Complaints exaggerated: Rackham (1986) 248–9.
99. Dere Street and A68: NT 60047 28230 to NT 59572 29750; Margary (1973) 485. Trans-Sahara routes: Symons (1938) 153; Thomas (1952) 272–3. Stanegate: NY 72632 66260 to NY 71564 66167; Margary (1973) 446. Chew Green: NT 81311 06387 to NT 80436 07277; ibid. 484. Multiple trackways: Hindle (1998) 46–9.
100. Highland military roads: Taylor (1996); Davies (2006) 59–61. Military Road: Spain (1937); Lawson (1966; 1973).
101. Turnpike Roads: Albert (1972); Davies (2006) 53–8. Macadamized roads: Codrington (1892) 3–9; Albert (1972) 141–8; Davies (2006) 85–7. Tarmac: Airey (2010) 209; Davies (2006) 87–9.

102. Telford: Albert (1972) 145–8; Hindle (2001) 116–17; Davies (2006) 84–5.
103. Watford Gap: Fisher (2009) 63.
104. Modern roads and motorways: Charlesworth (1984); Davies (2006) 69–73.

Chapter 5: Rediscovery

1. Horsley (1732) 428.
2. Margary's methodology: Margary (1973) 24–33. Remote sensing: Clark (1990); Wilson (1982); Barber (2011). Other methodologies: Sherman and Evans (2004) 5–6.
3. Straight stretches: Codrington (1918) 30.
4. Roadworks: e.g. Rushton (1995). Developer-funded archaeology: Greene and Moore (2010), 107–9. Fosse Way: Andrews and Harding (2012). Roman Ridge: Roberts (1998). Ermin Street: Mudd et al. (2000).
5. Cadw Roman Roads Project: Sherman and Evans (2004); Hopewell (2004; 2005; 2006; 2007; 2008).
6. Field boundaries: Margary (1973) 512; Bagshawe (1979) 24.
7. Place-names: Codrington (1918) 31–2; Margary (1973) 26, 507–8; Bagshawe (1979) 21–2.
8. Coldharbour: E.g. Viatores (1964) 351. Statistics: Ogden (1966); Briggs (2009). Antiquity of Coldharbour and Caldecote: Cole (2011) 58–61.
9. Royal itineraries: Hindle (1998) 17, 21–7; Gough (1900). No Roman predecessor: *contra* Hindle (1982) 204.
10. Alfred and Guthrun: Davis (1982). Osmanthorpe: Roy, J. in Bishop and Freeman (1993) 159–64.
11. Paris map: Lewis (1987) 364–72. Gough map: Hindle (1998) 31. Place-name evidence: Hussey (1853) 105–6. Sea-level change and alluviation: Burnham (1989). Canterbury to Southampton road: Hindle (1998) Fig 9. Royal itinerary: Hardy (1835) April 24–7, AD 1213 (Arundel – Lewes – Battle – Dover – Rye – Winchelsea). Gough's forty per cent: Colyer (1984) 60.
12. Richard of Westminster's map: Forbes and Burmester (1904) 194–6; cf. Codrington (1918) 24–5; Bagshawe (1979) 20.
13. Selkirk's roads: Selkirk (1983; 1995). Disputed: Poulter (2010) 62–3. Blackstone Edge: Brierley (1980); Pearson et al. (1985) 125–8.
14. OS and Roy's maps for Scotland: Hewitt (2010) 20–42. OS maps for England and Wales: Margary (1973) 510.
15. Margary dismissive of OS interpolations: e.g. Margary (1973) 160. Margary's own: e.g. ibid. 302.
16. OS record cards: Iredale (2003) 30. NMRs: Darvill (2004) 414 (note that the NMR for England has now been unhelpfully renamed the English Heritage Archive). HERs/SMRs: Wilkinson (2007) 10.
17. Aerial photography: Wilson (1982); Riley (1980; 1982); Barber (2011). Getmapping: www1.getmapping.com/Home accessed 17.12.12. Virtual globes: Myers (2010). Armchair archaeology: Handwerk (2006); cf. Summers (1950).
18. Lidar: Jones (2010).
19. Charterhouse: Jones (2010) 30–2.
20. Fieldwalking: Greene and Moore (2010) 57–8.
21. Probing: Margary (1973) 26; Greene and Moore (2010) 79.
22. Dowsing: Plummer (1976).
23. Geophysical survey: Bartlett (1976).
24. Sondages: Field (1992) 207–43; Waddelove (1999) *passim*.
25. Horsley: Macdonald (1933). Defoe's observations: Horn and Ransome (1969) 541–4. Background: Codrington (1892). Review: Haverfield (1918) 245–7. Acknowledgement: Margary (1973) 17.

26. Watkins and 'ley lines': Davies (2006) 36–7.
27. Green roads: Hippisley Cox (1944).
28. Monographs: Belloc 1913; Grant 1922; Winbolt 1936. Put-down: Grant (1922) 10.
29. First edition: Margary (1955; 1957). Second edition (Margary (1967). Third edition: Margary (1973). Reviews of the first edition: Richmond (1956; 1958); Rivet (1956; 1958).
30. Codrington: (1918) 232. South-West Scotland: Wilson (1994–5) especially Fig.1.
31. Misspelling: e.g. 'Cheese Hill Street' for 'Chesil Street' (Margary (1973) 91, or 'Black Oar' for 'Black Carr' (ibid. 271).
32. Margary and the Viatores: Viatores (1964) frontispiece; Margary (1973) 176. On the Viatores methodology: Poulter (2010) 60–2.
33. Field (1992); Waddelove (1999); Allan (1994).
34. Books: Selkirk 1983; 1995. Questionable routes: Poulter (2010) 62–3.
35. France: Chevallier (1997). Arabia: Graf (1995b); Kennedy (1982). Stanegate project: www.journallive.co.uk/north-east-news/todays-news/2012/11/16/hadrian-s-wall-community-archaeology-event-will-probe-legacy-61634-32242664/ accessed 13.2.13. Birmingham Roman Roads Project: Leather (1994).
36. OS Roman Britain maps: Margary (1973) 31.
37. *Tabula Imperii Romani*: TIR (1983; 1987).
38. Via Julia: Codrington (1918) 277. First edition, 6-inch OS map: Somerset sheet 6NE, published 1867. Third edition Roman Britain: OS (1956). Fourth edition: OS (1978). Revised fourth edition: OS (1994). TIR: (1983). Margary: (1955) 217.
39. Star rating system: www.nehhas.org.uk/RRAbstracts.html#rat accessed 7.3.12.
40. Summaries: www.nehhas.org.uk/RRAbstracts.html#contents accessed 7.2.12.
41. OCL: opencontent.org/opl.shtml accessed 13.2.13. Development tax: www.rescue-archaeology.freeserve.co.uk/manifest.html accessed 13.2.13
42. Winchester to London road: NEHHAS (2011). Aldborough: Wacher (1974) 401. Melton: Burnham (2005) 415.

Chapter 6: Conclusions
1. Belloc (1906) 220.

Appendix 1: Margary's Road Numbers
1. Numbering system: Margary (1973) 32–3; Viatores (1964).

Appendix 5: Possible Roman Roads in North-East England and South-East Scotland
1. 'Romanized': e.g. Margary (1973) 262, of the Icknield Way (Margary 333); cf. 18–19.
2. Codrington: (1918) 165; Hafemann (1956) 150; Bidwell and Holbrook (1989) 103. Newcastle: Bidwell and Snape (2002) 254; 260. Inveresk and Cramond: Bishop (2004) 175–7. Ogilby: (1675) Plate 9.
3. Roads in SE Scotland and NE England: Bishop (forthcoming a and b). Road north of Newcastle: Codrington (1918) 165; Bidwell and Holbrook (1989) 103. Malcolm III: Anderson (1908) 110–14. William I: Anderson (1908) 271–4. Edward I: Gough (1900) vol 2, 140; 166; 184.
4. Chester: NU 172 205. Chesters: NU 106 350. Chesterhill: NU 162 040. Coldharbour: NU 205 226. Causey: NZ 182 950. Morpeth: NZ 197 860. Hemelspeth: NZ 181 995.
5. Ogilby (1675) Plate 9. Helm: Harper (1901) 202.
6. Longshaws: St Joseph (1969) 105–6. Learchild: Taylor (1957) 206. Wooperton: Burnham (2004) 275. Pacified region: Hanson (1987) 91–2.
7. Published: Inglis (1915–16) 38–40.

8. Tweedmouth castle: F. Cowe, pers. comm.
9. Fords on the Tweed: J.L. Marlow pers. comm.
10. Route long known: Graham (1962–63). 1810 post road: Mackay (1998) 56; Inglis (1915–16) 39.
11. Kirklandhill: RCAHMS (1924) 131–2. Pencraig Hill: ibid. 99. Lamberton Moor: Anderson (1905). New post road: Mackay (1998) 55–6.
12. Norham: Welfare and Swan (1995) 118. East Learmouth: ibid. 95–6. Mindrum: ibid. 181. Carham: ibid. 82. Wooden House Farm: Jones (2011) 319. Maxton: ibid. 337. Milrighall: ibid. 278. Oakwood: ibid. 288. Eastcote: ibid. 195. Cavers Mains: ibid. 170. Innerleithen: ibid. 229. Eshiels: ibid. 200. Lyne: ibid. 268–9. Other evidence: Walter Elliot pers. comm.
13. Haddon Rigg and Kelso: Lindsay (1728) 169–70.
14. Holy Chesters: NT 875 421.
15. Duddo stone circle: NT 930 437.
16. Road to Otterburn: Tyson (1992) 76.
17. Northumberland at Alnwick: Ramsay (1913) 259.
18. Ferney Chesters: NZ 053 812. Raechester: NY 978 871.
19. See above, note 2.
20. Hotspur intercepts the Scots: Skene (1877) 259–60. Montagu: Kinross (1998) 62–3.
21. A697: see above, note 3.
22. Cornhill Castle: Bates (1891) 11–12. Ford: Home (1863) 458.
23. Bowchester: NT 979 291. Battle Stone: NT 968 294.
24. A697: Mackay (1998) 64–8.
25. Cornhill–Lennel ford: Home (1863) 458.
26. Darnchester: NT 815 427. Belchester: NT 794 435. Rowchester: NT 733 439. Chesters: NT 741 474.
27. B6397: Mackay (1998) 80–5.
28. Edward I: Gough (1900) 141. Jean de Vienne: Johnes (1901) 1:289.
29. Edward I: Gough (1900) 240.
30. Graham (1959–60) 223–6.
31. 1497: Graham (1959–60) 224–6.
32. Whitchester: NT 720 590. Chesters: NT 567 709. Stoneypath: NT 616 711.
33. Chester-le-Street: Bidwell and Hodgson (2009) 183–5. Newcastle: Breeze (2006) 144–8. Pons Aelius: Bidwell and Holbrook (1989) 99–103.

Bibliography

Abramson, P., Bishop, M.C., Evans, J., and Young, G. (forthcoming), 'Iron Age settlement and Roman pottery kilns near Crambeck, North Yorkshire'

Ackroyd, P. (2000), *London, the Biography*, London

Adams, C. and Laurence, R. (eds) (2002), *Travel and Geography in the Roman Empire*, London

Airey, G. (2010) 'Bituminous materials', in Domone, P.L.J. and Illston, J.M. (eds), *Construction Materials: Their Nature and Behaviour*, Abingdon, 209–46

Albert, W. (1972), *The Turnpike Road System in England 1663–1840*, Cambridge

Alcock, L. (1971), *Arthur's Britain*, Harmondsworth

Allan, M. (1994), *The Roman Route Across the Northern Lake District*, Lancaster

Allen, T. and Welsh, K. (1996), 'Eton rowing lake', *Current Archaeology* 13:4, 124–7

Anderson, A.O. (1908), *Scottish Annals from English Chroniclers AD 500 to 1286*, London

Anderson, J. (1905), 'Notes on a Romano-British hoard of bronze vessels and personal ornaments found in a moss on Lamberton Moor, Berwickshire, now exhibited to the Society by Mrs Michael Cochrane, through Rev. Robert Paul, FSAScot., Dollar', *Proceedings of the Society of Antiquaries of Scotland* 39, 367–76

Anderson, J.D. (1992), *Roman Military Supply in North-East England*, BAR British Series 224, Oxford

Andrews, P. and Harding, P. (2012), *Following the Fosse Way through Nottinghamshire. Archaeology and the A46*, Cirencester

Anonymous (1815), *History of Verulam and St Alban's: Containing an Historical Account of the Decline of Verulam and Origin of St. Alban's, and of the Present State of the Town, the Abbey, and other Churches*, St Albans

Anonymous (1995), 'All roads lead from Rome', *Trimontium Trumpet* 9, 21–3

Anonymous (1999), 'News', *British Archaeology* 46, 4–5

Armitt, M.L. (1916), *Rydal*, Kendal

Armstrong, P. (2006), *Otterburn 1388: Bloody Border Conflict*, Oxford

Austin, N.J.E. and Rankov, N.B. (1995), *Exploratio. Military and Political Intelligence in the Roman World from the Second Punic War to the Battle of Adrianople*, London

Baggs, A.P. and Siraut, M.C. (1992), 'Chedzoy', in Dunning, R.W. and Elrington C.R. (eds), *A History of the County of Somerset: Volume 6: Andersfield, Cannington, and North Petherton Hundreds (Bridgwater and neighbouring parishes)*, www.british-history.ac.uk/report.aspx?compid=18652 accessed 10.4.12

Bagshawe, R.W. (1979), *Roman Roads*, Princes Risborough

Barber, M. (2011), *A History of Aerial Photography and Archaeology: Mata Hari's Glass Eye and Other Stories*, Swindon

Barber, R. (2003), *Henry Plantagenet*, Woodbridge

Barr, N. (2001), *Flodden 1513: The Scottish Invasion of Henry VIII's England*, Stroud

Barrett, C.R.B. (1896), *Battles and Battlefields in England*, London

Barrett, J.G. (1996), *Sherman's March Through the Carolinas*, Chapel Hill

Bartlett, A.D.H. (1976), *Report on Geophysical Survey at Corbridge, Northumberland, April 1976*, Ancient Monuments Laboratory Report Series No. 2025, London

Bates, C.J. (1891), 'Border holds of Northumberland', *Archaeologia Aeliana*, series 2, 14, 1–448

Battlefields Trust (2012), *UK Battlefields Resource Centre*, www.battlefieldstrust.com/resource-centre/ accessed 17.8.12

Beeler, J.H. (1956), 'Castles and strategy in Norman and early Angevin England', *Speculum* 31, 581–601

Belloc, H. (1906), *Hills and the Sea*, London

Belloc, H. (1913), *The Stane Street: A Monograph*, London

Berry, C.A.F. (1949), 'Centuriation at Gloucester' *Transactions of the Bristol and Gloucestershire Archaeological Society* 68, 14–21

Bidwell, P. and Hodgson, N. (2009), *The Roman Army in Northern England*, South Shields

Bidwell, P.T. and Holbrook, N. (1989), *Hadrian's Wall Bridges*, HBMCE Archaeological Report 9, London

Bidwell, P. and Snape, M. (2002), 'The history and setting of the Roman fort at Newcastle upon Tyne', *Archaeologia Aeliana*, Series 5, 31, 251–83

Bishop, M.C. (1991), 'Soldiers and military equipment in the towns of Roman Britain' in V.A. Maxfield and M.J. Dobson (eds), *Roman Frontier Studies 1989*, Exeter, 21–7

Bishop, M.C. (1993), 'Excavations in the Roman fort at Chester-le-Street (Concangis), Church Chare 1990–91', *Archaeologia Aeliana* Ser.5, 21, 1993, 29–85

Bishop, M.C. (1995), 'A new Roman military site at Roecliffe, North Yorkshire' *YAS RAS Bulletin* No.12, 3–5

Bishop, M.C. (1996), *Finds from Aldborough: A Catalogue of Small Finds from the Romano-British Town of Isurium Brigantum*, Oxbow Monographs 65, Oxford

Bishop, M.C. (1999a), 'An Iron Age and Romano-British "Ladder" settlement at Melton, East Yorkshire', *Yorkshire Archaeological Journal* 71, 23–63

Bishop, M.C. (1999b), Praesidium: social, military, and logistical aspects of the Roman army's provincial distribution during the early principate, in A. Goldsworthy and I. Haynes (eds), The Roman Army as a Community, JRA Supplementary Series 34, Portsmouth RI, 111–18

Bishop, M.C. (2004), *Inveresk Gate: Excavations in the Roman Civil Settlement at Inveresk, East Lothian, 1996–2000*, STAR Monograph 7, Loanhead

Bishop, M.C. (2005), 'A new Flavian military site at Roecliffe, North Yorkshire', *Britannia* 36, 135–223

Bishop, M.C. (2011), *An Introduction to Hadrian's Wall. One Hundred Questions About the Roman Wall Answered*, Darlington

Bishop, M.C., forthcoming, Roads of NE England

Bishop, M.C., forthcoming, Roads of SE England

Bishop, M.C. and Dore, J.N. (1980), *Corbridge: Excavations of the Roman Fort and Town, 1947–80*, HBMCE Archaeological Report 8, London

Bishop, M.C. and Freeman, P.W.M. (1993), 'Recent work at Osmanthorpe, Nottinghamshire', *Britannia* 24, 159–89

Black, E.W. (1984), 'The Antonine Itinerary: aspects of government in Roman Britain', *Oxford Journal of Archaeology* 3:3, 109–21

Black, E.W. (1995), *Cursus Publicus. The Infrastructure of Government in Roman Britain*, BAR British Series 241, Oxford

Blair, P.H. (2003), *An Introduction to Anglo-Saxon England*, ed. 3, Cambridge

Bland, D.S. (1957), 'The maintenance of roads in medieval England', *Journal of Environmental Planning and Management* (Series 1) 4:2, 5–15

Boon, G.C. (1992), 'The early church in Gwent, I: the Romano-British church', *The Monmouthshire Antiquary* 8, 11–24

Branigan, K. (1976), *The Roman Villa in South-West England*, Bradford-on-Avon

Breeze, D.J. (2006), *J. Collingwood Bruce's Handbook to The Roman Wall*, ed 14, Newcastle upon Tyne

Breeze, D.J. and Dobson, B. (1985), 'Roman military deployment in north England', *Britannia* 16, 1–19

Breeze, D.J. and Dobson, B. (2000), *Hadrian's Wall*, ed 4, Harmondsworth

Brierley, F. (1980), *Romans in Littleborough and Rochdale*, Rochdale

Briggs, K. (2009), 'The distribution of distance of certain place-name types to Roman roads', *Nomina* 32, 43–57

Brodersen, K. (2002), 'The presentation of geographical knowledge for travel and transport in the Roman world: *itineraria non tantum adnotata sed etiam picta*', in Adams and Laurence (2002), 7–21

Brown, R.H. (1911), *History of Scotland to the Present Time*, Vol. II, Cambridge

Bruce, J. Collingwood (1886), 'On the discovery of five Roman milestones', *Archaeologia Aeliana* new series, 11, 130–6

Bund, J.W.W. (1905), *The Civil War in Worcestershire 1642–1646 and the Scotch Invasion of 1651*, Birmingham and London

Burl, A. (2002), *Prehistoric Avebury*, ed 2, Yale

Burl, A. (2005), *A Guide to the Stone Circles of Britain, Ireland and Brittany*, ed 2, Yale

Burnham, C.P. (1989), 'The coast of south-east England in Roman times', in Maxfield, V.A. (ed.), *The Saxon Shore: A Handbook*, Exeter 12–17

Burnham, B.C. (2004), 'Roman Britain in 2003 – 4. Northern Counties', *Britannia* 35, 275–86

Burnham, B.C. (2005), 'Roman Britain in 2004 – 4. Northern Counties', *Britannia* 36, 408–24

Burnham, B.C. and Johnson, H.B. (eds 1979), *Invasion and Response: the Case of Roman Britain*, BAR British Series 73, Oxford

Byrne, M.St C. (1961), *Elizabethan Life in Town and Country*, ed. 8, London

Cambridge, E. (1989), 'Why did the community of St Cuthbert settle at Chester-le-Street?', in Bonner, G., Rollason, D.W., and Stancliffe, C. (eds), *St Cuthbert: His Cult and His Community*, Woodbridge, 367–86

Campbell, B.C. (2000), *The Writings of the Roman Land Surveyors*, Journal of Roman Studies Monograph 9, London

Campbell, B.C. (2012), *Rivers and the Power of Rome*, North Carolina

Carrick, J.C. (1894), 'The Monks of New Battle and Inveresk', in Wilkie, J., *St Michael and Inveresk*, Edinburgh and London, 33–60

Carter, S. and Hunter, F. (2003), 'An Iron Age chariot burial from Scotland', *Antiquity* 77, 531–5

Carver, M. (1995), 'Roman to Norman at York Minster,' in Phillips, D. and Heywood, B., *Excavations at York Minster, Vol. I*, London, 177–95

Castleden, R. (1992). *Neolithic Britain: New Stone Age Sites of England, Scotland, and Wales*, London

Chadwick, A.M. (2007) 'Trackways, hooves and memory-days – human and animal movements and memories around the Iron Age and Romano-British rural landscapes of the English north midlands' in Cumings, V. and Johnston, R. (eds) *Prehistoric Journeys*, Oxford, 131–52

Charlesworth, G. (1984), *A History of British Motorways*, London

Chartres, J.A. (1977), 'Road carrying in England in the seventeenth century: myth and reality', *The Economic History Review*, New Series, 30, 73–94

Chevallier, R. (1997), *Les voies romaines*, Paris

Childs, W. (2005), *Vita Edwardi Secundi: the Life of Edward the Second*, Oxford

Church, S.D. (2003), *King John: New Interpretations*, Woodbridge

Churchill, W. (2002), *Struggle for the Land: Native North American Resistance to Genocide, Ecocide*, San Franciso

Clark, A. (1990), *Seeing Beneath the Soil. Prospecting Methods in Archaeology*, London

Clark, G.T. (1884), *Mediaeval Military Architecture in England*, Vol. I, London

Coarelli, F. (1982), *Guide Archeologiche Laterza. Lazio*, Roma-Bari

Coates, R. 1984: 'Coldharbour – for the last time?', *Nomina* 8, 73–8

Codrington, T. (1892), *The Maintenance of Macadamised Roads*, ed. 2, London

Codrington, T. (1918), *Roman Roads in Britain*, ed 3, London

Cole, A. (2011), 'Place-names as travellers' landmarks', in Higham, N.J. and Ryan, M. J. (eds), Place-Names, *Language and the Anglo-Saxon Landscape*, Woodbridge, 51–67

Coles, B. and J. (1986), *Sweet Track to Glastonbury. The Somerset Levels in Prehistory*, London

Collingwood, R.G. and Richmond, I.A. (1969), *The Archaeology of Roman Britain*, revised edition, London

Collingwood, R.G. and Wright, R.P. (1965), *The Roman Inscriptions of Britain. Volume 1, Inscriptions on Stone*, Oxford

Colville, J. (1825), *The Historie and Life of King James the Sext: Being an Account of the Affairs of Scotland, from the Year 1566, to the Year 1596*, Edinburgh

Colyer, R. (1984), *Roads and Trackways of Wales*, Ashbourne

Cooper, A. (2006), *Bridges, Law and Power in Medieval England: 700–1400*, Woodbridge

Copeland, T. (2009), *Akeman Street. Moving Through Iron Age and Roman Landscapes*, Stroud

Copinger, W.A. (1904), *County of Suffolk. Its History as Disclosed by Existing Records and other Documents, being Materials for the History of Suffolk*, V, London

Coulston, J. (2001), 'Transport and travel on the Column of Trajan', in Adams and Laurence (2001), 106-37

Coulston, J.C.N. (2000), '"Armed and belted men": the soldiery in imperial Rome', in Coulston, J.C.N. and Dodge, H. (eds), *Ancient Rome: the Archaeology of the Eternal City*, Oxford University School of Archaeology Monograph 54, 76–118

Cox, R. Hippesley (1944), *The Green Roads of England*, ed 5, London

Craster, H.H.E. (1914), *History of Northumberland, Vol X. The Parish of Corbridge*, Newcastle upon Tyne

Crompton, C.H. and Brooke, E.P.L. (1885), 'Recently discovered remains of a Roman bridge in the River Trent', *Journal of the British Archaeological Association* 41, 43 and 83

Curle (1911) *A Roman Frontier Post and its People. The Fort of Newstead in the Parish of Melrose*, Glasgow

Darvill, T. (2004), 'Public archaeology: a European perspective', in Bintliff, J. (ed.), *A Companion to Archaeology*, Oxford, 409–34

Davies, H.E.H. (1998), 'Designing Roman roads', *Britannia* 29, 1–16

Davies, H. (2002), *Roads in Roman Britain*, Stroud

Davies, H. (2006), *From Trackways to Motorways. 5000 Years of Highway History*, Stroud

Davies, H. (2009), *Roman Roads in Britain*, Oxford

Davies, J.S. (1856), *An English Chronicle of the Reigns of Richard II, Henry IV, Henry V, and Henry VI Written Before The Year 1471*, London

Davis, R.H.C. (1982), 'Alfred and Guthrum's frontier,' *English Historical Review* 97, 803–10

Dearne, M.J. (1993), *Navio: The Fort and Vicus at Brough-On-Noe, Derbyshire*, BAR British Series 234, Oxford

Deuel, L. (1969), *Flights Into Yesterday. The Story of Aerial Archaeology*, Harmondsworth

Dilke, O.A.W. (1985), *Greek and Roman Maps*, London

Divine, D. (1969), *The North-West Frontier of Rome: a Military Study of Hadrian's Wall*, London

Dodd, A.E. and E.M. (1980), *Peakland Roads and Trackways*, Ashbourne

Duncan, A.A.M. (1976), 'The Battle of Carham, 1018', *Scottish Historical Review* 55:159, 20–8

Elkington, D. (1976), 'The Mendip lead industry', in Branigan. K. and Fowler, P. (eds), *The Roman West Country. Classical Culture and Celtic Society*, Newton Abbott and London, 183–97

Ellis, H. (1844), *Three Books of Polydore Vergil's English History, Comprising the Reigns of Henry VI., Edward IV., and Richard III*, London

Field, N. (1992), *Dorset and the Second Legion. New Light on a Roman Campaign*, Tiverton

Fisher, S. (2009), *The Canals of Britain: A Comprehensive Guide*, London

Fleming, A. (1988), *The Dartmoor Reaves. Investigating Prehistoric Land Divisions*, London

Fleming, P. (2011), *Operation Sea Lion: Hitler's Plot to Invade England*, New York

Fleming, R. (1985), 'Monastic lands and England's defence in the Viking Age', *The English Historical Review* 100, 247–65

Florescu, F.B. (1959), *Monumental de la Adamklissi: Tropaeum Traiani*, Bucharest

Flower, C.T. (1923), *Public Works in Medieval Law*, Vol. 2, Selden Society 40, London

Foard, G. (2003a), *Boroughbridge Battle and Campaign*, www.battlefieldstrust.com/media/128. pdf accessed 23.3.12

Foard, G. (2003b), *Boroughbridge Battle and Campaign*, www.battlefieldstrust.com/media/128. pdf accessed 23.3.12

Foard, G. (2005a), *Falkirk I.*, www.battlefieldstrust.com/media/601.pdf accessed 20.3.12

Foard, G. (2005b), *Stirling Bridge*, www.battlefieldstrust.com/media/612.pdf accessed 20.3.12

Foard, G. (2006) *Bannockburn*, www.battlefieldstrust.com/media/672.pdf accessed 22.3.12

Foard, G. (2010) 'Discovering Bosworth', *British Archaeology* 112, 26–31

Foard, G. and Partida, T. (2005), 'Battle of Braddock Down 19th January 1643' www.battlefieldstrust. com/resource-centre/civil-war/battleview.asp?BattleFieldId=9 accessed 12.12.12

Foot, S. (2008), 'Where English becomes British: Rethinking contexts for Brunanburh' in Barrow, J. and Wareham, A. (eds), *Myth, Rulership, Church and Charters: Essays in Honour of Nicholas Brooks*, Aldershot, 127–44

Forbes, U.A. and Burmester, A.C. (1904) *Our Roman Highways*, London

Forester, T. (1854), *The Ecclesiastical History of England and Normandy by Ordericus Vitalis*, Vol. 2, London

Forster, R. (1881), *History of Corbridge and its Antiquities*, Newcastle

Forster, R.H. and Knowles, W.H. (1912), 'Corstopitum: report on the excavations in 1911', *Archaeologia Aeliana* series 3, 8, 137–263

Freeman, P.W.M. (2007), *The Best Training Ground for Archaeologists: Francis Haverfield and the Invention of Romano-British Archaeology*, Oxford

Frend, W.H.C. (1956), 'A third-century inscription relating to angareia in Phrygia', *Journal of Roman Studies* 46, 46–56

Frere, S.S. and Fulford, M.G. (2001), 'The Roman invasion of AD 43', *Britannia* 32, 45–55

Frere, S.S., and St Joseph, J.K. (1983), *Roman Britain from the Air*, Cambridge

Frere, S.S., Roxan, M., and Tomlin, R.S.O. eds (1990), *The Roman Inscriptions of Britain. II: Fasc. 1. The Military Diplomata; Metal Ingots; Tesserae; Dies; Labels; and Lead Sealings (RIB 2401–2411)*, Gloucester

Fuhrmann, C.J. (2012), *Policing the Roman Empire: Soldiers, Administration, and Public Order*, Oxford

Fulford, M.G. (1973), 'The distribution and dating of New Forest pottery', *Britannia* 4, 160–78

Gairdner, J. (1900), *Letters and Papers, Foreign and Domestic of the Reign of Henry VIII, Preserved in the Public Record Office, The British Museum, and Elsewhere in England*, London

Gardiner, S.R. (1893), *History of the Great Civil War*, 1642–1649, Vol. 2, London

Gardiner, V. (2001), 'An analysis of Romano-British lead pigs', *Institute for Archaeo-Metallurgical Studies Newsletter* 21, 11–13

Gibson, J.P. and Simpson, F.G. (1909), 'The Roman fort on the Stanegate at Haltwhistle Burn', *Archaeologia Aeliana* series 3, 5, 213–85

Giles, J.A. (1849), *Roger of Wendover's Flowers of History, Comprising the History of England from the Descent of the Saxons to AD 1235 Formerly Ascribed to Matthew Paris*, vol.2, London

Giles, J.A. (1914), *The Anglo-Saxon Chronicle*, London

Gilliver, C.M. (1999), *The Roman Art of War*, Stroud

Glover, J. (1865), *Le Livere de Reis de Brittanie e le Livere de Reis de Angleterre*, London

Goldsworthy, A. (2003), *The Complete Roman Army*, London

Goodyear, F.H. (1974), 'The Roman villa at Hales, Staffordshire: the final report', *North Staffordshire Journal of Field Studies* 14, 1–20

Gough, H. (1900), *Itinerary of King Edward the First Throughout His Reign, AD 1272–1307, Exhibiting His Movements from Time to Time, So Far As They Are Recorded*, Paisley

Graafstal, E.P. (2012), 'Hadrian's haste: a priority programme for the Wall', *Archaeologia Aeliana* series 5, 41, 123–84

Graf, D.F. (1995a), 'Milestones with uninscribed painted latin texts', in Hadidi, A. (ed), *Studies in the History and Archaeology of Jordan 5*, Amman, 417–25

Graf, D.F. (1995b), 'The Via Nova Traiana in Arabia Petraea', in *The Roman and Byzantine Near East: Recent Archaeological Research*, Journal of Roman Archaeology Supplementary Series 14, Ann Arbor, 241–67

Graham, A. (1959–60), 'More old roads in the Lammermuirs', *Proceedings of the Society of Antiquaries of Scotland* 93, 217–35

Graham, A. (1962–63), 'Archaeology on a great post road', *Proceedings of the Society of Antiquaries of Scotland* 96, 318–47

Graham, A. and Richmond, I.A. (1952–3), 'Roman communications in the Tweed Valley', *Proceedings of the Society of Antiquaries of Scotland* 87, 63–71

Gravett, C. (1992), *Hastings 1066: The Fall of Saxon England*, Oxford

Gravett, C. (2003), *Towton 1461: England's Bloodiest Battle*, Oxford

Greene, K. (1986), *The Archaeology of the Roman Economy*, London

Greene, K. and Moore, T. (2010), *Archaeology: An Introduction*, ed. 5, Abingdon

Gregory, J.W. (1931), *The Story of the Road from the Beginning Down to AD 1931*, Maclehose: London

Gregory, S. (1989) 'Not "why not playing cards?" but "why playing cards in the first place?"', in French, D.H. and Lightfoot, C.S. (eds), *The Eastern Frontier of the Roman Empire. Proceedings of a Colloquium held at Ankara in September 1988*, BAR S553, Oxford, 169–75

Grinsell, L.V. (1958), *The Archaeology of Wessex: An Account of Wessex Antiquities from the Earliest Times to the End of the Pagan Saxon Period with Special Reference to Existing Field Monuments*, London

Grünewald, T. (2004), *Bandits in the Roman Empire: Myth and Reality*, London

Hafemann, D. (1956), *Beiträge zur Siedlungsgeographie des römische Britannien, I: die militärischen Siedlungen*, Wiesbaden

Haines, R.M. (2003), *King Edward II: His Life, His Reign, and Its Aftermath, 1284–1330*, Montreal and Kingston

Halliwell, J.O. (1840), *The Chronicle of William de Rishanger, of The Barons' Wars. The Miracles of Simon de Montfort. Edited From Manuscripts In The Cottonian Library*, London

Handwerk, B. (2006), 'Google Earth, satellite maps boost armchair archaeology', *National Geographic News* November 7, news.nationalgeographic.com/news/2006/11/061107-archaeology.html accessed 26.3.12

Hardy, T.D. (1835), *A Description of the Patent Rolls in the Tower of London; to Which is Added an Itinerary of King John with Prefatory Observations*, London

Harper, C.G. (1901), *The Great North Road. The Old Mail Road to Scotland*, vol.2, London

Harrison, I. (2002), *British Battles*, London

Hart, C.R. (1984), *The North Derbyshire Archaeological Survey*, Sheffield

Hartshorne, C.H. (1861), *The Itinerary of King Edward the Second*, privately printed

Harvey, M. (2005). 'Travel from Durham to York (and back) in the fourteenth century', *Northern History* 42, 119–30

Haverfield, F. (1899–1900), 'Note of the antiquity of the Wheel Causeway', *Proceedings of the Society of Antiquaries of Scotland* 34, 139–40

Haverfield, F. (1918), 'Centuriation in Roman Britain', *English Historical Review* 131, 289–96

Hayes, R.H., Rutter, J.G., and Rimington, F.C. (1964), *Wade's Causeway: A Roman Road in North-East Yorkshire*, Scarborough Archaeological And Historical Society Research Report No 4, Scarborough

Hewitt, R. (2010), *Map of a Nation: A Biography of the Ordnance Survey*, London

Higham, N.J. (1993), *The Kingdom of Northumbria AD 350–1100*, Stroud

Hill, P. (2006), *The Construction of Hadrian's Wall*, Stroud

Hind, J.G.F. (1989), 'The invasion of Britain in AD 43 – an alternative strategy for Aulus Plautius', *Britannia* 20, 1–21

Hindle, P. (1998), *Medieval Roads and Tracks*, ed.3, Princes Risborough

Hindle, P. (2001), *Roads and Tracks for Historians*, Chichester

Hingley, R. (2012), *Hadrian's Wall: A Life*, Oxford

Hodgson, N. (2009), *Hadrian's Wall 1999–2009*, Kendal

Holmes, N. (2003), *Excavation of Roman Sites at Cramond, Edinburgh*, Edinburgh

Home, D.M. (1863), 'Notices of the remains of ancient camps on both banks of the River Tweed, near Milne-Graden', *Proceedings of the Berwickshire Naturalists' Club* 4, 454–5

Hooke, D. (2009), 'Trees in Anglo-Saxon charters: some comments and some uncertainties', in Pierbaumer, P and Klug, H W (eds), *Old Names – New Growth. Proceedings of the 2nd ASPNS Conference, University of Graz, Austria, 6–10 June 2007*, and Related Essays, Frankfurt

Hopewell, D. (2004), 'Roman Fort Environs and Roman Roads, Project No. 1632', tinyurl.com/cadwroads2004 accessed 13.3.12

Hopewell, D. (2005), 'Roman Roads, Project No. 1632', tinyurl.com/cadwroads2005 accessed 13.3.12

Hopewell, D. (2006), 'Roman Roads, Project No. 1632', tinyurl.com/cadwroads2006 accessed 13.3.12

Hopewell, D. (2007), 'Roman Forts and Roads, Project No. 1632', tinyurl.com/cadwroads2007 accessed 13.3.12

Hopewell, D. (2008), 'Roman Fort Environs and Roads, Project No. GAT1632', tinyurl.com/cadwroads2008 accessed 13.3.12

Horn, D.B. and Ransome, M. (eds) (1969), *English Historical Documents*, Vol. X, 1714–1783, Oxford

Horsley, J. (1732), *Britannia Romana: or, The Roman Antiquities of Britain*, London

Hussey, A. (1853), 'An enquiry after the site of Anderida or Andredesceaster', *Sussex Archaeological Collections* 6, 90–106

Hyland, A. (1990), *Equus: The Horse in the Roman World*, London

Inglis, H.R.G. (1915–16), 'The roads that led to Edinburgh', *Proceedings of the Society of Antiquaries of Scotland* 50, 18–49

Iredale, D. (2003), *Discovering Local History*, ed.2, Princes Risborough

Isaac, B. (1992) *The Limits of Empire: The Roman Army in the East*, Oxford

Jackman, W.T. (1916), *The Development of Transportation in Modern England*, Cambridge

Jackson, K.H. (1969), *The Gododdin: the Oldest Scottish Poem*, Edinburgh

Jackson, R.B. (2002), *At Empire's Edge. Exploring Rome's Egyptian Frontier*, New Haven

Johnes, T. (1901), *Chronicles of England, France, Spain and the Adjoining Countries*, 2 vols, New York and London

Johnston, D.E. (1979), *An Illustrated History of Roman Roads in Britain*, Bourne End

Johnston, D.E. (2004), *Roman Villas*, Princes Risborough

Jones, C. (2011) *Finding Fulford: The Search for the First Battle of 1066*, London

Jones, D.M. (2010), *The Light Fantastic. Using Airborne Lidar in Archaeological Survey*, Swindon www.english-heritage.org.uk/publications/light-fantastic/light-fantastic.pdf accessed 26.3.12

Jones, R. (1869), *The Battle of Flodden Field Fought September 9, 1513*, Coldstream

Jones, R.H. (2011), *Roman Camps in Scotland*, Edinburgh

Jones, M.W. (2000), *Principles of Roman Architecture*, New Haven

Kennedy, D.L. (1982), *Archaeological Explorations on the Roman Frontier in North-East Jordan. The Roman and Byzantine Military Installations and Road Network on the Ground and from the Air*, BAR S134, Oxford

Kennedy, D.L. and Riley, D.N. (1990), *Rome's Desert Frontier from the Air*, London

Keynes, S. and Lapidge, M. (1983), *Alfred the Great: Asser's Life of King Alfred and other Contemporary Sources*, Harmondsworth

Kinross, J. (1998), *Discovering Battlefields of England and Scotland*, Princes Risborough

Laurence, R. (2000), *The Roads of Roman Italy. Mobility and Cultural Change*, London

Laurence, R. (2002), 'The creation of geography. An interpretation of Roman Britain', in Adams and Laurence (2002), 67–94

Lawson, W. (1966), 'The origin of the Military Road from Newcastle to Carlisle', *Archaeologia Aeliana* 4th Series, 44, 185–207

Lawson, W. (1973), 'The construction of the Military Road in Northumberland 1751–1757', *Archaeologia Aeliana* series 5, 1, 177–93

Lay, M.G. and Vance, J.E. (1992) *Ways of the World: A History of the World's Roads and of the Vehicles That Used Them*, New Brunswick

Leather, P. (1994), 'The Birmingham Roman Roads Project', *West Midlands Archaeology* 37, 8–11

Lewis, M.J.T. (2009), *Surveying Instruments of Greece and Rome*, Cambridge

Lewis, S. (1987), *The Art of Matthew Paris in the Chronica Majora*, Berkeley and Los Angeles

Lindsay, R. (1728), *The History of Scotland, from 21 February, 1436 to March, 1565*, Edinburgh

Linford, N. (2008–9), 'Geophysical survey in the shadow of the Hill', *English Heritage Research News* 10, Winter, 10–13

Littlehales, H. (1896), *Some Notes on the Road from London to Canterbury in the Middle Ages*, London

Luttwak, E.N. (1976), *The Grand Strategy of the Roman Empire from the First Century* AD *to the Third*, Baltimore

Macdonald, G. (1933), 'John Horsley: Scholar and Gentleman', *Archaeologia Aeliana*, Fourth Series, 10, 1–57

Mackay, J.J. (1998), *Border Highways*, Kelso

Mackenzie, W.M. (1909), *The Bruce, Edited from the Best Texts with Literary and Historical Introduction, Notes, and Appendices, and a Glossary*, London

MacLauchlan, H. (1851), *Memoir Written During a Survey of the Watling Street, from the Tees to the Scotch Border, in the Years 1850 and 1851*, Newcastle upon Tyne

Macmullen, M.A. (1858), *Taunton; Or, The Town We Live In*, Taunton and London

Madry, S. and Crumley, C.L. (1990), 'An application of remote sensing and GIS in a regional archaeological survey' in Allen, K., Green, S., and Zubrow, E. (eds) *Interpreting Space: GIS and Archaeology*, London, 364–80

Magilton, J. (1977), *The Doncaster District: an Archaeological Survey*, Doncaster

Malim, T. and Hayes, L. (2011), 'The Roman road that was', *British Archaeology* 120, 14–19

Mann, J.C. (1979), 'Power, force and the frontiers of the Empire', *Journal of Roman Studies* 69, 175–83

Marcy, R.B. (1861), *The Prairie Traveler. A Hand-book for Overland Expeditions*, New York

Margary, I.D. (1955), *Roman Roads in Britain*, vol 1, London

Margary, I.D. (1957), *Roman Roads in Britain*, vol 2, London

Margary, I.D. (1967), *Roman Roads in Britain*, rev ed, London

Margary, I.D. (1973), *Roman Roads in Britain*, ed 3, London

Marren, P. (1990), *Grampian Battlefields: the Historic Battles of North East Scotland from* AD 84 *to 1745*, Aberdeen

Marsh, S. (2005), *Battle of Brentford*, www.battlefieldstrust.com/resource-centre/medieval/battleview.asp?BattleFieldId=53 accessed 22.7.13

Marsh, S. (2008), *Battle of Turnham Green*, www.battlefieldstrust.com/resource-centre/medieval/battleview.asp?BattleFieldId=83 accessed 22.7.13

Marwood, J. (1995) *History of Gilling* www.apl385.com/gilling/history/gilling.htm

Mason, D.J.P. (2001), *Chester: City of the Eagles*, Stroud

Matthews, J. (1984), 'The tax law of Palmyra: Evidence for economic history in a city of the Roman East', *Journal of Roman Studies* 74, 157–80

Maxfield, V.A. (1987), 'The army and the land in the Roman South West', in Higham, R (ed.), *Security and Defence in South-West England Before 1800*, Exeter, 1–25

Maxwell, G.S. (1986), 'Sidelight on the Roman military campaigns in North Britain', in Unz, C. (ed), *Studien zu den Militärgrenzen Roms III*, Stuttgart, 60–3

Maxwell, G.S. (1989), *The Romans in Scotland*, Edinburgh

Maxwell, H. (1913), *The Chronicle of Lanercost, 1272–1346*, Glasgow

Merrifield, R. (1983), *Roman London*, London

Millea, N. (2007), *The Gough Map: The Earliest Road Map of Great Britain?*, Oxford

Mills, P. (1996), 'The Battle of London 1066', *London Archaeologist* 8:3, 59–62

Milne, G. (1982), 'Further evidence for Roman London Bridge?', *Britannia* 13, 271–6

Mitchell, S. (1976), 'Requisitioned transport in the Roman empire. A new inscription from Pisidia', *Journal of Roman Studies* 66, 106–31

Moffat, A. (1985), *Kelsae. A History of Kelso from Earliest Times*, Edinburgh

Morgan, T.O. (1851), 'Historical and traditional notices of Owain Glyndwr,' *Archaeologia Cambrensis* 2, 24–41

Morillo, S. (1996), *The Battle of Hastings: Sources and Interpretations*, Woodbridge

Morris, J. (1975–1992), *Domesday Book*, Chichester

Morris, J.E. (1901), *The Welsh Wars of Edward I*, Oxford

Morris, M. (2012), *The Norman Conquest*, London

Mudd, A., Lupton, A. and Williams, R.J. (2000), *Excavations Alongside Roman Ermin Street, Gloucestershire and Wiltshire: The Archaeology of the A419/A417 Swindon to Gloucester Road Scheme*, Oxford

Munby, J.T. (1990), *Portchester Castle, Hampshire*, London

Muir, R. (1985), *Reading the Celtic Landscapes*, London

Myers, A. (2010), 'Field work in the age of digital reproduction: a review of the potentials and limitations of Google Earth for archaeologists', *The SAA Archaeological Record* 10:4, 7–11

Nash-Williams, V.E. (1969), *The Roman Frontier in Wales*, ed. 2, revised by Jarret, M.G., Cardiff

NEHHAS (2011), *Finding the Road*, Journal of the North-East Hampshire Historical and Archaeological Society 3, Fleet

Neilson, G. (1910), '*Brunanburh* and *Burnswork*', *Scottish Historical Review* 7, 37–55, 435–6

Newall, F. (1976), 'The Roman signal fortlet at Outerwards, Ayrshire,' *Glasgow Archaeological Journal* 4, 111–23

Noort, R. van de and Ellis, S. eds (1997), *Wetland Heritage of the Humberhead Levels: An Archaeological Survey*, Hull

Noort, R. van de and Lillie, M. (1997), 'Scaftworth: a timber and turf Roman road', *Current Archaeology* 151, 272–3

Northern Archaeological Associates (2005), *Iron Age Settlement and Roman Pottery Kilns near Crambeck, North Yorkshire. Publication Report Draft*, NAA Report 05/41, Barnard Castle

Ogden, T. (1966), 'Coldharbour and Roman roads,' *Durham University Journal* 59, 13–24

Ogilby, J. (1675), *Britannia*, London

Ogilby, J. (1699), *The Traveller's Guide, or, a Most Exact Description of the Roads of England*, London

OS (1956), *Map of Roman Britain*, ed 3, Southampton

OS (1978), *Map of Roman Britain*, ed 4, Southampton

OS (1994), *Map of Roman Britain*, ed 4 rev, Southampton

Partridge, E. (1966), *Origins. A Short Etymological Dictionary of Modern English*, London

Pearson, B., Price, J., Tanner, V. and Walker, J. (1985), 'The Rochdale Borough survey', *The Greater Manchester Archaeological Journal* 1, 103–31 www.gmau.manchester.ac.uk/pdfs/gmac13.pdf accessed 16.12.12

Peddie, J. (1998), *Conquest: The Roman Invasion of Britain*, Stroud

Pennant, T. (1813), *Some Account of London*, ed 5, London

Peterson, J.W.M. (1990), 'Roman cadastres in Britain II. Eastern A. Signs of a large System in the northern English home counties', *Dialogues d'histoire ancienne* 16, 233–72

Peterson, J.W.M. (2002), 'Le réseau centurié "Kent A"', in Clavel-Lévêque, M. and Orejas, A. (eds), *Atlas Historique des cadastres d'Europe*. 2, Dossier 8, Luxembourg

Peterson, J.W.M. (2006) 'Planned military landscape in Roman Britain', in Lévêque, L., M.R. del Árbol, L. Pop & C. Bartels (eds), *Journeys through European Landscapes*, Ponferrada, 153–6

Piggott, S. (1949), 'A wheel of Iron Age type from Co Durham', Proceedings of the Prehistoric Society 15, 191

Plummer, J. (1976), 'Dowsing for Roman roads', *Journal of the British Society of Dowsers* 25:174, 205–14

Pollard, A.F. (1903), *Tudor Tracts, 1532–1588*, London

Poulter, J. (2010), *The Planning of Roman Roads and Walls in Northern Britain*, Stroud

Pounds, N.J.G. (2000), *A History of the English Parish: The Culture of Religion from Augustine to Victoria*, Cambridge

Prestwich, M. (1988), *Edward I*, Berkeley and Los Angeles

Purton, R.C. (1901), 'Historical notes relating to the parish of Kempsey', *Architectural Society* 25, 592–601

Quiller-Couch, A.T. (1918), *Studies in Literature*, Cambridge

Rackham, O. (1986), *The History of the Countryside*, London

Raftery, B. (1991), 'The early iron age', in Ryan, M. (ed), *The Illustrated Archaeology of Ireland*, Dublin, 107–12

Ramm, H. (1978), *The Parisi*, London

Ramsay, J.H. (1913), *Genesis of Lancaster: The Three Reigns of Edward II, Edward III, and Richard II, 1307–1399*, Oxford

Rankov, B. (1999), 'The governor's men: the *officium consularis* in provincial administration', in Goldsworthy, A. and Haynes, I. (eds), *The Roman Army as a Community*, JRA Supplementary Series 34, 15–34

Rendel, V. (1967), 'The meaning of "Coldharbour"', *Kent Archeological Review* 7, 7

Reno, F.D. (1996), *The Historic King Arthur: Authenticating the Celtic Hero of Post-Roman Britain*, Jefferson

Reno, F.D. (2000), *Historic Figures of the Arthurian Era: Authenticating the Enemies and Allies of Britain's Post-Roman King*, Jefferson

Richmond, I.A. (1956), Review of Margary (1955), *Journal of Roman Studies* 46, 198–9

Richmond, I.A. (1958), Review of Margary (1957), *Journal of Roman Studies* 48, 218–19

Richmond, I.A. and McIntyre, J. (1934), 'The Roman marching camps at Reycross and Crackenthorpe', *Transactions of the Cumberland and Westmorland Antiquarian Archaeological Society* series 2, 34, 50–61

Riley, D.N. (1980), *Early Landscape from the Air*, Sheffield

Riley, D.N. (1982), *Aerial Archaeology in Britain*, Princes Risborough

Rivet, A.L.F. (1956), Review of Margary (1955), *Antiquity* 30: 117, 43–5

Rivet, A.L.F. (1958), Review of Margary (1957), *Antiquity* 32: 125, 51–2

Rivet, A.L.F. (1970), 'The British section of the Antonine Itinerary', *Britannia* 1, 34–82

Rivet, A.L.F. and Smith, C. (1979), *The Place-Names of Roman Britain*, London

Robb, G. (2013) *The Ancient Paths: Discovering the Lost Map of Celtic Europe*, London

Roberts, I. (1998) 'New link to the past. The archaeology of the M1-A1 Link Road', *Archaeology in West Yorkshire* 6, 4–6

Roth, J.P. (1998), *The Logistics of the Roman Army at War (264 BC–AD 235)*, Leiden

Rowland, T.H. (1984), *The Devil's Causeway. A Roman Road Corbridge via Bewclay to Berwick*, Alnwick

Royal Commission on Ancient and Historical Monuments in Wales (1976), *An Inventory of the Ancient Monuments in Glamorgan Volume 1: Pre-Norman. Part II: The Early Christian Period*, Cardiff

Royal Commission on the Ancient and Historical Monuments and Constructions of Scotland (1924), *Eighth Report with Inventory of Monuments and Constructions in the County of East Lothian*, Edinburgh

Rushton, S. (1995), 'The Stanegate at Fourstones', *Archaeology in Northumberland 1994–1995*, 41

St Joseph, J.K. (1952), 'The roads to Nithsdale', in Clarke, J. et al. (eds), *The Roman Occupation of South-Western Scotland*, Glasgow, 48–9

St Joseph, J.K. (1969), 'Air reconnaissance in Britain, 1965–68', *Journal of Roman Studies* 59, 104–28

St Joseph, J.K. (1983), 'The Roman fortlet at Gatehouse of Fleet, Kirkcudbright', in Hartley, B. and Wacher, J. *Rome and her Northern Provinces. Papers Presented to Sheppard Frere in Honour of his Retirement from the Chair of Archaeology of the Roman Empire, University of Oxford*, Gloucester, 222–34

Salisbury, C. (1995), 'An 8th-century Mercian bridge over the Trent at Cromwell, Nottinghamshire, England', *Antiquity* 69:266, 1015–18

Salway, P. (1981), *Roman Britain*, Oxford

Salway, B. (2002), 'Travel, *itineraria et tabellaria*', in Adams and Laurence (2002), 22–66

Sartre, M. (2005), *The Middle East Under Rome*, Cambridge MA and London

Schenk, D. (1930), 'Flavius Vegetius Renatus; die Quellen der Epitoma rei militaris' *Klio* 22 (1930)

Sedgley, J.P. (1975), *The Roman Milestones of Britain: Their Petrography and Probable Origin*, BAR British Series 1, 41–2

Selkirk, R. (1983), *The Piercebridge Formula*, Cambridge

Selkirk, R. (1995), *On the Trail of the Legions*, Ipswich

Sharpe, M. (1918) 'Centuriation in Middlesex', English Historical Review 131, 489–62

Sheridan, A. (1996), 'The oldest bow... and other objects', *Current Archaeology* 149, 188–90

Sherman, A. and Evans, E. (2004), *Roman Roads in Southeast Wales. Desk-based Assessment with Recommendations for Fieldwork*, GGAT report no. 2004/073, Swansea

Simpson, G. (1972), 'Samian pottery and a Roman road at Corbridge', *Archaeologia Aeliana* series 4, 50, 217–34

Skene, W.F. (1872), *The Historians of Scotland I. John of Fordun's Chronicle of the Scottish Nation*, Edinburgh

Skene, W.F. (1877), *The Historians of Scotland VII. Liber Pluscardensis*, Edinburgh

Smith, C. (2000), 'Early and archaic Rome', in Coulston, J. and Dodge, H. (eds), *Ancient Rome. The Archaeology of the Eternal City*, Oxford, 16–41

Snape, M. and Bidwell, P. (2002), 'Excavations at Castle Garth, Newcastle upon Tyne, 1976–92 and 1995–6: the excavation of the Roman fort', *Archaeologia Aeliana* (5th ser), 31, 1–249

South, T.J. (ed.) (2002), *Historia De Sancto Cuthberto*, Cambridge

Spain, G.R.B. (1937), 'The original survey for the Newcastle-Carlisle military road', *Archaeologia Aeliana* 4th Series, 14, 17–21

Speidel, M.P. (1994), *Riding for Caesar: The Roman Emperors' Horse Guards*, London

Stenton, F. (1936), 'The road system of medieval England', *Economic History Review* 7, 1–21

Stevenson, J. (1855), *The Church Historians of England Vol.III Part II. The Historical Works of Simeon of Durham*, London

Sturt, J. (1987), *Revolt in the West: the Western Rebellion of 1549*, Tiverton

Summers, R. (1950), 'Armchair archaeology', *The South African Archaeological Bulletin* 5:19, 101–04

Symons, H.E. (1938), 'Two trans-Saharan motor routes', *Geographical Journal* 91, 153–5

Talbert, R.J.A. (2010), *Rome's World. The Peutinger Map Reconsidered*, Cambridge

Taylor, C. (1979), *Roads and Tracks of Britain*, London

Taylor, M.V. (1957), 'Roman Britain in 1956: sites explored', *Journal of Roman Studies* 47, 198–226

Taylor, W. (1996), *The Military Roads in Scotland*, revised edition, Colonsay

Thomas, B.E. (1952), 'Modern trans-Saharan routes', *Geographical Review* 42, 267–82

Thomas, E. (1916), *The Icknield Way*, London

Thomas, N. (1955), 'The Thornborough circles, near Ripon, North Riding', *Yorkshire Archaeological Journal* 38, 425–45

Thomas, T. (1822), *Memoirs of Owen Glendower, (Owain Glyndwr)*, Haverfordwest

Thomson, T. (1819), *The Auchinleck Chronicle*, Edinburgh

TIR (1983), *Tabula imperii romani. Condate–Glevum–Londinium–Lutetia* (London)

TIR (1987), *Tabula imperii romani. Britannia Septentrionalis* (London)

Tomlin, R.S.O., Wright, R.P., and Hassall, M.W.C. (2009), *The Roman Inscriptions of Britain. Volume III, Inscriptions on Stone*, Oxford

Troyano, L.F. (2003) *Bridge Engineering: A Global Perspective*, London

Twemlow, F.R. (1912), *The Battle of Bloreheath*, Wolverhampton

Tyson, C. (1992), 'The Battle of Otterburn: when and where was it fought?', in Goodman, A. (ed.), *War and Border Societies in the Middle Ages*, London, 65–93

Viatores (1964), *Roman Roads in the South-East Midlands*, London

Vyner, B. (2001), *Stainmore, the Archaeology of a North Pennine Pass*, Tees Archaeology Monograph Series 1, Hartlepool

Wacher, J. (1974), *The Towns of Roman Britain*, London

Waddelove, E. (1999), *The Roman Roads of North Wales: Recent Discoveries*, Ruthin

Waldman, C. (2009), *Atlas of the North American Indian*, ed 3, New York

Walters, B. (1999), 'Swindon: Blunsdon Rodge', *Current Archaeology* 163, 256–8

Ward, G.C. (1996), *The West. An Illustrated History*. Little Brown, Barton–New York–Toronto–London

Watkins, A. (1925), *The Old Straight Track. Its Mounds, Beacons, Moats, Sites, and Mark Stones*, London

Webster, G. (1980), *The Roman Invasion of Britain*, London

Webster, G. (1981), *Rome against Caratacus. The Roman Campaigns in Britain AD 48–58*, London

Welfare, H. and Swan, V. (1995), *Roman Camps in England: The Field Archaeology*, London

Weller, J.A. (1999), *Roman Traction Systems* www.humanist.de/rome/rts/index.html accessed 24.7.12

Westwood, J.O. (1858), 'Further notices of the early inscribed stones of Wales', *Archaeologia Cambrensis* series 3, 4, 405–8

White, R. (1857), *History of the Battle of Otterburn Fought in 1388*, London

White, R. and Barker, P. (1998), *Wroxeter. Life and Death of a Roman City*, Stroud

Wilkinson, P. (2007), *Archaeology: What It Is, Where It Is, and How to Do It*, ed.2, Oxford

Wilson, A. (1994–5), 'Roman penetration in Strathclyde south of the Antonine Wall. Part one: the topographical framework', *Glasgow Archaeological Journal* 19, 1–30

Wilson, D.R. (1982), *Air Photo Interpretation for Archaeologists*, London

Wilson, R.J.A. (2004), 'The Roman "Officer's Tomb" at High Rochester revisited', *Archaeologia Aeliana* series 5 33, 25–33

Winbolt, S.E. (1936), *With a Spade on Stane Street*, London

Witcher, R. (1997), 'Roman roads that reshaped the land', *British Archaeology* 27, 4–7

Witcher, R. (1998), 'Roman roads: phenomenological perspectives on roads in the landscape', in Forcey, C., Witcher, R., and Hawthorne, J. (eds), *TRAC 97: Proceedings of the Seventh Annual Theoretical Roman Archaeology Conference, Nottingham 1997*, Oxford, 60–70

Wood, M. (1999), *In Search of England: Journeys Into the English Past*, London

Wood, M. (2010) *The Story of England*, London

Woolliscroft, D.J. (2001), *Roman Military Signalling*, Stroud

Woolliscroft, D.J. and Hoffmann, B. (2006), *Rome's First Frontier: The Flavian Occupation of Northern Scotland*, Stroud

Wright, G.N. (1992), *Turnpike Roads*, Princes Risborough

Wylie, J.H. (1894), *History of England under Henry the Fourth*, vol.2, London

Wylie, J.H. (1896), *History of England under Henry the Fourth*, vol.3, London

Index

References to figures are *italicized* and plates **emboldened**. The Margary numbers of named roads are in square brackets